The Historical Atlas of State Power in Congress, 1790–1990

The Historical Atlas of State Power in Congress, 1790–1990

KENNETH C. MARTIS

West Virginia University

GREGORY A. ELMES

West Virginia University

CQ CONGRESSIONAL QUARTERLY INC.

Washington, D.C.

TO OUR PARENTS
Arthur and Christine
Joseph and Elizabeth

Printed in the United States of America

Book and jacket design: Kachergis Book Design

Acknowledgments: Tables 1-1 and 1-5 were adapted with permission of The Free Press, a Division of Macmillan, Inc., from *The Historical Atlas of United States Congressional Districts: 1789–1983* by Kenneth C. Martis. Copyright © 1982 by The Free Press.

Library of Congress Cataloging-in-Publication Data

Martis, Kenneth C.
  The historical atlas of state power in Congress,
1790-1990 / Kenneth C. Martis, Gregory A. Elmes.
      p.   cm.
  Includes bibliographical references and index.
  ISBN 0-87187-742-2
  1. Election districts—United States—History—Maps.   2. United States. Congress House—Election districts—Maps.
3. Apportionment (Election law)—United States—Maps.   4. United States—Census.   I. Elmes, Gregory A.   II. Congressional Quarterly, Inc.   III. Title.
G1201.F7M3   1993 <G&M>
328.73'07345'022—dc20   92-46583
                                                                                    CIP
                                                                                    MAP

Contents

Tables

Maps

Preface

The U.S. Constitution stipulates that a census of population be taken every ten years to determine the size of each state delegation to the House of Representatives. Since the first census in 1790, a reapportionment of House seats and a resultant shift of state power has occurred every ten years, except in 1920. Different population growth rates, immigration rates, and especially interstate migration patterns are the primary demographic factors that increase or decrease the size of a state's congressional delegation and the proportion of a state's political influence. If neighboring states have similar demographic characteristics then regional or sectional groups of states may show similar shifts in congressional power. The objective of this atlas is to illustrate and analyze the state, regional, and sectional shifts in power in decennial congressional apportionments.

The Historical Atlas of State Power in Congress, 1790–1990 is the first work to present in one volume maps of every apportionment change for each state and region for all apportionments throughout history. Thirty-three apportionment maps are the centerpiece of this work. From 1790 through 1910 the House increased in size every decade, except in 1840 (when it decreased in size). To analyze and illustrate the shift of state power from 1790 through 1910, two apportionment maps are required for each decade. The first map illustrates the increase or decrease in the number of House seats for each state. The second map illustrates the relative proportional increase or decrease in House power by percentage for each state. The second map is needed because many states, when the size of the House increased, gained one or more seats in Congress, but nevertheless decreased their total proportion in the House. From 1930 on, with the size of the House fixed at 435 members, one map per decade is sufficient to illustrate both the shifts of seats and relative power. This atlas is the first work to calculate and map these relative gains and losses of congressional power.

Decennial apportionments determine not only the strength of a state in Congress but also the power of a state in the election of the president. The Constitution stipulates that the electoral college vote for each state is equal to the number of senators and representatives. As states, regions, and sections increase or decrease in House membership, their power in both Congress and presidential elections also increases or decreases. The maps in this atlas, while specifically illustrating shifting state and regional power in the House of Representatives, also reflect changing state and regional power in electing the president.

Neighboring states that have similar demographic characteristics plus similar historical, geographical, agricultural, industrial, cultural, and social traits predictably have similar economic interests and political agendas. In fact, throughout American history contiguous states have banded together as regional and sectional blocs. These regional blocs have been obvious in presidential elections, congressional elections, and congressional roll-call voting behavior. Therefore, it is critical to understand fully the state, regional, and sectional shifts in power generated by the decennial census apportionments. This is the primary goal of this work.

Organization

The Historical Atlas of State Power in Congress, 1790–1990 has been organized to facilitate its use as a general, as well as cartographic, reference. The atlas is divided into three parts. Part 1 is an overview that discusses the constitutional origins of the House and looks at the changes in apportionment law and the size of Congress through history. This introduction concludes with a short discussion of the effect of apportionment on the redistricting of congressional seats within the states.

Part 2 examines each of the twenty congressional apportionments as an individual event. Each decennial section contains one or two apportionment maps and tables of apportionment statistics. The primary apportionment table includes for each state: (1) the change in House seats; (2) the new seat allocation; (3) the proportion of the total House expressed as a percentage; and (4) the percentage change from the previous Congress. Additional bar charts organize the apportionment statistics by regional divisions. The discussion of each decade includes significant census population figures and the apportionment law and allocation formula that translated the census figures into state delegation size. The core of the section is the analysis of the geographic pattern of the decade's apportionment map(s). This analysis explains the decennial shifts in power with respect to specific events during the preceding decade and long-term trends.

Part 3 discusses apportionment within the context of broad historical eras, discussing the theoretical and practical impacts of shifting state, regional, and sectional strength. Four case studies provide specific examples of how changing population geography and its resultant apportionment adjustments have had enormous political impacts on American history.

The first example of apportionment changing the nature of Congress and the nation is the development of the West as a separate region. After the American Revolution large numbers of people began migrating west of the Appalachian Mountains, and within decades an entirely new region developed with an economic and political agenda of its own. The old North-South division turned into a tripartite North-South-West division. This case study discusses the factors of population change and the economic and political differences that arose between the original Atlantic Coast states and the new trans-Appalachian states.

The second case study examines factors of different North-South population growth in the context of apportionment and impact on the political differences leading up to the Civil War. One of the most significant regional apportionment shifts in political power occurred between the slave and free states in the first half of the nineteenth century. Beginning at relative parity, the population of the Northeast and Northwest grew at a rate greater than that of the Southeast and Southwest, and eventually the North was able to dominate in Congress and in the election of the president.

The third case study looks at the transition of America from a rural agricultural society to an urban industrial one. Again, an analysis of the elements causing urbanization helps explain some of the more sweeping geographic apportionment changes occurring in the United States. Increasing urbanization sparked a rural-urban conflict that came to a head in 1920 when the census reported that the United States was, for the first time, over 50 percent urban. The only time the U.S. Congress was not apportioned as mandated by the Constitution was after the 1920 census. This case study also examines this nonapportionment and its relationship to the urban-rural conflict.

The last case study deals with contemporary migration to the Sunbelt. Over the last thirty years there has been a profound shift in American geopolitical power. Most of the old industrial northeastern manufacturing cities are declining or growing at a rate lower than the national average. Regional interstate migration patterns are flowing from the North and Northeast to the South and Southwest/Pacific. This section discusses the factors contributing to recent apportionments in the context of both long-term trends and the present Sunbelt shift. The final apportionment maps vividly display the political consequences of Sunbelt migration.

In both the case studies and the decade analyses the focus is on the apportionment maps. These maps and the accompanying statistics fill an important gap in the historical, political, and geographical record of the United States. American history takes place in both time and space. The geographical units of counties, congressional districts, states, regions, and sections have all played an important role in the American experience. The year 1990 was the two-hundredth anniversary of the first census and the first apportionment. This atlas elucidates the nature and impact of the changing geographical allocation of congressional and presidential political power in U.S. history.

Background and Acknowledgments

This atlas began in Kenneth C. Martis's research on the geographical aspects of the U.S. Congress. Two other atlases preceded this work—*The Historical Atlas of United States Congressional Districts: 1789–1983* and *The Historical Atlas of Political Parties in the United States Congress: 1789–1989.* These works confirmed the importance of studying the geographical aspects of Congress and also of developing a fuller geographical understanding of all of American political history. Kenneth C. Martis wrote Parts 1 and 3 of this atlas and is responsible for its general concept and format.

Gregory A. Elmes wrote Part 2. His participation in this work is connected with his long-term interest in the development and use of Geographic Information Systems (GIS). As part of a spring 1991 GIS graduate seminar, his students put apportionment statistics into an automated format. Dr. Elmes composed digital versions of the apportionment maps using ESRI's ARC-INFO software. The work was done through the facilities of West Virginia University's Department of Geology and Geography Laboratory for GIS and Spatial Analysis. Original versions of all maps were generated on a color electrostatic plotter using Arc Macro Language (AML). Research assistants Boian Koulov and Deborah Bennet helped in the actual coding and statistical manipulation of the data in the INFO relational database. K. Douglas Brown collaborated in drafting historically correct U.S. national boundaries and in map editing. Mark Mattson and Chris Salvatico of the Department of Geography and Urban Studies at Temple University reformatted the data and cartography for production into color negatives for the final printing process.

In the writing stage of the atlas, one of research assistant Reed Durbin's many tasks was to reconstitute the apportionment statistics along regional lines and compile virtually all the tables in this work after the completion of the original set of apportionment statistical tables. Reed was supported, in part, by an undergraduate research assistantship from the West Virginia University Regional Research Institute. We are grateful to all those in the Department of Geology and Geography (especially Hope Dennis), the Regional Research Institute, and West Virginia University who have made this research possible.

A special thanks to Jeanne Ferris, Jon Preimesberger, and the Congressional Quarterly staff for their help, encouragement, and patience. They saw the additional insight that cartographic illustration and analysis brings to the understanding of Congress, and we thank them for their support.

KENNETH C. MARTIS
GREGORY A. ELMES

Part 1

Introduction

Introduction

Historical Overview of Congressional Apportionment

Constitutional Apportionment

In 1788 the Constitution of the United States established a federal government with three distinct branches: legislative, executive, and judicial. Article I, Section 1, vests all legislative powers ". . . in a Congress of the United States, which shall consist of a Senate and House of Representatives." Approximately half of the original Constitution is devoted to creating and defining Congress, the branch the framers believed central to true representative democracy.

House of Representatives

Article I, Section 2, of the Constitution establishes the House of Representatives, the chamber of Congress designed to be the voice of the individual citizen. House members are elected directly by qualified voters every two years. The Constitution stipulates that a decennial census be taken to determine the population of the individual states.[1] After the census, House seats are divided among—that is, apportioned to—each state based on population. The total number of House seats and the statistical formula to allocate seats are determined by Congress.

Representation in the House is apportioned to the states based on

---

1. The original constitution determined ". . . those bound to service . . ." (slaves) shall be counted as three-fifths of a person. This remained legally in effect until the 1868 adoption of the Fourteenth Amendment. The Constitution expanded the ranks of qualified voters with the Fifteenth Amendment (addressing the rights of racial groups), the Nineteenth Amendment (enfranchising women), and the Twenty-sixth Amendment (lowering the voting age to eighteen years).

population. Although congressional power can be measured and exercised in many ways, the size of a state's delegation is one of the most basic measures of political power and influence. Population growth rates, immigration, and especially interstate migration are the primary determinants that increase or decrease the size of a state's congressional delegation and the relative proportion of a state's political influence. If neighboring states have similar economic, social, historical, and demographic characteristics, then these larger areas may share not only similar population growth rates and migration patterns but predictably similar political interests and agendas. Throughout U.S. history, contiguous states with one or more similar characteristics have been considered regional blocs and have banded together as such. Indeed, regional similarities have been demonstrated many times in presidential elections, congressional elections, and roll-call voting patterns within Congress.[2] These regional groupings may be large sections such as the South, North, or West, or smaller regions such as New England, Appalachia, the Midwest, or the Great Plains. Different growth rates, different immigration patterns, and interregional population migration patterns, then, determine the increase or decrease in regional influence in Congress and the relative proportion of regional power.[3]

Table 1-1 contains the central data for this atlas. This table enumerates the size of the House of Representatives and the size of each state delegation after each apportionment in American history. These numbers are taken from the primary source documents—the actual decennial apportionment laws and census reports. States entering the Union in between apportionments are listed in the following period.[4] This allows a more accurate analysis of the changes in House size from apportionment to apportionment. Most other published apportionment tables list new states with the preceding decade. In Part 2, corresponding maps of every apportionment change for each state for all reapportionments from 1790 through 1990 are provided.[5] These maps depict for the first time the shifting state and regional power in the House of Representatives during the entire course of the first two hundred years of U.S. history.

Since the House of Representatives changed size after each census apportionment from 1790 to 1910, two calculations and two maps are required to understand fully the changing distribution of state and regional power in the House. The first calculation and map show the gain or loss of seats for each state for each apportionment based on the data in Table 1-1. These maps are always designated as the "A" map for each apportionment from 1790 through 1910 and are Maps 1A–13A in the atlas. The second calculation and map show the gain or loss of House power, calculated by percentage for each state for each apportionment. These maps are always designated as the "B" map for each apportionment from 1790 through 1910 and are Maps 1B–13B in the atlas.

For example, the 1800 census apportionment expanded the House from 105 seats to 141 seats. The state of Virginia was apportioned twenty-two seats, an increase in three seats from its previous nineteen. Although this is an increase in seats given to Virginia, the state *decreased* in its proportion of total House membership. Virginia's nineteen seats of the 1790 apportionment constituted 18.1 percent of all the seats in the House. However, the twenty-two seats of the 1800 apportionment constituted only 15.6 percent of the House, a decrease of 2.5 percentage points. Virginia declined in relative power in spite of an increase in actual seats. This is a common occurrence in the 1800 apportionment and all the other apportionments in the period when the size of the House was increasing.[6] Using the above example, Virginia is depicted on the 1800 apportionment map of seat change in blue, with a 3, indicating an increase of three in the number of House seats (see Map 2A, p. 41). However, on the 1800 apportionment map of percentage change in power, Virginia is depicted in orange, with a -2.5, indicating the amount of percentage decrease in congressional strength (see Map 2B, p. 41).

Table 1-2 gives the percentage of House membership for each state for

2. J. Clark Archer and Peter J. Taylor, *Section and Party* (Chichester, UK: Research Studies Press, 1981); Richard F. Bensel, *Sectionalism and American Political Development, 1880–1980* (Madison: University of Wisconsin Press, 1984); Kenneth C. Martis, "Sectionalism and the United States Congress," *Political Geography Quarterly* 7 (April 1988): 99–109.

3. For example, see the regional analysis of the 1970 and 1980 apportionment in Larry M. Schwab, *The Impact of Congressional Reapportionment and Redistricting* (Landam, Md.: University Press of America, 1988), 15–52.

4. This is the case since most secondary source publications use and repeat the readily available standard public domain source, specifically the apportionment tables in *Biographical Directory of the United States Congress, 1774–1989* (Washington, D.C.: Government Printing Office, 1989), 47 (and previous directories), and U.S. Department of Commerce, Bureau of the Census, *Historical Statistics of the United States Colonial Times to 1970* (Washington, D.C.: Government Printing Office, 1975), part 2, 1085.

5. There was no reapportionment after the 1920 census. This is the only time in U.S. history this occurred. For an in-depth discussion of this nonapportionment, see the case study on rural and urban places and the 1920 nonapportionment in Part 3.

6. For example, the original thirteen states in the 1800 apportionment fared as follows: (1) six states increased in seats, but declined in proportion; (2) three states remained the same and they, of course, declined in proportion; and (3) four states increased enough in seats to increase also in proportion of the House (see statistical tables accompanying Maps 2A and 2B).

Table 1–1. Apportionment of the House of Representatives After Each Decennial Census

Census Apportionment

States	1788[a]	1790	1800	1810	1820	1830	1840	1850	1860	1870	1880	1890	1900	1910	1930	1940	1950	1960	1970	1980	1990
Alabama					3	5	7	7	6	8	8	9	9	10	9	9	9	8	7	7	7
Alaska																		1	1	1	1
Arizona														1	1	2	2	3	4	5	6
Arkansas							1	2	3	4	5	6	7	7	7	7	6	4	4	4	4
California								2	3	4	6	7	8	11	20	23	30	38	43	45	52
Colorado											1	2	3	4	4	4	4	4	5	6	6
Connecticut	5	7	7	7	6	6	4	4	4	4	4	4	5	5	6	6	6	6	6	6	6
Delaware	1	1	1	2	1	1	1	1	1	1	1	1	1	1	1	1	1	1	1	1	1
Florida								1	1	2	2	2	3	4	5	6	8	12	15	19	23
Georgia	3	2	4	6	7	9	8	8	7	9	10	11	11	12	10	10	10	10	10	10	11
Hawaii																		2	2	2	2
Idaho												1	1	2	2	2	2	2	2	2	2
Illinois					1	3	7	9	14	19	20	22	25	27	27	26	25	24	24	22	20
Indiana					3	7	10	11	11	13	13	13	13	13	12	11	11	11	11	10	10
Iowa								2	6	9	11	11	11	11	9	8	8	7	6	6	5
Kansas									1	3	7	8	8	8	7	6	6	5	5	5	4
Kentucky		2	6	10	12	13	10	10	9	10	11	11	11	11	9	9	8	7	7	7	6
Louisiana					3	3	4	4	5	6	6	6	7	8	8	8	8	8	8	8	7
Maine					7	8	7	6	5	5	4	4	4	4	3	3	3	2	2	2	2
Maryland	6	8	9	9	9	8	6	6	5	6	6	6	6	6	6	6	7	8	8	8	8
Massachusetts	8	14	17	20	13	12	10	11	10	11	12	13	14	16	15	14	14	12	12	11	10
Michigan							3	4	6	9	11	12	12	13	17	17	18	19	19	18	16
Minnesota									2	3	5	7	9	10	9	9	9	8	8	8	8
Mississippi					1	2	4	5	5	6	7	7	8	8	7	7	6	5	5	5	5
Missouri					1	2	5	7	9	13	14	15	16	16	13	13	11	10	10	9	9
Montana												1	1	2	2	2	2	2	2	2	1
Nebraska										1	3	6	6	6	5	4	4	3	3	3	3
Nevada										1	1	1	1	1	1	1	1	1	1	2	2

Table 1–1. Apportionment of the House of Representatives After Each Decennial Census (continued)

Census Apportionment

States	1788[a]	1790	1800	1810	1820	1830	1840	1850	1860	1870	1880	1890	1900	1910	1930	1940	1950	1960	1970	1980	1990
New Hampshire	3	4	5	6	6	5	4	3	3	3	2	2	2	2	2	2	2	2	2	2	2
New Jersey	4	5	6	6	6	6	5	5	5	7	7	8	10	12	14	14	14	15	15	14	13
New Mexico														1	1	2	2	2	2	3	3
New York	6	10	17	27	34	40	34	33	31	33	34	34	37	43	45	45	43	41	39	34	31
North Carolina	5	10	12	13	13	13	9	8	7	8	9	9	10	10	11	12	12	11	11	11	12
North Dakota												1	2	3	2	2	2	2	1	1	1
Ohio				6	14	19	21	21	19	20	21	21	21	22	24	23	23	24	23	21	19
Oklahoma														8	9	8	6	6	6	6	6
Oregon									1	1	1	2	2	3	3	4	4	4	4	5	5
Pennsylvania	8	13	18	23	26	28	24	25	24	27	28	30	32	36	34	33	30	27	25	23	21
Rhode Island	1	2	2	2	2	2	2	2	2	2	2	2	2	3	2	2	2	2	2	2	2
South Carolina	5	6	8	9	9	9	7	6	4	5	7	7	7	7	6	6	6	6	6	6	6
South Dakota												2	2	3	2	2	2	2	2	1	1
Tennessee			3	6	9	13	11	10	8	10	10	10	10	10	9	10	9	9	8	9	9
Texas								2	4	6	11	13	16	18	21	21	22	23	24	27	30
Utah													1	2	2	2	2	2	2	3	3
Vermont		2	4	6	5	5	4	3	3	3	2	2	2	2	1	1	1	1	1	1	1
Virginia	10	19	22	23	22	21	15	13	11	9	10	10	10	10	9	9	10	10	10	10	11
Washington												2	3	5	6	6	7	7	7	8	9
West Virginia										3	4	4	5	6	6	6	6	5	4	4	3
Wisconsin								3	6	8	9	10	11	11	10	10	10	10	9	9	9
Wyoming												1	1	1	1	1	1	1	1	1	1
Total	65	105	141	181	213	240	223	234	241	292	325	356	386	435	435	435	435	435	435	435	435

[a]Constitutional apportionment.

Note: States specifically mentioned in the decennial apportionment law or report are listed for that year. Several territories were counted in the census and admitted after the census year, but before the apportionment law. These states are included in that apportionment decade. The remaining states were admitted during the decade after an apportionment law or report. All new states were admitted with one seat unless noted. These states were, after the 1790 apportionment, Tennessee; after the 1800 apportionment, Ohio; after the 1810 apportionment, Alabama, Illinois, Indiana, Louisiana, and Mississippi; after the 1830 apportionment, Arkansas and Michigan; after the 1840 apportionment, California (2 seats), Florida, Iowa (2 seats), Texas (2 seats), and Wisconsin (2 seats); after the 1850 apportionment, Minnesota (2 seats) and Oregon; after the 1860 apportionment, Nebraska and Nevada; after the 1870 apportionment, Colorado; after the 1880 apportionment, Idaho, Montana, North Dakota, South Dakota (2 seats), Washington, and Wyoming; after the 1890 apportionment, Utah; after the 1900 apportionment, Oklahoma (5 seats); after the 1950 apportionment, Alaska and Hawaii.

each apportionment from 1790 through 1990. This statistic is derived by dividing the number of each state's allocated members by the total allocated seats.[7] The decade that peak congressional strength is initially reached for each state is highlighted in blue. For example, the 1790 apportionment gave Virginia 18.1 percent of all the members of the House of Representatives. This 18.1 percent not only makes the 1790s the peak period of Virginia's congressional strength but also happens to be the highest percentage of strength for any single state in U.S. history to date. Virginia's smallest proportion of state power, highlighted in orange on Table 1-2, was initially reached after the 1930 apportionment when its delegation constituted 2.1 percent of the House.

The bottom row of Table 1-2 gives a decade-by-decade breakdown of the number of peaks and lows of state power. Because of their position, the first and last apportionments are notable. In the 1790 apportionment, nine of the original thirteen states registered their peak proportion of power, and one, Georgia, began at its lowest proportion. In the last apportionment in 1990, five states reached their peak power: Arizona, California, Florida, Texas, and Washington. Six states reached their lowest percentage of state power in their history in 1990: Kentucky, Massachusetts, Montana, New York, Pennsylvania, and West Virginia.

As the U.S. population expanded in the nineteenth century and more and more states came into the Union, the population became more dispersed and the percentage of the House controlled by any one state was reduced. The House of Representatives has remained at 435 members since 1910; therefore, the 1930 to 1990 apportionments can be compared in a number of ways. In this modern era, 1930–1990, California has surpassed other states to assume the largest proportion of state power, 12.0 percent of the House after the 1990 census. This is the largest percentage of the House allocated to any state since the 1860 apportionment. All states allocated the minimum one seat since the House size was fixed at 435 share the unenviable distinction of the smallest proportion of congressional strength in U.S. history, with 0.2 percent each.

Since the size of the House of Representatives has remained fixed at 435 seats since 1910, the apportionments from 1930 through 1990 need only one map each to illustrate the changing state and regional power. Maps 14–20 illustrate the geographic pattern of apportionment gains and losses from 1930 through 1990. Again, the orange indicates a state with a decline in power and the number inside the state indicates the number of seats lost; the blue indicates a state with an increase in power and the number inside the state indicates the number of seats gained.

Table 1-3 gives the gain or loss of proportional state power for each apportionment from 1790 to 1990. This statistic is derived by comparing the difference in percentage allocation for each state from the previous apportionment. This is the statistic given within each state on Maps 1B–13B. Each time a state increases its relative strength in the House, it is highlighted in blue and contains a number indicating the percentage gained. Each time it decreases its relative strength, it is highlighted in orange and contains a number indicating the percentage lost preceded by a negative sign.[8] States that have no change are in cream.

The greatest loss in congressional strength in U.S. history occurred in the 1810 apportionment when Virginia's House delegation fell from 15.6 percent to 12.7 percent, a reduction of 2.9 percentage points. Ohio experienced the greatest gain in congressional strength for any state in 1820 when its House delegation increased by 3.3 percentage points.[9] As the United States expanded in population and in number of states the statistical probability of large gains or losses decreased. Again, examining the gains and losses of state power just in the modern era, 1930–1990, California registered the largest gain, 2.1 percentage points, after the 1930 apportionment and New York the greatest loss, 1.2 percentage points, after the 1980 census.

The bottom rows of Table 1-3 summarize the number of states whose House percentage increased, decreased, or did not change for each

7. The total in each Congress may not add up to 100 percent because of rounding calculations.

8. We (the authors) conducted research to determine the most appropriate statistical range to designate relative gain, loss, or no change in for each state. For example, we considered making the no change category -0.1 percent through +0.1 percent, or -0.2 through +0.2, or -0.3 through +0.3, and so on. We also considered various statistical procedures for deviation. In the end we decided to let the data speak for itself. All negative numbers are mapped as losses, all positive numbers are mapped as relative gains, irrespective of size. This is a problem common to choropleth mapping and careful judgment is urged in interpreting the relative map patterns. All numbers are rounded off to the nearest tenth using the common procedures.

The maps illustrate only those states mentioned in the decade apportionment law. When a new state enters the Union, its gain or loss of proportional power is calculated on a base of zero; therefore, every new state entering the Union has a positive number at least for that initial Congress.

9. Ohio also has a 3.3 percentage point increase in 1810. However, since this is Ohio's first apportionment, and all new states are assigned a base allocation of zero, this and other initial state statistics are not used in this particular calculation. See footnote 8.

Table 1–2. Percentage of the House of Representatives for Each State After Each Apportionment

Census Apportionment

States	1790	1800	1810	1820	1830	1840	1850	1860	1870	1880	1890	1900	1910	1930	1940	1950	1960	1970	1980	1990
Alabama				1.4	2.1	3.1	3.0	2.5	2.7	2.5	2.5	2.3	2.3	2.1	2.1	2.1	1.8	1.6	1.6	1.6
Alaska[a]																	0.2	0.2	0.2	0.2
Arizona													0.2	0.2	0.5	0.5	0.7	0.9	1.1	1.4
Arkansas						0.4	0.9	1.2	1.4	1.5	1.7	1.8	1.6	1.6	1.6	1.4	0.9	0.9	0.9	0.9
California							0.9	1.2	1.4	1.8	2.0	2.1	2.5	4.6	5.3	6.9	8.7	9.9	10.3	12.0
Colorado										0.3	0.6	0.8	0.9	0.9	0.9	0.9	0.9	1.1	1.4	1.4
Connecticut	6.7	5.0	3.9	2.8	2.5	1.8	1.7	1.7	1.4	1.2	1.1	1.3	1.1	1.4	1.4	1.4	1.4	1.4	1.4	1.4
Delaware	1.0	0.7	1.1	0.5	0.4	0.4	0.4	0.4	0.3	0.3	0.3	0.3	0.2	0.2	0.2	0.2	0.2	0.2	0.2	0.2
Florida							0.4	0.4	0.7	0.6	0.6	0.8	0.9	1.1	1.4	1.8	2.8	3.4	4.4	5.3
Georgia	1.9	2.8	3.3	3.3	3.8	3.6	3.4	2.9	3.1	3.1	3.1	2.8	2.8	2.3	2.3	2.3	2.3	2.3	2.3	2.5
Hawaii[a]																	0.5	0.5	0.5	0.5
Idaho											0.3	0.3	0.5	0.5	0.5	0.5	0.5	0.5	0.5	0.5
Illinois				0.5	1.3	3.1	3.8	5.8	6.5	6.2	6.2	6.5	6.2	6.2	6.0	5.7	5.5	5.5	5.1	4.6
Indiana				1.4	2.9	4.5	4.7	4.6	4.5	4.0	3.7	3.4	3.0	2.8	2.5	2.5	2.5	2.5	2.3	2.3
Iowa							0.9	2.5	3.1	3.4	3.1	2.8	2.5	2.1	1.8	1.8	1.6	1.4	1.4	1.1
Kansas								0.4	1.0	2.2	2.2	2.1	1.8	1.6	1.4	1.4	1.1	1.1	1.1	0.9
Kentucky	1.9	4.3	5.5	5.6	5.4	4.5	4.3	3.7	3.4	3.4	3.1	2.8	2.5	2.1	2.1	1.8	1.6	1.6	1.6	1.4
Louisiana				1.4	1.3	1.8	1.7	2.1	2.1	1.8	1.7	1.8	1.8	1.8	1.8	1.8	1.8	1.8	1.8	1.6
Maine				3.3	3.3	3.1	2.6	2.1	1.7	1.2	1.1	1.0	0.9	0.7	0.7	0.7	0.5	0.5	0.5	0.5
Maryland	7.6	6.4	5.0	4.2	3.3	2.7	2.6	2.1	2.1	1.8	1.7	1.6	1.4	1.4	1.4	1.6	1.8	1.8	1.8	1.8
Massachusetts	13.3	12.1	11.0	6.1	5.0	4.5	4.7	4.1	3.8	3.7	3.7	3.6	3.7	3.4	3.2	3.2	2.8	2.8	2.5	2.3
Michigan						1.3	1.7	2.5	3.1	3.4	3.4	3.1	3.0	3.9	3.9	4.1	4.4	4.4	4.1	3.7
Minnesota								0.8	1.0	1.5	2.0	2.3	2.3	2.1	2.1	2.1	1.8	1.8	1.8	1.8
Mississippi				0.5	0.8	1.8	2.1	2.1	2.1	2.2	2.0	2.1	1.8	1.6	1.6	1.4	1.1	1.1	1.1	1.1
Missouri				0.5	0.8	2.2	3.0	3.7	4.5	4.3	4.2	4.1	3.7	3.0	3.0	2.5	2.3	2.3	2.1	2.1
Montana												0.3	0.3	0.5	0.5	0.5	0.5	0.5	0.5	0.2
Nebraska									0.3	0.9	1.7	1.6	1.4	1.1	0.9	0.9	0.7	0.7	0.7	0.7

Percent of House Peak Representation  Lowest Representation

[a]*Alaska and Hawaii retained the same percentage since their first census apportionment in 1960.*

Table 1–2. Percentage of the House of Representatives for Each State After Each Apportionment *(continued)*

Census Apportionment

States	1790	1800	1810	1820	1830	1840	1850	1860	1870	1880	1890	1900	1910	1930	1940	1950	1960	1970	1980	1990
Nevada									0.3	0.3	0.3	0.3	0.2	0.2	0.2	0.2	0.2	0.2	0.5	0.5
New Hampshire	3.8	3.5	3.3	2.8	2.1	1.8	1.3	1.2	1.0	0.6	0.6	0.5	0.5	0.5	0.5	0.5	0.5	0.5	0.5	0.5
New Jersey	4.8	4.3	3.3	2.8	2.5	2.2	2.1	2.1	2.4	2.2	2.2	2.6	2.8	3.2	3.2	3.2	3.4	3.4	3.2	3.0
New Mexico													0.2	0.2	0.5	0.5	0.5	0.5	0.7	0.7
New York	9.5	12.1	14.9	16.0	16.7	15.2	14.1	12.9	11.3	10.5	9.6	9.6	9.9	10.3	10.3	9.9	9.4	9.0	7.8	7.1
North Carolina	9.5	8.5	7.2	6.1	5.4	4.0	3.4	2.9	2.7	2.8	2.5	2.6	2.3	2.5	2.8	2.8	2.5	2.5	2.5	2.8
North Dakota											0.3	0.5	0.7	0.5	0.5	0.5	0.5	0.2	0.2	0.2
Ohio			3.3	6.6	7.9	9.4	9.0	7.9	6.8	6.5	5.9	5.4	5.1	5.5	5.3	5.3	5.5	5.3	4.8	4.4
Oklahoma													1.8	2.1	1.8	1.4	1.4	1.4	1.4	1.4
Oregon								0.4	0.3	0.3	0.6	0.5	0.7	0.7	0.9	0.9	0.9	0.9	1.1	1.1
Pennsylvania	12.4	12.8	12.7	12.2	11.7	10.8	10.7	10.0	9.2	8.6	8.4	8.3	8.3	7.8	7.6	6.9	6.2	5.7	5.3	4.8
Rhode Island	1.9	1.4	1.1	0.9	0.8	0.9	0.9	0.8	0.7	0.6	0.6	0.5	0.7	0.5	0.5	0.5	0.5	0.5	0.5	0.5
South Carolina	5.7	5.7	5.0	4.2	3.8	3.1	2.6	1.7	1.7	2.2	2.0	1.8	1.6	1.4	1.4	1.4	1.4	1.4	1.4	1.4
South Dakota											0.6	0.5	0.7	0.5	0.5	0.5	0.5	0.5	0.2	0.2
Tennessee		2.1	3.3	4.2	5.4	4.9	4.3	3.3	3.4	3.1	2.8	2.6	2.3	2.1	2.3	2.1	2.1	1.8	2.1	2.1
Texas							0.9	1.7	2.1	3.4	3.7	4.1	4.1	4.8	4.8	5.1	5.3	5.5	6.2	6.9
Utah												0.3	0.5	0.5	0.5	0.5	0.5	0.5	0.7	0.7
Vermont	1.9	2.8	3.3	2.3	2.1	1.8	1.3	1.2	1.0	0.6	0.6	0.5	0.5	0.2	0.2	0.2	0.2	0.2	0.2	0.2
Virginia	18.1	15.6	12.7	10.3	8.8	6.7	5.6	4.6	3.1	3.1	2.8	2.6	2.3	2.1	2.1	2.3	2.3	2.3	2.3	2.5
Washington											0.6	0.8	1.1	1.4	1.4	1.6	1.6	1.6	1.8	2.1
West Virginia									1.0	1.2	1.1	1.3	1.4	1.4	1.4	1.4	1.1	0.9	0.9	0.7
Wisconsin							1.3	2.5	2.7	2.8	2.8	2.8	2.5	2.3	2.3	2.3	2.3	2.1	2.1	2.1
Wyoming											0.3	0.3	0.2	0.2	0.2	0.2	0.2	0.2	0.2	0.2
Number of states at peak percentage	9	1	2	2	3	2	1	1	2	4	2	3	5	1	0	0	1	0	5	5
Number of states at lowest percentage	1	0	1	5	1	2	6	2	2	1	3	2	7	3	0	1	1	2	1	6
Total number of states at peak and lowest	10	1	3	7	4	4	7	3	4	5	5	5	12	4	0	1	2	2	6	11

Percent of House Peak Representation ▢ Lowest Representation ▢

Table 1–3. Gain or Loss of Proportional Power for Each State After Each Apportionment

Census Apportionment

States	1790	1800	1810	1820	1830	1840	1850	1860	1870	1880	1890	1900	1910	1930	1940	1950	1960	1970	1980	1990
Alabama				1.4	0.7	1.0	-0.1	-0.5	0.2	-0.2	0.0	-0.2	0.0	-0.2	0.0	0.0	-0.3	-0.2	0.0	0.0
Alaska																	0.2	0.0	0.0	0.0
Arizona													0.2	0.0	0.3	0.0	0.2	0.2	0.2	0.3
Arkansas						0.4	0.5	0.3	0.2	0.1	0.2	0.1	-0.2	0.0	0.0	-0.2	-0.5	0.0	0.0	0.0
California							0.9	0.3	0.2	0.4	0.2	0.1	0.4	2.1	0.7	1.6	1.8	1.2	0.4	1.7
Colorado										0.3	0.3	0.2	0.1	0.0	0.0	0.0	0.0	0.2	0.3	0.0
Connecticut	-1.0	-1.7	-1.1	-1.1	-0.3	-0.7	-0.1	0.0	-0.3	-0.2	-0.1	0.2	-0.2	0.3	0.0	0.0	0.0	0.0	0.0	0.0
Delaware	-0.5	-0.3	0.4	-0.6	-0.1	0.0	0.0	0.0	-0.1	0.0	0.0	0.0	-0.1	0.0	0.0	0.0	0.0	0.0	0.0	0.0
Florida							0.4	0.0	0.3	-0.1	0.0	0.2	0.1	0.2	0.3	0.4	1.0	0.6	1.0	0.9
Georgia	-2.7	0.9	0.5	0.0	0.5	-0.2	-0.2	-0.5	0.2	0.0	0.0	-0.3	0.0	-0.5	0.0	0.0	0.0	0.0	0.0	0.2
Hawaii																	0.5	0.0	0.0	0.0
Idaho											0.3	0.0	0.2	0.0	0.0	0.0	0.0	0.0	0.0	0.0
Illinois				0.5	0.8	1.8	0.7	2.0	0.7	-0.3	0.0	0.3	-0.3	0.0	-0.2	-0.3	-0.2	0.0	-0.4	-0.5
Indiana				1.4	1.5	1.6	0.2	-0.1	-0.1	-0.5	-0.3	-0.3	-0.4	-0.2	-0.3	0.0	0.0	0.0	-0.2	0.0
Iowa							0.9	1.6	0.6	0.3	-0.3	-0.3	-0.3	-0.4	-0.3	0.0	-0.2	-0.2	0.0	-0.3
Kansas								0.4	0.6	1.2	0.0	-0.1	-0.3	-0.2	-0.2	0.0	-0.3	0.0	0.0	-0.2
Kentucky	1.9	2.4	1.2	0.1	-0.2	-0.9	-0.2	-0.6	-0.3	0.0	-0.3	-0.3	-0.3	-0.4	0.0	-0.3	-0.2	0.0	0.0	-0.2
Louisiana				1.4	-0.1	0.5	-0.1	0.4	0.0	-0.3	-0.1	0.1	0.0	0.0	0.0	0.0	0.0	0.0	0.0	-0.2
Maine				-0.6	0.0	-0.2	-0.5	-0.5	-0.4	-0.5	-0.1	-0.1	-0.1	-0.2	0.0	0.0	-0.2	0.0	0.0	0.0
Maryland	-1.6	-1.2	-1.4	-0.8	-0.9	-0.6	-0.1	-0.5	0.0	-0.3	-0.1	-0.1	-0.2	0.0	0.0	0.2	0.2	0.0	0.0	0.0
Massachusetts	1.0	-1.2	-1.1	-1.1	-1.1	-0.5	0.2	-0.6	-0.3	-0.1	0.0	-0.1	0.1	-0.3	-0.2	0.0	-0.4	0.0	-0.3	-0.2
Michigan						1.3	0.4	0.8	0.6	0.3	0.0	-0.3	-0.1	0.9	0.0	0.2	0.3	0.0	-0.3	-0.4
Minnesota								0.8	0.2	0.5	0.5	0.3	0.0	-0.2	0.0	0.0	-0.3	0.0	0.0	0.0
Mississippi				0.5	0.3	1.0	0.3	0.0	0.0	0.1	-0.2	0.1	-0.3	-0.2	0.0	-0.2	-0.3	0.0	0.0	0.0
Missouri				0.5	0.3	1.4	0.8	0.7	0.8	-0.2	-0.1	-0.1	-0.4	-0.7	0.0	-0.5	-0.2	0.0	-0.2	0.0
Montana											0.3	0.0	0.2	0.0	0.0	0.0	0.0	0.0	0.0	-0.3
Nebraska									0.3	0.6	0.8	-0.1	-0.2	-0.3	-0.2	0.0	-0.2	0.0	0.0	0.0

Percentage Change Gain ▢   Loss ▢   No change ▢

Table 1–3. Gain or Loss of Proportional Power for Each State After Each Apportionment *(continued)*

Census Apportionment

States	1790	1800	1810	1820	1830	1840	1850	1860	1870	1880	1890	1900	1910	1930	1940	1950	1960	1970	1980	1990
Nevada									0.3	0.0	0.0	0.0	-0.1	0.0	0.0	0.0	0.0	0.0	0.3	0.0
New Hampshire	-0.8	-0.3	-0.2	-0.5	-0.7	-0.3	-0.5	-0.1	-0.2	-0.4	0.0	-0.1	0.0	0.0	0.0	0.0	0.0	0.0	0.0	0.0
New Jersey	-1.4	-0.5	-1.0	-0.5	-0.3	-0.3	-0.1	0.0	0.3	-0.2	0.0	0.4	0.2	0.4	0.0	0.0	0.2	0.0	-0.2	-0.2
New Mexico													0.2	0.0	0.3	0.0	0.0	0.0	0.2	0.0
New York	0.3	2.6	2.8	1.1	0.7	-1.5	-1.1	-1.2	-1.6	-0.8	-0.9	0.0	0.3	0.4	0.0	-0.4	-0.5	-0.4	-1.2	-0.7
North Carolina	1.8	-1.0	-1.3	-1.1	-0.7	-1.4	-0.6	-0.5	-0.2	0.1	-0.3	0.1	-0.3	0.2	0.3	0.0	-0.3	0.0	0.0	0.3
North Dakota											0.3	0.2	0.2	-0.2	0.0	0.0	0.0	-0.3	0.0	0.0
Ohio			3.3	3.3	1.3	1.5	-0.4	-1.1	-1.1	-0.3	-0.6	-0.5	-0.3	0.4	-0.2	0.0	0.2	-0.2	-0.5	-0.4
Oklahoma													1.8	0.3	-0.3	-0.4	0.0	0.0	0.0	0.0
Oregon								0.4	-0.1	0.0	0.3	-0.1	0.2	0.0	0.2	0.0	0.0	0.0	0.2	0.0
Pennsylvania	0.1	0.4	-0.1	-0.5	-0.5	-0.9	-0.1	-0.7	-0.8	-0.6	-0.2	-0.1	0.0	-0.5	-0.2	-0.7	-0.7	-0.5	-0.4	-0.5
Rhode Island	0.4	-0.5	-0.3	-0.2	-0.1	0.1	0.0	-0.1	-0.1	-0.1	0.0	-0.1	0.2	-0.2	0.0	0.0	0.0	0.0	0.0	0.0
South Carolina	-2.0	0.0	-0.7	-0.8	-0.4	-0.7	-0.5	-0.9	0.0	0.5	-0.2	-0.2	-0.2	-0.2	0.0	0.0	0.0	0.0	0.0	0.0
South Dakota											0.6	-0.1	0.2	-0.2	0.0	0.0	0.0	0.0	-0.3	0.0
Tennessee		2.1	1.2	0.9	1.2	-0.5	-0.6	-1.0	0.1	-0.3	-0.3	-0.2	-0.3	-0.2	0.2	-0.2	0.0	-0.3	0.3	0.0
Texas							0.9	0.8	0.4	1.3	0.3	0.4	0.0	0.7	0.0	0.3	0.2	0.2	0.7	0.7
Utah												0.3	0.2	0.0	0.0	0.0	0.0	0.0	0.2	0.0
Vermont	1.9	0.9	0.5	-1.0	-0.2	-0.3	-0.5	-0.1	-0.2	-0.4	0.0	-0.1	0.0	-0.3	0.0	0.0	0.0	0.0	0.0	0.0
Virginia	2.7	-2.5	-2.9	-2.4	-1.5	-2.1	-1.1	-1.0	-0.2	0.0	-0.3	-0.2	-0.3	-0.2	0.0	0.2	0.0	0.0	0.0	0.2
Washington											0.6	0.2	0.3	0.3	0.0	0.2	0.0	0.0	0.2	0.3
West Virginia									-0.3	0.2	-0.1	0.2	0.1	0.0	0.0	0.0	-0.3	-0.2	0.0	-0.2
Wisconsin							1.3	1.2	0.2	0.1	0.0	0.0	-0.3	-0.2	0.0	0.0	0.0	-0.2	0.0	0.0
Wyoming											0.3	0.0	-0.1	0.0	0.0	0.0	0.0	0.0	0.0	0.0
Number of states increasing	8	6	7	10	9	10	12	12	17	14	13	16	18	11	7	7	10	5	11	8
Number of states decreasing	7	9	10	13	14	15	17	17	16	18	17	22	22	21	9	9	16	9	10	13
Number of states with no change		1		1	1	1	2	5	4	6	14	7	8	16	32	32	24	36	29	29

Percentage Change Gain ▢ Loss ▢ No change ▢

decade. The rows across for each state indicate patterns of change in each state's history. For example, California is colored blue for all its history, indicating continual relative increases; New Hampshire is colored orange for a long period of decline before stabilizing, and Alabama is colored blue and orange for many changes in direction.

Table 1-4 gives the number and percentage of seats shifted at each apportionment since the House size was fixed at 435. The greatest interstate shift in power in the modern era occurred in the 1930 apportionment. In 1930 twenty-one states lost one or more seats, eleven gained seats, and sixteen had no change. There was a net interstate transfer of twenty-seven seats, 6.2 percent of the House. This large interstate shift occurred in 1930 because 1920 was the only time in U.S. history in which there was not a decennial census reapportionment; therefore, the 1930 allocations represented two decades of population change (see the case study on rural and urban places and the 1920 nonapportionment in Part 3).

Table 1-4. Interstate Transfer of House Seats, 1930–1990

	1930	1940	1950	1960	1970	1980	1990
Number of states losing seats	21	9	9	16	9	10	13
Number of states gaining seats	11	7	7	10	5	11	8
Number of states with no change in seats	16	32	32	24	36	29	29
Number of seats shifted	27	9	14	21	11	17	19
Percentage of House shifted	6.2%	2.1%	3.2%	4.8%	2.5%	3.9%	4.4%

Senate

Article I, Section 3, of the Constitution creates the Senate of the United States. The framers intended the Senate to be the legislative chamber representing state interests in the federal government. The size of the Senate is fixed—each state receiving two seats irrespective of population. In the original Constitution, senators were elected every six years by the state legislatures. In 1912 the Seventeenth Amendment to the Constitution changed the method of electing senators to today's practice of general election by all qualified voters.

Representative power in the Senate, then, is significantly malapportioned—that is, the state with the smallest population has as much power as the state with the largest population. For example, the 1990 census reported that California had a population of approximately 29,760,000 and Wyoming had 454,000, but both states have two senators. The framers accepted this distribution of power in the Senate as part of the Connecticut or Great Compromise in order to ratify the Constitution and to establish a relatively strong central government.

Presidential Elections

Decennial apportionment has an additional significance since it also affects the election of the president of the United States. Article II of the Constitution establishes and defines the executive branch and outlines how the chief executive, the president, shall be elected. Article II, Section 1, outlines a method of indirect presidential selection by way of "electors" chosen from each state. By the middle of the 1800s virtually all the states selected their presidential electors by the ballot of qualified voters. The majority or plurality winner of the state general election for president usually wins the entire number of presidential electors.[10] When the electors from each state meet, the majority of all the states' presidential electors legally elect the president.[11] The combined membership of electors from all the states has been given the name electoral college.[12] Article II, Section 1, of the Constitution states the number of electors from each state is ". . . equal to the whole Number of Senators and Representatives to which each State may be entitled in the Congress. . . ." Since the Senate is quite malapportioned with respect to population, the electoral college is somewhat malapportioned. Nevertheless, the larger a state or regional delegation in the House of Representatives, the larger its role in electing the president.[13] For example, since 1964 the size of the electoral college has been 538, allocated for the 435 House members,

10. States have the option of allocating electoral votes in different ways, for example: (1) by winner take all; (2) proportionally; and (3) by winner of each congressional district, with the two electors for the senators going to the individual winning the state. Today, some states are considering alternative methods other than the winner-take-all option. For example, in the 1992 presidential election Maine and Nebraska used method three.

11. This point was clarified by the Twelfth Amendment.

12. Wallace S. Sayre and Judith H. Parris, *Voting for President: The Electoral College and the American Political System* (Washington, D.C.: Brookings Institution, 1970).

13. Indeed, the larger a state's delegation in the House of Representatives, the larger the state's role in nominating presidential candidates since participation in political parties' quadrennial presidential nominating conventions is roughly based on state population.

100 senators, and 3 additional electors given to the District of Columbia. To win the presidency an individual must attain at least 270 electoral college votes. The 1990 census apportioned 52 House seats to the state of California. California, then, has 54 electors in the electoral college, 20 percent of all the votes needed to elect the president. This is the largest number of House seats and electoral college members in U.S. history.[14] As states and regions increase or decrease in House membership their relative power in both the House and presidential elections also increases or decreases. The maps in this atlas, while specifically illustrating changing state and regional power in the House of Representatives, also reflect changing state and regional power in electing the president.

Federal Apportionment Law

The Constitution stipulates that seats in the House of Representatives be divided among the states according to population after each decennial census. However, Congress is given the power to determine the final size of the House and the specific formula of apportioning these seats to the states. The result has been a series of laws, which historically have been included in apportionment acts passed after each decennial census. These laws, listed in Table 1-5, have been the statutes implementing the changing state and regional power in the United States.

Changes in the Size of the House of Representatives

During the Constitutional Convention in 1787, the size of the House of Representatives was hotly debated. The Anti-Federalists desired a large number of representatives so members would come from small districts and thereby be close to the people. The Anti-Federalists also believed a large House would prevent possible corruption and dominance of the federal government by a small band of elite politicians. The Federalists, on the other hand, argued that a smaller House would run more efficiently and that the new system of constitutional checks and balances effectively dispersed political power.[15] In the end, Article I, Section 2, of the Constitution distributed sixty-five representative seats among the thirteen original states, a smaller size than the Anti-Federalists desired. Article I also directed that an actual count of the population be conducted within three years for a more definitive apportionment of representa-

Table 1–5. Summary of Major Federal Apportionment Laws

Apportionment Law	United States Statutes at-Large Citation	Size of House Specified	Method of Apportionment
April 14, 1792	1 Stat. 253	105	Fixed ratio with rejected fractions
January 14, 1802	2 Stat. 128	141	Fixed ratio with rejected fractions
December 21, 1811	2 Stat. 669	181	Fixed ratio with rejected fractions
March 7, 1822	3 Stat. 651	213	Fixed ratio with rejected fractions
May 22, 1832	4 Stat. 516	240	Fixed ratio with rejected fractions
June 25, 1842	5 Stat. 491	223	Fixed ratio with major fractions
May 23, 1850	9 Stat. 428	233	Vinton method
July 30, 1852	10 Stat. 25	234	Vinton method
March 4, 1862	12 Stat. 353	241	Vinton method
July 14, 1862	12 Stat. 572		Vinton method
February 2, 1872	17 Stat. 28	283	Vinton method
May 30, 1872	17 Stat. 192	292	Vinton method
February 25, 1882	22 Stat. 5	325	Vinton method
February 7, 1891	25 Stat. 735	356	Vinton method
January 16, 1901	31 Stat. 733	386	Vinton method
August 8, 1911	37 Stat. 13	435[a]	Major fractions
June 18, 1929	46 Stat. 21		Major fractions
April 25, 1940	54 Stat. 162		Major fractions
November 15, 1941	55 Stat. 761		Equal proportions

[a]*The apportionment law stipulated 433 seats with a provision that allowed Arizona and New Mexico one seat each if they became states before the next apportionment.*

14. Although this is the greatest number of seats it is still not the greatest proportion of seats in American history (see Table 1-2).

15. Bruce A. Ragsdale, ed., *Origins of the House of Representatives: A Documentary Record* (Washington, D.C.: Government Printing Office, 1990), 83–106.

tives. The first census was taken in 1790 and one has been taken every ten years as stipulated in the Constitution.

The House of Representatives during the First Congress (1789–1791) had the constituted sixty-five seats. During the Second Congress, the House (1791–1793) had four additional seats after the states of Vermont and Kentucky were admitted to the Union and allotted two representatives each by Congress. After the results of the first census were tabulated, Congress debated the first apportionment law. Again, the size of the House was central to the discussion.[16] The specifics of the debate centered on the so-called ratio of representation. The Constitution specified that "the Number of Representatives shall not exceed one for every thirty Thousand, but each State shall have at Least one Representative. . . ." Those arguing for a large House size wanted the smallest possible ratio, 30,000 to 1; those arguing for a smaller House wanted a larger ratio. The debate once again pitted Anti-Federalist philosophy against Federalist. Those arguing for a large House size suggested that representative democracy could only exist where those elected had an intimate knowledge of those represented. A large House would "secure the liberties" of the common people so hard fought for in the American Revolution. An extensive Republic, with such a large diversity of physical and human geography, needed a large number of representatives to speak for these various interests.[17] Those arguing for a smaller House suggested that too many members would make the House unwieldy, hindering the conduct of legislation and unnecessarily increasing the cost and size of government.

This philosophical aspect of the debate was eventually overshadowed by the perceived distribution of state power in Congress. The smaller, less populous states perceived a greater and greater loss of power as the House grew larger. The small states realized this loss of power was due to their small fixed geographical area and, more importantly, the resultant lack of potential for future population expansion and growth. These states usually had the most to lose, especially with the method of apportionment that divided the population of each state by a fixed ratio and rejected any remaining fraction. Indeed, many members of Congress argued against the fairness of this apportionment formula itself, irrespective of philosophical or state power arguments. The amount of lost representation under the rejected fractions method for the small states was usually proportionately much greater than the loss for large, more popu-lous states.[18] The core of the small-state coalition was made up of New Jersey, Connecticut, Rhode Island, and New Hampshire. The core of the large-state coalition was Pennsylvania, Georgia, North Carolina, New York, South Carolina, and Virginia.[19] While the tendency was for small states to have a large rejected fraction, all states examined different pos-sible ratios to maximize the greatest assignment of representatives and minimize their rejected fraction. Thus, the struggle between states with big populations and those with small populations, and between states with large rejected fractions and those with small rejected fractions un-derlined the entire debate.[20]

After lengthy debate on apportionment ratio and resultant House size, eighteen major roll-call votes, and a presidential veto, Congress fi-nally passed the first apportionment law on April 14, 1792.[21] This law simply set the ratio of representation of 33,000 to 1 "computed accord-ing to the rule prescribed in the Constitution. . . " (interpreted as fixed ratio with rejected fractions) and gave the specific numbers of represen-tatives for each state. A ratio of 33,000 to 1 was agreed to because of the insistence of the Senate, where the small, less populous states had pro-portionally more power. This ratio still significantly increased the size of the House to 105 members.[22] Ironically, one consequence of the in-

16. *The Debates and Proceedings of the Congress of the United States, Second Congress: October 24, 1791 to March 2, 1793* (Washington, D.C.: Gales and Seaton, 1849), 150–1360.

17. Rosemarie Zagarri, *The Politics of Size* (Ithaca, N.Y.: Cornell University Press, 1987), 84–94.

18. One example of the small-state problem in the first apportionment is Delaware. Delaware's apportionment population was 55,540. Under the 33,000-to-1 ratio, Delaware would be assigned one representative and have a rejected fraction of 22,540 "unrepresented" individuals. Since a ratio of 30,000 to 1 would not change the final apportionment results, Delaware was not consistent in supporting its fellow small states in voting on congressional apportionment. Rudolf M. Bell, *Party and Faction in American Politics: The House of Representatives, 1789–1801* (Westport, Conn.: Greenwood Press, 1973), 276, n24.

19. Zagarri, *Politics,* 158.

20. Ibid., 134–140.

21. The first presidential veto in U.S. history was against an apportionment bill sent to President George Washington in March 1792. From the very first census the size of the House, representation ratio, and apportionment formula were significant issues. Congres-sional Quarterly, *Guide to U.S. Elections* (Washington, D.C.: Congressional Quarterly, 1985), 685.

22. One additional member to the House was added when Tennessee was admitted to the Union during the Fourth Congress (1795–1797). Because no additional state was admit-ted during the remainder of the decade, the size of the House remained at 106 members until after the second census in 1800. Throughout congressional history the size of the House increased as new states were admitted between decennial apportionments. States were usually admitted with one representative, and this number remained until the next

creased size of the House was to ensure that virtually all states, whether large or small, retained at least the same number of seats or even increased the number of representatives, even though their proportion of the population was found to be less than originally allocated in the Constitution.[23] The new size and accompanying apportionment went into effect for the elections to the Third (1793–1795) through Seventh (1801–1803) Congresses. Maps 1A and 1B (see p. 37) indicate the actual and relative change of state power in the House from the Constitution distribution to the first census apportionment (see Part 2 for detailed discussion of this and all other apportionments).[24] The second federal apportionment bill was approved January 14, 1802, and was effective for the elections for the Eighth (1803–1805) through Twelfth (1811–1813) Congresses. Congress settled on the same representation ratio of 33,000 to 1; however, since the population of the United States had grown, the size of the House of Representatives significantly increased to 141 members. Again, this ratio and increased size ensured that most states would at least retain the same number of representatives even though their proportion of the population decreased from the first census. Once more, much of the congressional debate centered around the small-state versus large-state struggle. Indeed, these intersectional state coalitions based on population size held up during subsequent reapportionments through the 1840s and possibly until 1850.[25] By the 1840s and 1850s, the North-South sectional conflict began to play a larger role in apportionment battles. However, it should be noted again that all states, irrespective of size or section of the country, examined the possible representation ratios after each decennial census in order to maximize their position.

Specific apportionment laws were also passed in 1811 (35,000 to 1), 1822 (40,000 to 1), and 1832 (47,700 to 1) increasing the size of the House to 181, 213, and 240 seats, respectively. The very specific ratio of 47,700 to 1 in 1832 indicates how carefully each state examined the ratio of representation to maximize state power. Coalitions of states had to be put together in both the House and Senate to pass these specific apportionment bills.

The apportionment population of the United States at the first census was 3,615,920 and after the 1830 census was 11,928,731.[26] The 1840 census showed another large increase with the population reaching 15,908,376. The debate over apportionment after the 1840 census again centered on the eventual size of the House. This debate brought out once more the political, philosophical, and small-state versus large-state arguments mentioned above. In addition to each state examining its particular situation of rejected fractions and the ratio of representation, regional groupings, such as New England and the original thirteen states, also analyzed their gains and losses. Of course, the inevitable North-South—that is, free versus slave—sectional group ratios were also calculated (see the case study on free and slave states in Part 3). However, the House was now so large that there was serious concern about its ability to conduct business. In the end, the 1842 apportionment law fixed the very specific ratio of representation of 70,680 to 1, a ratio much higher than in previous laws. The result was the first reduction in House size in U.S. history, from 240 to 223 members.

In 1850 the apportionment rules were integrated into the enabling law for the 1850 census, and for the first time a separate postcensus apportionment law was not used. This integration was partially instituted to stop the haggling over the distribution of seats and power after the census. Rather than fixing a ratio of representation, the 1850 act fixed the size of the House at 233 members, the very same size calculated by the ratio of representation after the 1840 census.[27] The 1860s apportionment was also based on the general 1850 census law and, therefore, continued to fix the size of the House at 233 members. However, after the

---

apportionment. Several states were admitted with two representatives (California, Iowa, Minnesota, South Dakota, Texas, and Wisconsin) and Oklahoma with five. Maine was admitted with seven representatives and West Virginia with three, but these were taken from the states from which they were created, Massachusetts and Virginia, respectively (see Table 1-1). The only variance from this regular admittance/apportionment process was when California was given one additional representative for the Thirty-seventh Congress (1861–1863).

23. In spite of the large increase in the size of the House, Georgia still lost one seat (see Maps 1A and 1B).

24. As explained above, in the era of changing size of the House, 1790–1910, two apportionment maps must be displayed, one illustrating gain and losses of seats, and one illustrating gains and losses in power (see maps and apportionment tables covering 1790–1910).

25. Zagarri, *Politics*, 142–144.

26. The "apportionment population" is different than the "total population" for the period 1790–1860. During this period the Constitution mandated that the slave population of each state be counted as three-fifths and added to the free population to obtain the apportionment population. Since the 1870 census the total population of the state is the number used to calculate apportionment. For tables enumerating the apportionment population of the slave states and free states from 1790–1860, see Lawrence F. Schmeckebier, *Congressional Apportionment* (Washington, D.C.: Brookings Institution, 1941), 227–228.

27. After the census, Congress passed a supplemental bill increasing the size of the House to 234 to ensure that California did not lose a seat due to incomplete census returns.

census a supplemental bill was passed giving eight additional seats to eight northern states.

After the 1870 census, Congress began to pass specific apportionment acts again, and the size of the House began to increase once more. The 1872 apportionment law originally provided for a House of 283 members, but membership was later increased to 292 by a supplemental law. Specific apportionment laws were also passed in 1882, 1891, 1901, and 1911, increasing the House total to 325, 356, 386, and 433 (with a planned adjustment to 435), respectively. These increases ensured that virtually no state lost actual seats during the 1870–1910 period (see Maps 9A–13A, pp. 69–85). The decennial debate over the size of the House continued to bring up most of the same issues as had been discussed since 1790. The House membership was increased each time under the powerful pressure of states and individual incumbents who faced possible defeat at the polls if the House was reduced in size or even kept at the same size.

The decade of the 1920s is the only time in U.S. history when seats in the House of Representatives were not redistributed among the states after the population census (see the case study on rural and urban places and the 1920 nonapportionment in Part 3). Numerous apportionment laws were brought before Congress during the 1920s, but all failed to pass both the House and Senate. Many of these proposals included provisions to increase the size of the House further. The 1920 census reflected the continued rapid growth of American cities caused by immigration from abroad and from rural areas. States that were to lose House seats, led by rural representatives, delayed House reapportionment legislation for almost a decade.[28] In effect, the 1920s were the first time that, contrary to the intention of the framers of the Constitution, changes in population did not cause changes in state power in the House.[29]

The inability of Congress to pass a reapportionment law was widely seen at the time as not only unconstitutional, but undemocratic.[30] Reformers, led by urban representatives, began a movement to make the next and succeeding apportionments again automatic (as in 1850 and 1860) by inclusion in the census law. Automatic reapportionment was included in a 1929 law enabling the 1930 census. This law required the director of the census to submit to the Congress, by way of the president, population data and the appropriate reapportionment figures after each decennial census. This law also stated that the size of the House should be fixed at 435 members, the number determined after the 1910 apportionment. The House of Representatives has had 435 members since the 1912 election of the Sixty-eighth Congress (1913–1915), except for a brief period during the Eighty-sixth (1959–1961) and the entire Eighty-seventh (1961–1963) Congresses when the number was temporarily increased to 437 with the admission of Alaska and Hawaii.

Apportionment Formulas

As discussed above, the Constitution directs that the membership in the House of Representatives be apportioned among the states according to population. However, the specific method of apportionment is determined by Congress. There are several statistical methods and mathematical formulas capable of dividing a certain number of states, each with a certain number of citizens, by a certain number of seats. Ideally, the most unbiased and mathematically sound method should be used in dividing representation among the states. However, each method has its strengths and weaknesses, and perhaps more importantly for political purposes, each has the possibility of apportioning a different number of seats to the same state.[31] Five methods of House apportionment have been used in U.S. history:

1. The fixed ratio with rejected fractions (1792, 1802, 1811, 1822, and 1832) produced considerable inequality in representation for states with large rejected fractions.

2. The fixed ratio with major fractions (1842) divided the population of each state by a fixed ratio and then allotted an additional representative for each fraction over one-half.

28. Charles W. Eagles, *Congressional Reapportionment and Urban-Rural Conflict in the 1920s* (Athens: University of Georgia Press, 1990).

29. Additionally, most state legislatures, without the motivation of an apportionment law, did not change the congressional districts within their states according to changing population patterns.

30. Eagles, *Conflict,* 151–155.

31. Schmeckebier, *Apportionment,* 109–110. See Table 1-5 for all the dates and legal citations for the federal apportionment and congressional electoral procedure laws. U.S. Congress, Committee on Commerce, Apportionment of Representatives in Congress, Hearings, before a subcommittee of the Committee on Commerce, Senate on H.R. 2665, *An Act to Provide for Apportioning Representatives in Congress Among the Several States by the Equal Proportions Method,* 77th Cong., 1st sess., 1941, 107–126.

3. The Vinton method (1850, 1860, 1872, 1882, 1891, 1901)—named after Rep. Samuel F. Vinton of Ohio—first fixed the size of the House and then determined the ideal ratio of representation. This ratio was then divided into the population of each state. States having the highest leftover fractions were assigned representatives in order until the predetermined size of the House was reached.

4. The major fractions method (1911 and 1929) was based on the Vinton method with the use of additional calculations and a ranking system to make the distribution fairer.

5. The equal proportions method (1941 to the present) involved more sophisticated mathematical formulas designed to make the proportional differences in the average district in any two states as small as possible.[32]

The apportionments for the 1930s and 1940s illustrate how different formulas can produce a different result. The general 1929 apportionment law included in the 1930 census enabling act specified that apportionment should be calculated by two methods, major fractions and equal proportions. With the 1930 census data, the two apportionment formulas produced exactly the same result. However, in 1940 the two methods apportioned a different number of representatives to two states. Under the major fractions formula, Michigan would have gained one seat and Arkansas lost one seat. Under the equal proportions formula, both states retained the previous number of representatives. Since Arkansas was a solidly Democratic state and Michigan historically a Republican state, the Democratic-controlled Congress directed that the equal proportions results be used and later permanently adopted this formula, which is still in use today.

Apportionment Within the States

Establishing Single-Member Districts

The first five federal apportionment laws (1792–1832) simply contained the ratio of representation and the resultant number of representatives for each state. The Constitution spells out how senators should be elected but not how representatives should be. After apportionment, the job of actually developing the electoral procedures for U.S. representatives was left up to each state legislature. Although the framers intended the states to divide into districts in proportion to population, just as the Constitution divided House membership proportionally, several different electoral methods emerged in the states. Four electoral and representative forms were used in different states for House elections in the early decades of congressional history:

1. The single-member district method elected one representative from each geographically defined House district.

2. The general ticket method, used from 1789–1971, elected the entire state delegation by statewide voting for all candidates.

3. The plural district method, used from 1793–1843, elected two, three, or four representatives from one geographically defined district.

4. The at-large method, used from 1853–1967, elected the majority of the state delegation from single-member districts and one or more additional representatives (the at-large members) in statewide voting.[33]

To achieve the intentions of the framers, electoral equity, and a systematic form of representation, Congress passed a series of provisions throughout U.S. history, mostly included in apportionment laws, mandating electoral procedures for representatives.

The first concern was the election of representatives by single-member geographically defined districts. After several unsuccessful attempts in the early nineteenth century to institute districts in all states, the apportionment act of June 25, 1842, finally included the mandate that representatives be ". . . elected by districts composed of contiguous territory equal in number to the representatives to which said state may be entitled. . . ." Although this provision was only in effect until the next apportionment, this act began the legal precedent that codified the geographically defined single-member district as part of the American political system. The last in this series of laws mandating districts was passed December 14, 1967, and remains in effect today. The last Congress to elect representatives by plural district was the Twenty-seventh Congress (1841–1843), the last at-large representatives were elected to the Eighty-ninth Congress (1965–1967), and the last state to elect its entire delegation statewide by general ticket was Hawaii for the Ninety-first Congress (1969–1971).

32. Schmeckebier, *Apportionment,* 107–126; Congressional Quarterly, *Guide to Congress* (Washington, D.C.: Congressional Quarterly, 1991), 739–745.

33. Kenneth C. Martis, *The Historical Atlas of United States Congressional Districts: 1789–1983* (New York: Free Press, 1982), 2–5.

Drawing District Boundaries

Congress has established the single-member geographically defined congressional district as the desired form of representation. Since the very first law mandating districts, Congress has given directives to the states with respect to the drawing of district boundaries. The 1842 apportionment law not only mandated single-member districts, but also stated that these districts must be "contiguous." This eliminated, temporarily, the practice of creating districts with geographically separated portions.[34] The 1872 apportionment law was the first to require that each district within a state should contain ". . . as nearly as practicable an equal number of inhabitants. . . ." This law also set the first Tuesday in November as a national election date for the president and representatives, a practice generally followed since 1876. The 1901 apportionment law added the words "compact territory" to "contiguous" to describe how the congressional districts should be drawn. This addressed the practice of gerrymandering, which is the drawing of congressional districts to favor the party or group in power, often using odd or peculiar shapes.[35] In spite of the past good intentions of Congress, neither the currently standing 1929 apportionment law nor its amendments address the question of gerrymandering congressional district boundaries. Hence, congressional redistricting since the 1930s contains numerous examples of gerrymandered and even split districts.

Although the actual state delegation size and electoral procedures are mandated by the federal government, it is usually the legislatures of the states that finally define and draw congressional district boundaries. State legislators have been the political cartographers of U.S. history.[36] After each decennial national apportionment, each state having more than one representative is confronted with the congressional redistricting question. As discussed above, past electoral provisions allowed the states to fulfill their reapportionment in a variety of ways. Table 1-6 outlines the situations states confronted and possible courses of action prior to the 1960s.

After the 1929 general apportionment law was enacted, congressional directives for contiguous, compact, and equal population districts were no longer in effect. If a state lost one or more House seats, the legislature usually was forced to redistrict, although the general-ticket election was sometimes used for an election or two. If a state retained the same num-

Table 1–6. Apportionment Changes and State Options Before the 1960s

Decrease in number of House seats:
      1. Elect entire delegation by general ticket
      2. Redistrict

No change in number of House seats:
      1. Retain the same districts
      2. Redistrict

Increase in number of House seats:
      1. Retain the same districts and elect additional members at-large
      2. Redistrict
      3. Elect entire delegation by general ticket

ber of seats, even for a long period of time, the legislature often did not redistrict, especially if the same party retained power and the incumbents wished to keep the same district boundaries. The longest example of this in American history is the New Hampshire congressional district law of February 19, 1881, which remained in effect until court-mandated redistricting on July 3, 1969.[37] Even if a state gained in House seats, legislatures could still avoid redistricting by electing the additional representative(s) at-large.

The failure to redistrict over a long period of time can cause malapportionment—that is, districts being substantially unequal in population. State legislatures sometimes ignored census data and intentionally created malapportioned districts. Historically, malapportionment and the gerrymander were practiced hand in hand to give the greatest possible partisan advantage to the state legislators in power. In the 1960s two events occurred that changed congressional redistricting practices. In 1964 the Supreme Court, in *Wesberry v. Sanders,* applied the "one-person, one-vote" principle to congressional districts, effectively eliminating

34. See, for example, the map for the Eighth Congress (1803–1805), eleventh district of New York, in Martis, *Atlas of Districts,* 57.

35. Kenneth C. Martis, "gerrymandering," in *Encyclopedia of Congress* (New York: Simon & Schuster, 1993).

36. For virtually all of U.S. history, it has been the duty of the state legislators to debate, draft, and pass the statutes legally defining congressional districts. In 1973, the state of Montana established a commission to prepare redistricting plans. This is the first significant variation from the state legislative redistricting system. Common Cause, *Toward a System of "Fair and Effective Representation"* (Washington, D.C.: Common Cause, 1977), 106. Since the 1970s, several other states have implemented various forms of nonpartisan or bipartisan redistricting commissions.

37. Martis, *Atlas of Districts,* 8–9, 246–247.

quantitative population malapportionment.[38] In 1967 Congress passed a law mandating that all representatives be elected by districts. This law and the *Wesberry v. Sanders* ruling effectively require state legislatures to redraw congressional districts after every apportionment based on internal population changes even if the state retains the same number of representatives.

After the question of malapportionment was settled in the 1960s, gerrymandering became a prime target of redistricting reform. In the 1970s the Supreme Court ruled racial gerrymandering unconstitutional. In the 1980s the Supreme Court took a legally significant step with respect to congressional redistricting by ruling that intentional partisan gerrymandering is subject to judicial review.[39]

A new set of questions with respect to gerrymandering, however, arose in the 1990s. Congressional redistricting after the 1990 census was substantially affected by a 1982 amendment to the Voting Rights Act mandating the drawing of "minority-majority districts." This law requires the drawing of House districts in which minority groups, African-Americans and/or Hispanics, constitute the majority of the population. These districts would then have an opportunity to elect minority representatives. The drawing of these districts, however, has resulted in the most elongated, convoluted, circuitous, and oddly shaped districts in U.S. history.[40] These districts, as the racial and partisan gerrymandered districts of the past, call into question the meaning of representation in a democratic society and the role of single-member geographic districts in achieving democratic representation. The United States is now in an era of evolving standards of how congressional districts should be drawn and the provision of an equitable distribution of power in the House of Representatives.

38. Gordon E. Baker, *The Reapportionment Revolution* (New York: Random House, 1966), 14–22.

39. Chandler Davidson, ed., *Minority Vote Dilution* (Washington, D.C.: Howard University Press, 1984) and Bernard Grofman, ed., *Political Gerrymandering and the Courts* (New York: Agathon Press, 1990).

40. "Advantage Shifts to G.O.P. in 1992 Redistricting Battle," *New York Times*, December 30, 1991, A1, A11; *CQ's Guide to 1990 Congressional Redistricting* (Washington, D.C.: Congressional Quarterly, 1993).

Part 2

Congressional Apportionment by Decade

Introduction

Analysis of Decennial Changes

A representative democracy has the responsibility to enfranchise its citizens so that they are as equal as possible in their vote and voice, given the constraints of the population size, its geographical distribution, and the size of the elected legislature. One of the most contentious issues at the Constitutional Convention of 1787 in Philadelphia was how states were to be represented in a national government (see Part 1). From the debate emerged two compromises directly affecting the calculation, duration, and the distribution of representation in the new U.S. Congress. The Great Compromise resolved the tensions pertaining to democratic representation that arose between the large populous states, such as Virginia, and small populous states, such as New Jersey. The more nationalistic components of the Virginia Plan proposed a democratically elected lower house with delegations based on state population. An upper house would be elected by the lower. Conversely the New Jersey Plan proposed equality among the states so as to preserve their identity and political power. The resulting compromise created a bicameral national legislature, comprising an upper chamber, the Senate, with equal membership from the states, and a lower chamber, the House of Representatives, with membership proportional to population size.

A second compromise of the Philadelphia convention centered on the fundamental basis for enumeration, the issue of counting free and enslaved people. Profound differences existed between the regional factions on the definition of the individual for census purposes. As a significant portion of the South's population consisted of slaves, the southerners were anxious to have slaves enumerated fully for the purpose of representation in the House. Certain direct federal taxes, however, were levied according to population size, and counting slaves as persons in this case would have been detrimental to the southern states. Eventually the slave states compromised with the northern free states whereby slaves were counted as three-fifths of a person.[1] While the issue of slavery has been settled for more than a century, other issues of equal representation persist due to the problems of enumerating fully the population of the United States. Although mandated by the Constitution, this task is considered by many to be impossible, and unnecessary by others given the accuracy of statistical sampling.

This part of the atlas examines the two hundred years of reapportionment history decade by decade. The analysis of the redistribution of political representation in the diverse and expanding United States begins with an understanding of the size and distribution of the population. Thus each of the following decennial sections starts with census statistics and highlights. The census is the driving force of reapportionment. But as a human institution, census taking has always been subject to error, mismanagement, and criticism, no more so with the first census of 1790 than with the twenty-first census of 1990. A final section on the discussion of the 1990 census emphasizes the consequences of enumeration of a plural society in a continental-sized nation.

The census figures establish the demographic basis for reallocation. Each decennial analysis then reviews the passage of the apportionment law and how it translated the census numbers into delegation size. Considerable debate occurred in Congress after each new census until the mid-twentieth century when a politically acceptable formula was adopted to minimize the rancor over apportionment law. Despite six decades of automatic redistribution of House districts, contentious political feeling over the number and distribution of seats has been the norm and may reemerge as an issue of debate in response to the changing geography of population.

The geographical trends of apportionment are analyzed using an array of maps and tables that form the reference of this work. To the extent possible each decade is treated independently, but human events in time and in space do not lend themselves to natural partitions of ten years. The analytical emphasis is geographical in the sense of accounting for population distributions over the country, but a full accounting of the integration and diversity of the forces of political, social, and economic geography requires deeper and more subtle explanations than are feasible within the scope of this atlas.

Each apportionment from 1790 to 1910 is presented in two maps; the first map illustrates the changes in seats between the apportionment and the preceding one; the second map illustrates the percentage change in House power. The changing size of the House requires that maps and tables of actual change be interpreted with care as the power of any state's delegation is measured with respect to the size of all the others. Therefore, maps and tables of relative change record the increase or decrease in political representation expressed as a proportion of the whole, regardless of size. Some geographical patterns conform to established historical explanations such as the western expansion, the conflict over slavery, and the migration to the Sunbelt. These important trends are given a separate emphasis through tables with appropriate regional groupings (see the full discussion of each of these major trends in the case studies in Part 3). After the House size was fixed for the 1930 apportionment, the actual change in seats is sufficient for analysis and only one map is presented for each decade.

The final section of each decennial analysis describes some of the underlying forces and processes that give rise to the demographic changes that themselves are translated to political representation. Trends are addressed in the social, political, and economic sweep of affairs and are discussed as to their influence on the variations in the maps. Again a caveat is necessary that a complete explanation of social and political relations is not the focus of the work and only the most significant processes behind these maps can be addressed. The statewide level of the maps limits the information content and care must be taken not to overinterpret the patterns, particularly on maps of relative change. Sufficient references are provided to enable the reader to follow specific aspects in greater depth. Each decade analysis stands alone but will benefit from an understanding of previous and succeeding apportionments given the persistent nature of many social and economic processes. The concluding section to Part 2 briefly speculates on the reapportionment in the year 2000.

1. U.S. Constitution, Article I, Section 2.

1790 CENSUS APPORTIONMENT

In accordance with Article I, Section 2, of the Constitution, the first U.S. census law was signed on March 1, 1790, to enumerate the population in order to allocate members to the House of Representatives. The census, begun in 1790, was completed in eighteen months under difficult conditions, producing results that foreshadowed the difficulties of counting the population that would be experienced persistently in subsequent decades. Census assistants, under the authority of U.S. marshals, sought answers to six questions relating to population size, sex, age, and the free or enslaved status of individuals. Transportation was difficult, census geography uncertain at best, and the widely dispersed population was distrustful of the agents of central authority. The census recorded a population of 3,929,214 Americans, somewhat fewer than the four million that the public had been led to expect. Errors of overestimation and omission in the initial enumeration were compounded by arithmetic mistakes when the apportionment populations were calculated.[2]

The first apportionment act prescribed a ratio of one House representative for every 33,000 persons on the basis of figures reported by Thomas Jefferson, then secretary of state. It was passed only after the first apportionment bill had been vetoed by President George Washington on the grounds that the allotment of representatives was not based on a single proportion, and also that the number of representatives exceeded one for every 30,000 in eight states (which was contrary to the Constitution).[3] Using the fixed ratio with rejected fractions method of calculation and a proportion of 1:33,000, the House of Representatives increased from the sixty-five members of the constitutional apportionment to one hundred and five members. As projected under the Virginia Plan, the states with the largest populations received the greatest number of members. Virginia added nine representatives, Massachusetts gained six, North Carolina and Pennsylvania each added five, and New York received four additional seats. Because its constitutional population had been overestimated, Georgia lost a seat under the 1790 census figures, the only state to do so. Early concerns, expressed during the Constitutional Convention, that the disparity between state population sizes would result in a federation dominated by its largest members were allayed to the extent that the three largest delegations, Virginia, Massachusetts, and Pennsylvania, accounted for a minority of forty-six seats (43 percent of the House) to fifty-nine seats for the other thirteen states (57 percent). Thus the House could not be dictated to on issues related to population size alone. The disparity between Virginia, the largest state with nineteen members, and Delaware, the smallest with one, produced a spread somewhat larger than had been foreseen during the debate leading to the Great Compromise. The two new states admitted to the Union in this period—Vermont on March 4, 1791, and Kentucky on June 1, 1792—were each allotted two members as provided for under the apportionment act.[4]

The relative changes in states' power, depicted in Map 1B, were more extensive than the seat changes shown in Map 1A. Eight states show relative gains in power. A breakdown of this percentage change in Table 2-1 indicates that the larger Atlantic Coast states increased in power while seven of the original signatories of the Constitution decreased in relative strength, including five geographically small coastal states. The persistence of heterogeneous regional groupings, such as New England or the Middle Atlantic states, through the first apportionment partially offset the threat of subordination of the smallest states. New England had 28 percent of the House, the Middle Atlantic states had 27 percent, and the southern states controlled 46 percent.[5]

The initial proportions of power allocated in the federal government were largely an inheritance of colonial development. The disparate wealth and populations of the original states were tied to the size, resources, and history of the colonies. Prior to the first attempt to count the American population, the British government and colonial administrators had conducted nearly forty surveys of population.[6] Such estimates were hindered by the lack of expertise of colonial officials in demographic surveys and compounded by the fears and superstitions of the people. The changes observed between the original constitutional allocation of delegates and the first census ap-

portionment mostly represent differences between contemporary estimates and the 1790 census that was in many ways subject to the same errors as previous surveys. Nevertheless, as the first systematic count of the American population the 1790 census is the basis for determining the changes of states' power in Congress. Tables 2-2 and 2-3 divide the states into different regional components and are included here primarily as a baseline against which similar partitions from subsequent reapportionments may be compared. Note that the issues of western expansion and slavery had both been pertinent in the debates preceding the Constitution on the grounds of maintaining political equilibrium between the factions.

2. The population of the states as first reported to Congress on October 27, 1791, contained certain arithmetical errors in the summation of various segments of the populations of Delaware, New Jersey, and Vermont. Corrected figures would not have influenced the apportionment. Subsequently, Jefferson also made arithmetical errors with respect to New York and New Jersey apportionment populations. Neither error would have resulted in changes in the allotted membership. Laurence F. Schmeckebier, *Congressional Apportionment* (Washington, D.C.: Brookings Institution, 1941), 109–111.

3. See *Annals of Congress*, 2d Cong., 1st sess., 539.

4. Vermont and Kentucky were allowed two representatives until the enumeration under provisions of an act adopted on February 25, 1791 (1 Stat. L. 191). Vermont's delegation took their seats before the apportionment act was passed in April 1792. Kentucky's delegation was seated after the admission of the state on June 1, 1792.

5. Proportions reported here are based on the following groupings of states: (1) New England: Massachusetts, Connecticut, New Hampshire, Rhode Island, and Vermont; (2) Middle Atlantic: New Jersey, New York, and Pennsylvania; (3) South: Delaware, Georgia, Kentucky, Maryland, North Carolina, South Carolina, and Virginia. Slightly different ratios among these commonly accepted regional groupings are reported in D. W. Meinig, *The Shaping of America*, vol. 1, *Atlantic America 1492–1800* (New Haven: Yale University Press, 1986), 390, where New England is listed at 26 percent, the "middle states" at 29 percent, and the southern states at 45 percent.

6. W. S. Rossiter, *A Century of Population Growth in the United States, 1790–1900*, prepared for the U.S. Department of Commerce, Bureau of Census (Washington, D.C.: Government Printing Office, 1909), 4.

Table 2-1. 1790 Apportionment Statistics

State	Change in Seats	Seats Apportioned	Percent of House	Percentage Change
Connecticut	2	7	6.7	-1.0
Delaware	0	1	1.0	-0.5
Georgia	-1	2	1.9	-2.7
Kentucky	2	2	1.9	1.9
Maryland	2	8	7.6	-1.6
Massachusetts	6	14	13.3	1.0
New Hampshire	1	4	3.8	-0.8
New Jersey	1	5	4.8	-1.4
New York	4	10	9.5	0.3
North Carolina	5	10	9.5	1.8
Pennsylvania	5	13	12.4	0.1
Rhode Island	1	2	1.9	0.4
South Carolina	1	6	5.7	-2.0
Vermont	2	2	1.9	1.9
Virginia	9	19	18.1	2.7
Total	40	105		

Table 2-2. Percentage Change for Original and New States, 1790

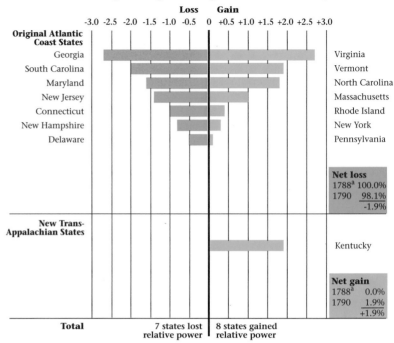

a Constitutional apportionment.

Table 2-3. Percentage Change for Slave and Free States, 1790

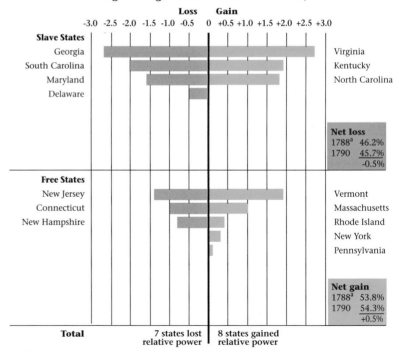

a Constitutional apportionment.

Map 1A. Change in Seats–1790

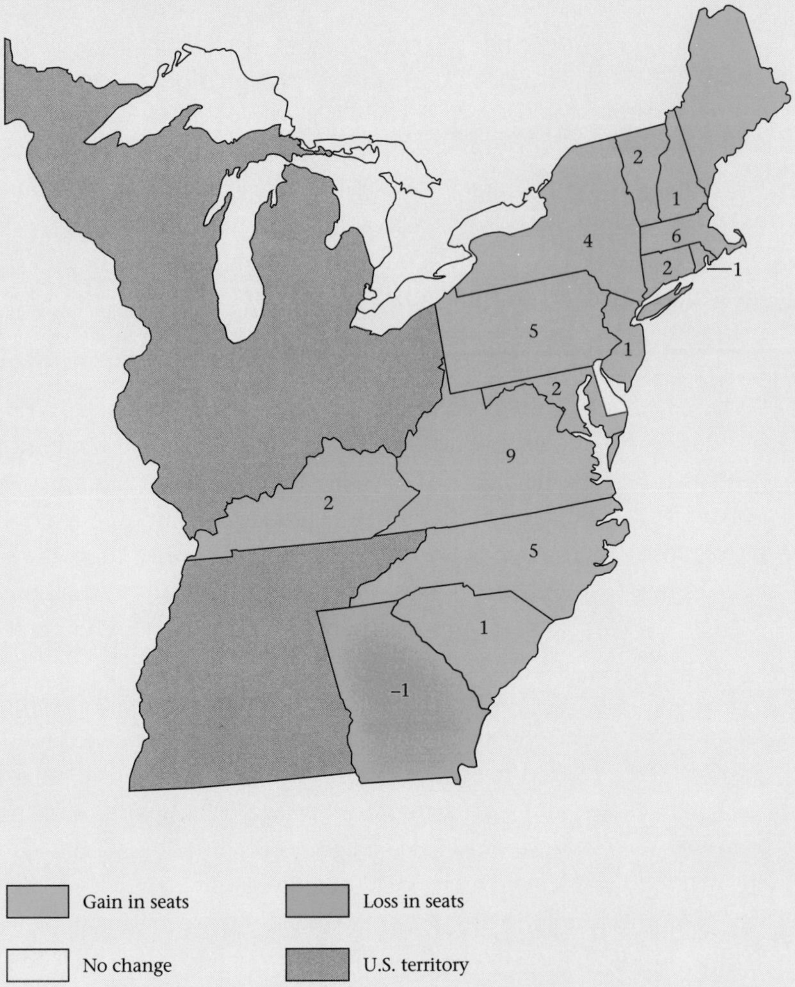
2
1
4
6
2
1
5
1
2
9
2
5
1
–1
Gain in seats
Loss in seats
No change
U.S. territory

Map 1B. Percentage Change in Power–1790

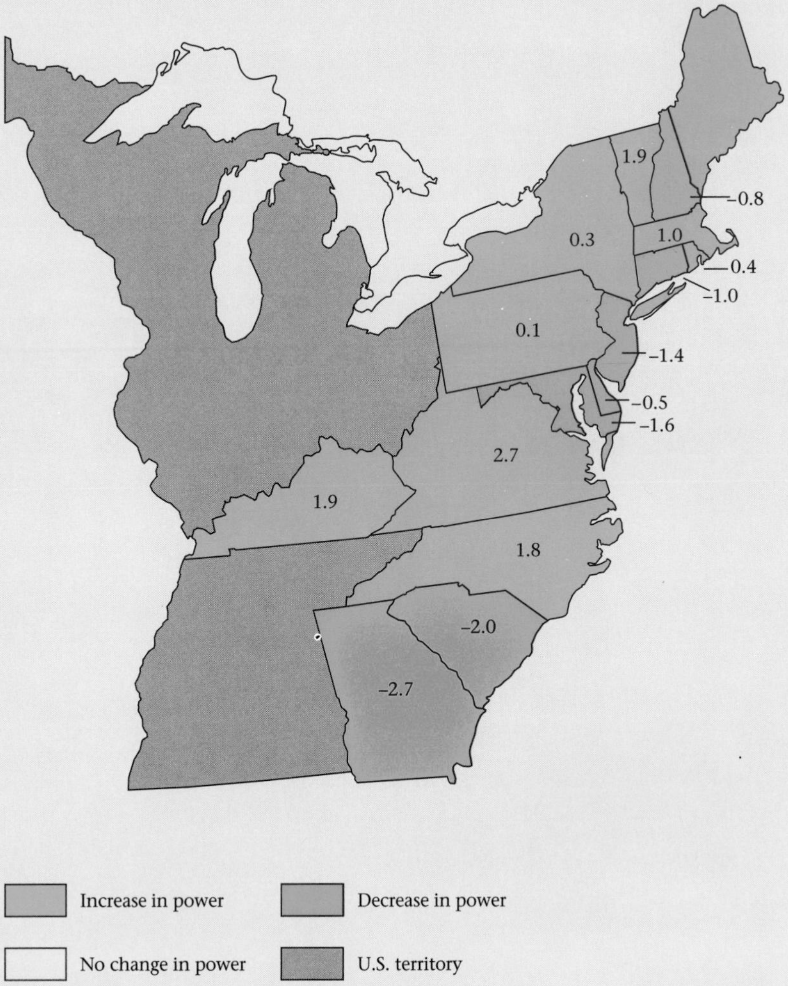
1.9
–0.8
0.3
1.0
0.4
–1.0
0.1
–1.4
–0.5
–1.6
2.7
1.9
1.8
–2.0
–2.7
Increase in power
Decrease in power
No change in power
U.S. territory

1800 CENSUS APPORTIONMENT

Exhibiting a remarkable growth rate of 35 percent, the population of the United States grew by 1,379,264 between the first census of 1790 and the second census of 1800. Immigration from Europe had been negligible in this period so the population growth of the new nation was almost entirely due to natural increase—that is, an excess of births over deaths.[7] Slave trading, still practiced in the southern states in spite of the declining economic value of slaves, continued the enforced migration from Africa of unknown numbers. However the increase of 244,829 in the black population can primarily be attributed to natural increase. Of the total U.S. population of 5,308,473, 90 percent lived in the maritime states, although important pockets of settlement were expanding west of the Appalachians in the more accessible, fertile valleys of the upper Ohio River and its tributaries. A backbone of population densities between forty-five and ninety people per square mile extended from Boston to Philadelphia, supporting a broad belt of lower density from Maine to the North Carolina border.[8] In 1800 Virginia had the largest total population (880,200) and Delaware had the smallest (64,273).

The apportionment act of 1802 provided for a ratio of one representative for every 33,000 persons using the same rule of fixed proportions with rejected fractions as in 1790.[9] Since the population of the United States was by now considerably larger, the apportionment increased the House size to 141 members. The gain of thirty-six seats ensured most states of an increase in their delegation.

The large Atlantic Coast states gained the most seats, which is evident in Map 2A. New York increased by seven members to a total delegation of seventeen, Pennsylvania gained five to increase to eighteen, Virginia and Massachusetts added three each to total twenty-two and seventeen, respectively (see Table 2-4). With twenty-two members (15.6 percent of the House), Virginia's delegation remained the largest. The new state of Tennessee, admitted to the Union in 1796 with one member, was allotted three by the apportionment. Because of the widespread increase in population, no states lost seats in the House.

Map 2B shows that New York also had the largest increase in relative House power (2.6 percent), a gain that was closely matched by Kentucky (2.4 percent) and the new state of Tennessee (2.1 percent).[10] Georgia and Pennsylvania had small percentage gains. All of the remaining nine original states lost relative strength, led by Virginia (2.5 percent). As indicated in Table 2-5, six states gained relative power and nine states lost relative power resulting in a net shift of 4.5 percent to the new trans-Appalachian states. An East-to-West, old-to-new, geographical distribution of this shift of power was beginning to develop as seen in Table 2-5. In 1800 the original Atlantic Coast states held 93.6 percent of the membership of the House of Representatives. Although the issue of slavery was far from being politically explosive, some southern states were already beginning to lose ground in terms of representatives in the House (see Table 2-6). In 1800 the slave states overall showed a slight net gain, but the relative decline in power of Delaware, Maryland, North Carolina, and Virginia indicated a net loss of power that was to come and continue until the Civil War.

During the decade immediately prior to 1800, the most characteristic population shifts were from New England and from the southern Atlantic Coast states towards the interior. Virginia contributed thousands of trans-Appalachian migrants to the upper Ohio. Inland Virginia, the Carolinas, and Georgia benefited from migration streams extending along the Great Valley west of the Blue Ridge Mountains in Pennsylvania and Virginia, and across the Piedmont as settlers sought new lands either to replace lands already becoming less fertile or to gain land for the first time.[11] The migrants from the Middle Atlantic states and New England who settled in western Pennsylvania and New York carried along a strong Yankee influence. In the trans-Appalachian regions, settlers moving down the Ohio River or migrating overland through the Cumberland Mountains from Virginia and the South were of more mixed cultural background.[12] These diverse movements to the frontier were the basis for the beginning of redistribution of political strength within the House, forming patterns that would endure long after 1800.

7. Donald Bogue attributes the decline of immigration between 1770 and 1830 largely to insecurity and uncertainty created by the Revolutionary War, the establishment of the Republic, and the War of 1812. Donald J. Bogue, *The Population of the United States* (Glencoe, Ill.: Free Press, 1959), 349. Bogue also comments on the lack of official immigration records before 1820 and the difficulty of assessing the volume and origin of immigrants, free or enslaved. Of 1,002,037 blacks recorded in the 1800 census, 893,602 (89 percent) were slaves. The slave population increased by 195,921 from 1790 to 1800. (p. 14). See also Ralph H. Brown, *Mirror for Americans,* Special Publication No. 27 (New York: American Geographical Society, 1943), 31. Brown summarizes contemporary accounts of the growth of the American population in the immediate post–Revolutionary War period until 1810, noting the birth rate of 5.75 percent and death rate of 2.5 percent and the minor role of foreign immigration, estimated at 4,000 to 5,000 per year gross. Contemporary estimates of emigration to Canada and overseas offset immigration almost completely.

8. While no contemporary maps of population distribution exist, the best available historical population maps are found in C. O. Paullin, *Atlas of the Historical Geography of the United States* (New York: Carnegie Institution of Washington and the American Geographical Society, 1932).

9. The apportionment act was approved January 14, 1802, the first statute passed by the Seventh Congress (2 Stat. L. 128).

10. Statistical calculations in this atlas are based on the data in the decennial apportionments. All new states entering the Union have a positive seat and percentage gain for the first apportionment since the states' representation numbers in the previous apportionment are considered to be zero. Numbers of representatives assigned by Congress to new states upon admission are not included in the calculations. For example, Tennessee was not mentioned in the first apportionment act. In 1796 Tennessee was admitted to the Union with one representative. In the second apportionment act, Tennessee was allocated 3 seats, 2.1 percent of the total House. This is presented as a change of +3 seats and +2.1 percent from the previous apportionment (see Table 2-4 and Maps 2A and 2B). In each subsequent apportionment, of course, Tennessee and all other new states' calculations are based on population changes as measured by the census and allocated by the appropriate apportionment formula.

11. The push-pull effects of agricultural soils were important at this time in the patterning of the U.S. population. Commenting on the attraction of the "mulatto" and "gray" soils of Piedmont South Carolina and Georgia, Brown simultaneously notes the decline of rice and indigo production in coastal regions. See R. H. Brown, *Historical Geography of the United States* (New York: Harcourt, Brace and Co., 1948), 1146. In addition, Brown notes the negative effects of tobacco culture on soil fertility and its contribution to erosion (p. 133). Elsewhere on the same theme, he draws on contemporary accounts showing that coastal sandy soils could sustain tobacco for at most eight to ten seasons. See Brown, *Mirror for Americans,* 69.

12. See Meinig, *Shaping of America,* 360–361.

Table 2-4. 1800 Apportionment Statistics

State	Change in Seats	Seats Apportioned	Percent of House	Percentage Change
Connecticut	0	7	5.0	-1.7
Delaware	0	1	0.7	-0.3
Georgia	2	4	2.8	0.9
Kentucky	4	6	4.3	2.4
Maryland	1	9	6.4	-1.2
Massachusetts	3	17	12.1	-1.2
New Hampshire	1	5	3.5	-0.3
New Jersey	1	6	4.3	-0.5
New York	7	17	12.1	2.6
North Carolina	2	12	8.5	-1.0
Pennsylvania	5	18	12.8	0.4
Rhode Island	0	2	1.4	-0.5
South Carolina	2	8	5.7	0.0
Tennessee	3	3	2.1	2.1
Vermont	2	4	2.8	0.9
Virginia	3	22	15.6	-2.5
Total	36	141		

Table 2-5. Percentage Change for Original and New States, 1800

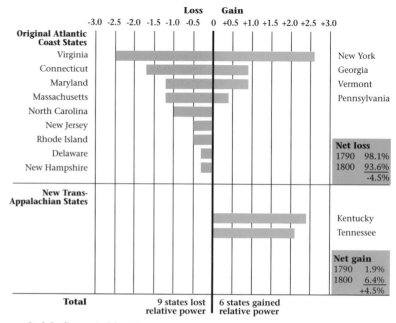

South Carolina remained the same.

Table 2-6. Percentage Change for Slave and Free States, 1800

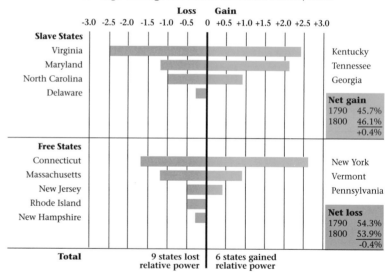

South Carolina remained the same.

Map 2A. Change in Seats–1800

Map 2B. Percentage Change in Power–1800

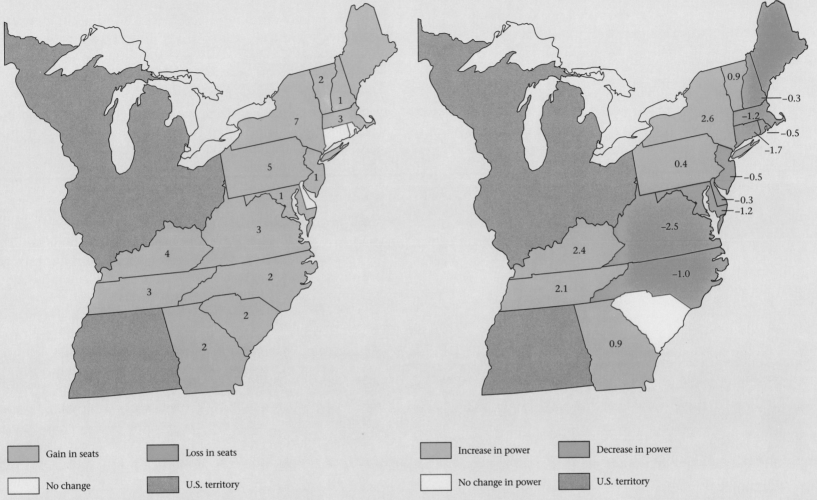

Legend (Map 2A):
- Gain in seats
- Loss in seats
- No change
- U.S. territory

Legend (Map 2B):
- Increase in power
- Decrease in power
- No change in power
- U.S. territory

1810 CENSUS APPORTIONMENT

The third census in 1810 recorded a U.S. population of 7,239,881. The national growth rate was an exceptional 36.4 percent, the highest decennial increase in American demographic history to date. This population growth was almost entirely the result of natural increase. European immigration continued to be limited by persistent uncertainty overseas about the viability of the new Republic and deteriorating political relationships between the United States, Great Britain, and Europe. Although the importation of slaves was banned in 1808 (an agreement from the Constitutional Convention), the practice continued illicitly at much reduced levels. Thus the exceptional population growth rate resulted from the high fertility rates of resident Americans and relatively low rates of mortality, especially as a consequence of sufficient food.[13] With a population of 72,674, Delaware remained the smallest state. At the other extreme, Virginia retained the largest population with 974,600 inhabitants, but it recorded a population growth rate only half that of the national rate.

The fastest growth rates occurred in frontier areas. Internal migration led to spectacular relative growth rates of population in some regions of expansion. On the frontier Kentucky grew at twice the national rate between 1800 and 1810; Tennessee grew at three times the rate, more than doubling its population. Mississippi Territory, starting from a relatively small base population, grew at more than seven times the average. The territory that later became Alabama experienced a growth rate of more than sixteen times the national average, albeit from very small initial numbers.

In 1803 Ohio was admitted to the Union with one member until the apportionment. Ohio grew at ten times the national average from 1800 to 1810 and was allotted six seats under the apportionment act of 1811. The act provided for a House based on a ratio of one member for every 35,000 people, a prescription that produced a House of 181 members, an increase of 40 over the 1801 apportionment.[14] As in 1801 the increase in House size ensured that most states gained representatives (see Map 3A). New York gained ten members to form a total delegation of twenty-seven representatives. Pennsylvania gained five seats to match Virginia's membership of twenty-three, and Massachusetts added three seats to make up a delegation of twenty seats (see Table 2-7). New York's delegation became the largest in the House supplanting the dominance that Virginia had possessed during the formative period of the Republic.[15]

Map 3B of percentage change in House power clearly shows the solidification of a frontier and the division between the growth of the new states and the relative losses in power among the original thirteen states. In line with its population growth, the new state of Ohio had the largest increase in power at 3.3 percent.[16] New York gained 2.8 percent, followed by gains in Kentucky (1.2 percent) and Tennessee (1.2 percent). Ten Atlantic Coast states lost relative strength, lead by Virginia (2.9 percent). In total, seven states gained and ten states lost relative power, resulting in a net shift of 5.8 percent to the new trans-Appalachian states as detailed in Table 2-8.

Land laws relating to territorial expansion in the last decade of the eighteenth century stimulated population growth, especially in the Northwest Territory, as people took up various options on military tracts, purchased public lands from the federal government, squatted on unsurveyed public lands, or expropriated lands ceded to Native Americans.[17] Land purchases and westward expansion were further assisted in 1804 by the reduction of minimum parcel size from a half section (320 acres) to a quarter section (160 acres). Transportation and accessibility on the one hand, and land availability and fertility on the other were the dominant influences over the redistribution of population within the United States and its territories. Colonial patterns continued and intensified in the young Republic. As before, westward expansion was hindered in Virginia by difficult terrain in the Appalachian Mountains, and in New England by the Green, White, and Taconic Mountains.

In the North, expansion via Braddock's and Forbes Roads in Pennsylvania and especially along the Hudson-Mohawk corridor in New York not only assisted development in the western portions of those states but channeled migrants to the rapidly growing state of Ohio and the Northwest Territory. The sources and pathways of settlers and the various forms in which land was available were shaping the cultural and political landscape.[18] Thus northern Pennsylvania, much of upstate New York, and the Western Reserve on the shores of Lake Erie in Ohio were strongly influenced by colonists from New England, whereas Kentucky and Tennessee were settled by Virginians, Marylanders, and North Carolinians. The drive westward was encouraged by a growing availability of land in systematic land surveys under the Public Land Survey System and in available tracts supplied by commercial land companies. The promise of the West contrasted with high land prices in the maritime regions, relatively dense populations, and the widespread decline of soil fertility.

Growth in the South continued patterns established in colonial times out of the Great Valley of the Shenandoah and across the Piedmont, but the South lagged relative to the Northwest as indicated by Table 2-9. As quality land in the core regions became scarce, southern migrants moved west through the Appalachians and the Kentucky Bluegrass, extending across Cherokee lands of the Cumberland Plateau to northern Tennessee and western Kentucky. The frontier had already reached the Mississippi with some pockets of settlement beginning to coalesce above St. Louis.[19]

13. Epidemic diseases were nevertheless rampant. Yellow fever had struck New York City, Philadelphia, New Haven, and Charleston repeatedly at the end of the eighteenth and early nineteenth century. See Brown, *Mirror for Americans*, 18. As a result of high vital rates the median age of the American population in 1810 may have been below 16.7 years. See Bogue, *Population*, 95. Mortality rates are not officially recorded but are estimated to be in the range of 25 to 33 per thousand. Ibid., 172. For other estimates of vital rates in the early nineteenth century, see also Conrad Taeuber and Irene B. Taeuber, *The Changing Population of the United States* (New York: John Wiley & Sons, 1958), 270.

14. The apportionment act was passed on December 21, 1811 (2 Stat. L. 669).

15. The total population of Virginia reported in the 1810 census was reduced by the three-fifths compromise for apportionment purposes. Of a total population of 974,600, only 817,615 were included in the apportionment population, a reduction of 17 percent. New York, on the other hand, had a census total of 959,049 and an apportionment population of 953,043 (99 percent of the state's total population), thus New York became entitled to more seats than Virginia. Figures are from Schmeckebier, *Congressional Apportionment*, Appendix C, 227.

16. See footnote 10.

17. There were three major legislative acts influencing settlement. The Ordinance of 1785 established the system for the surveying and selling of trans-Appalachian land. Under the system, public land was divided into thirty-six square-mile townships, which were in turn subdivided into sections of one square mile, or 640 acres. The "Seven Ranges" extending south and west from the intersection of the Pennsylvania boundary and the Ohio River was the first land so parceled. The Northwest Ordinance Act of 1787 applied settlement rules to all the Northwest Territories. The Land Sale Act of 1796 enabled the official sales of surveyed lands.

18. For example, see Meinig, *Shaping of America*, 357.

19. The exact extent of the frontier has been subject to debate. Twenty counties in Georgia, Kentucky, Mississippi Territory, and Tennessee formed the southern frontier in 1810; and 22 counties in Indiana, New York, Ohio, and Pennsylvania were on the northern frontier. For further details, see J. E. Davis, *Frontier America, 1800–1840: A Comparative Demographic Analysis of the Frontier Process* (Glendale, Calif.: Arthur Clarke Co.: 1977), 28.

Table 2-7. 1810 Apportionment Statistics

State	Change in Seats	Seats Apportioned	Percent of House	Percentage Change
Connecticut	0	7	3.9	-1.1
Delaware	1	2	1.1	0.4
Georgia	2	6	3.3	0.5
Kentucky	4	10	5.5	1.2
Maryland	0	9	5.0	-1.4
Massachusetts	3	20	11.0	-1.1
New Hampshire	1	6	3.3	-0.2
New Jersey	0	6	3.3	-1.0
New York	10	27	14.9	2.8
North Carolina	1	13	7.2	-1.3
Ohio	6	6	3.3	3.3
Pennsylvania	5	23	12.7	-0.1
Rhode Island	0	2	1.1	-0.3
South Carolina	1	9	5.0	-0.7
Tennessee	3	6	3.3	1.2
Vermont	2	6	3.3	0.5
Virginia	1	23	12.7	-2.9
Total	40	181		

Table 2-8. Percentage Change for Original and New States, 1810

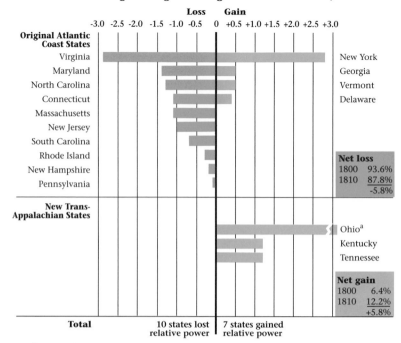

[a]Ohio gained 3.3% in relative power.

Table 2-9. Percentage Change for Slave and Free States, 1810

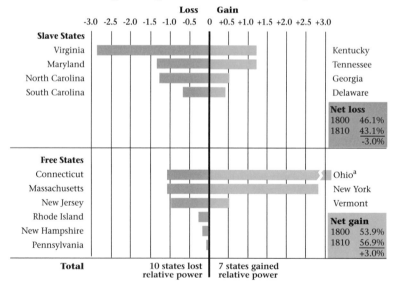

[a]Ohio gained 3.3% in relative power.

Map 3A. Change in Seats–1810

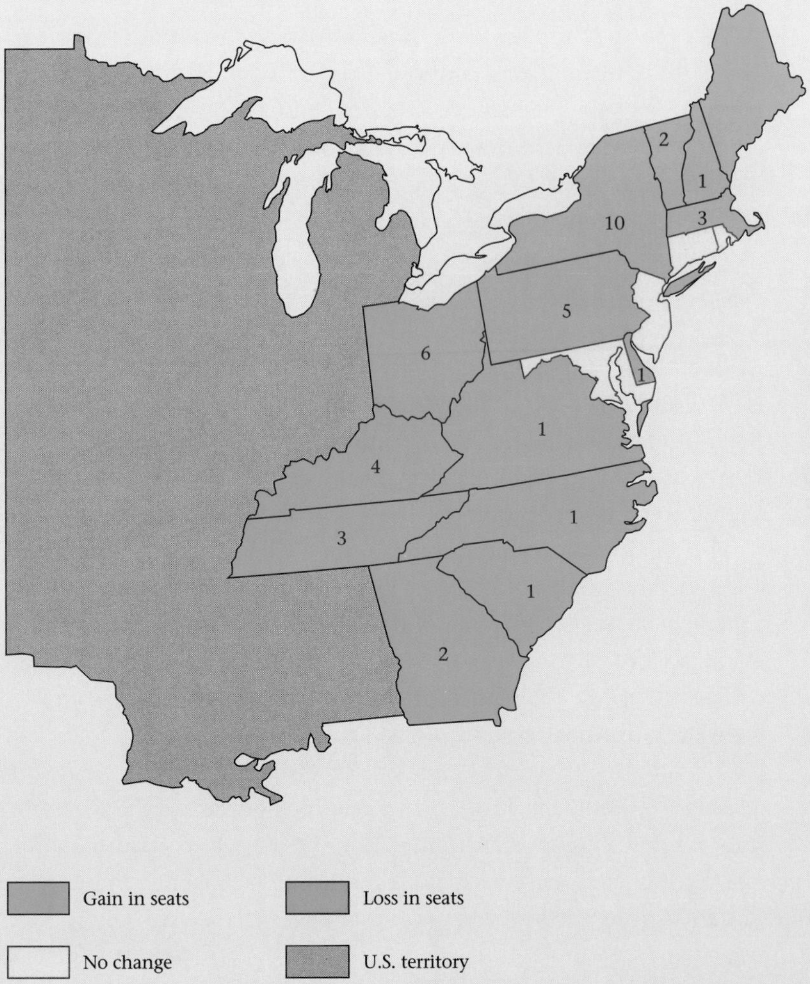
2
1
3
10
5
6
1
1
4
3
1
1
2
Gain in seats
Loss in seats
No change
U.S. territory

Map 3B. Percentage Change in Power–1810

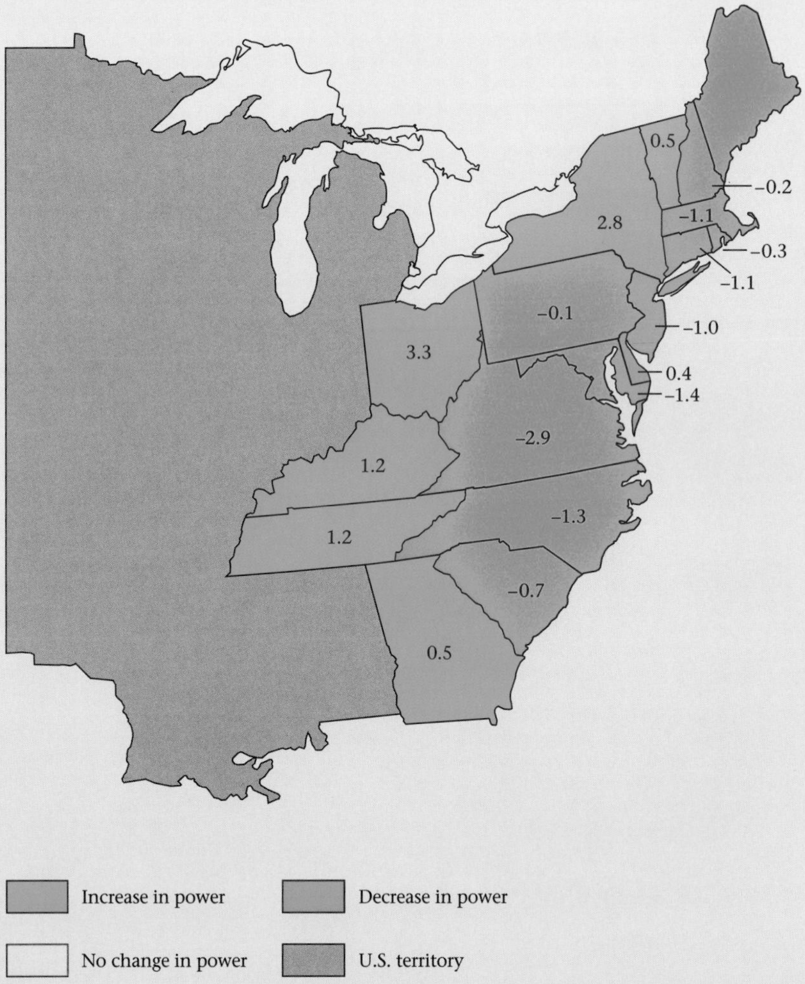
0.5
−0.2
−1.1
2.8
−0.3
−1.1
−0.1
−1.0
3.3
0.4
−1.4
−2.9
1.2
1.2
−1.3
−0.7
0.5
Increase in power
Decrease in power
No change in power
U.S. territory

1820 CENSUS APPORTIONMENT

Between the third census in August 1810 and the fourth in August 1820, the United States continued its rapid growth, increasing its population by 33.1 percent. The fourth census registered a total population of 9,638,453, an increase of 2,398,572 people. Three state population totals exceeded one million—those of New York, Virginia, and Pennsylvania. At 1,372,812, New York had the largest total population in 1820; Illinois was the smallest with 55,211 inhabitants. Between the third and fourth apportionments no less than seven states were admitted to the Union: Louisiana (1812), Mississippi (1817), and Alabama (1819) in the South; Indiana (1816), Illinois (1818), Maine (1820), and Missouri (1821) in the North and Northwest. Maine separated from Massachusetts in 1820 and was initially allocated seven of Massachusetts' twenty members. The allocation was confirmed under the subsequent apportionment act.

The apportionment act based on the 1820 census was adopted in 1822.[20] Using a ratio of 40,000 persons for each seat, the sum of the states' quotas placed the size of the House of Representatives at 213, an increase of 32 members over the previous apportionment (see Map 4A for change in seats). Because Ohio increased its membership by eight, a trans-Appalachian state had the largest increase in seats and relative power for the first time in congressional history. New York added seven seats but increased its relative position in the House by only 1.1 percent compared with 3.3 percent for Ohio. Alabama, Indiana, Louisiana, Pennsylvania, and Tennessee each gained three representatives, but their corresponding changes in relative power were not equal (see Table 2-10).

As a consequence of low rates of population growth, Virginia, Connecticut, Vermont, and Delaware each lost a seat. Neither Delaware nor Vermont have ever regained their loss because of consistent low growth relative to the nation. New York continued to be the largest House delegation with thirty-four members, followed by Pennsylvania with twenty-six seats. Virginia fell to third in rank with twenty-two representatives. Its population was expanding at only one-fifth as fast as the national average. In addition Virginia had an apportionment population 15 percent smaller than its total population because of the implementation of the three-fifths ruling regarding slaves.

In conjunction with Table 2-11, Map 4B of percentage change in power illustrates the marked shift of emphasis away from the original states. With the exception of New York, which gained relative power, and of Georgia, which remained on even par, all the Atlantic Coast states lost ground to the new states. Nine new states gained power, a net increase of 10 percent in the West. Gouverneur Morris's apprehension during the Constitutional Convention that the power of the original states would be eroded in favor of new western states was being confirmed by the fourth apportionment.[21] Similar concerns were later expressed by John C. Calhoun who perceived the decline and fall of slavery following rapid growth of the free West.[22] Likewise many legislators of the original thirteen states shared misgivings over the rise to power of the new states and the consequences for the political power of their own jurisdictions (see Table 2-11).

Greatly expanding the initial land holdings of the United States, the Louisiana Purchase raised additional questions relating to the sectional allegiances of states. The relative decline in power of the slave states was an emerging trend of major political significance (see Table 2-12). Sectional interests were pitted against each other over the wording of the enabling acts of states formed from territories acquired after the Constitution was ratified. These disputes were especially intense as to whether slavery would be permitted in Louisiana and Missouri.

In 1817 there were eleven free states and ten slave states and balance between the factions in the Senate was to be achieved through the admittance of Alabama. Of the original thirteen states, seven had abolished slavery and six had retained it. Of the states admitted after the original thirteen, five permitted slavery and four were free. But in terms of representation, the population of the free states had grown far in excess of that of the slave states. By 1820 the North had a total population of 5,144,000, while the South had 4,372,000 inhabitants. The difference was compounded by the three-fifths compromise under which five slaves were counted as three free men in apportioning seats.[23] Comparison of Table 2-12 with Table 2-3 indicates the continuing shift in power from 1790, when the North controlled 54 percent of the House of Representatives, to 58 percent in 1820, despite the compromise admitting Missouri as a slave state.

The pattern of change in the apportionment of the House in 1820 continued to be a result of the migration streams identified in the last section. The importance of water transport along the Ohio River cannot be underestimated and was accentuated by the building of the first steamboat on the Ohio in 1811. More than eighty steamboats had been built by 1820, carrying thousands of passengers each year. The frontier extended west from settled parts of Ohio and Kentucky through southern Indiana, Illinois, and up the Mississippi. Other pockets of settlement appeared west of the Mississippi in the Missouri, Arkansas, and the Red River valleys. In the Southwest, new Alabama and Mississippi cotton lands began to attract an influx of migrants from Georgia, the Carolinas, and Tennessee. The largest absolute growth was, of course, not on the frontier edge but in the infilling of the area behind it, on lands that had been surveyed and from which the Native American population had been removed or pacified. Hence the population growths of New York, Pennsylvania, Ohio, Kentucky, and Tennessee were highest in absolute numbers, having the combined advantages of well-established base populations and plentiful lands for expansion of settlement.

20. The apportionment act was approved on March 7, 1822 (3 Stat. L. 651).

21. Morris argued that the entry of new states or acquisitions should not be on equal terms with the original thirteen, which he considered to be eminently qualified to prevail in national governments. An underlying concern was that new states might destabilize the Republic through self-interest and a propensity to become involved in wars, for which the original states would have to pay. Meinig, *Shaping of America,* 390–391, 393. Congress decided the issue with the declaration that the territories to the west would be "settled and formed into distinct republican states, which shall become members of the federal union, and have the same rights of sovereignty, freedom and independence, as the other states" (p. 341). A measure of control over the formation of new states was maintained by the eastern establishment in the Ordinance of 1787, which set out a three-stage process through which a territory could attain full and equal statehood and specified the boundaries of three of the states to be formed in the Northwest Territory.

22. Cited in G. Carson and B. A. Weisberger, "The Great Countdown," *American Heritage* 7 (1989): 5.

23. The apportionment population of the slave states in 1820 amounted to 3,833,867 as opposed to 5,135,947 in free states. In total population, the ratio of North to South was 55:45; in apportionment population the ratio was 57:43.

Table 2-10. 1820 Apportionment Statistics

State	Change in Seats	Seats Apportioned	Percent of House	Percentage Change
Alabama	3	3	1.4	1.4
Connecticut	-1	6	2.8	-1.1
Delaware	-1	1	0.5	-0.6
Georgia	1	7	3.3	0.0
Illinois	1	1	0.5	0.5
Indiana	3	3	1.4	1.4
Kentucky	2	12	5.6	0.1
Louisiana	3	3	1.4	1.4
Maine	0[a]	7	3.3	-0.6
Maryland	0	9	4.2	-0.8
Massachusetts	0[a]	13	6.1	-1.1
Mississippi	1	1	0.5	0.5
Missouri	1	1	0.5	0.5
New Hampshire	0	6	2.8	-0.5
New Jersey	0	6	2.8	-0.5
New York	7	34	16.0	1.1
North Carolina	0	13	6.1	-1.1
Ohio	8	14	6.6	3.3
Pennsylvania	3	26	12.2	-0.5
Rhode Island	0	2	0.9	-0.2
South Carolina	0	9	4.2	-0.8
Tennessee	3	9	4.2	0.9
Vermont	-1	5	2.3	-1.0
Virginia	-1	22	10.3	-2.4
Total	32	213		

[a]*Maine was a part of Massachusetts until March 1820. In the 1810 apportionment, this area was allotted twenty representatives. Seven of these representatives were given districts in the Maine portion of the state. In the 1820 apportionment Maine received seven representatives and Massachusetts thirteen for a total of twenty. Maine and Massachusetts are assigned a seat change of zero for this apportionment.*

Table 2-11. Percentage Change for Original and New States, 1820

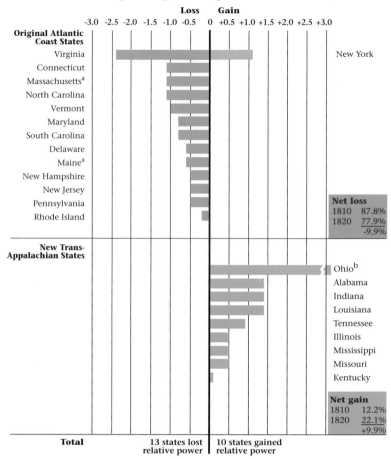

Georgia remained the same.
[a]*Maine had been part of original Massachusetts state boundaries.*
[b]*Ohio gained 3.3% in relative power.*

Table 2-12. Percentage Change for Slave and Free States, 1820

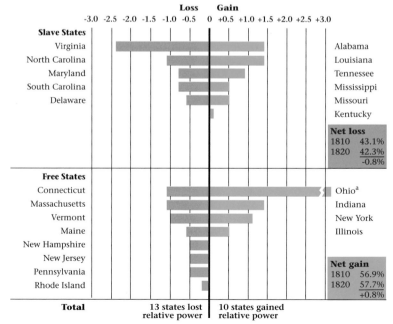

Georgia remained the same.
[a]*Ohio gained 3.3% in relative power.*

Map 4A. Change in Seats–1820

Map 4B. Percentage Change in Power–1820

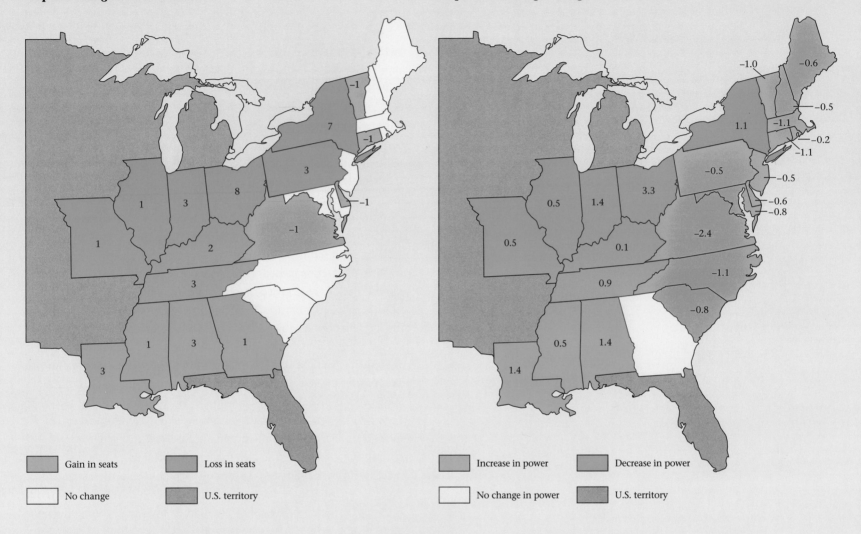

Map 4A legend:
- Gain in seats
- Loss in seats
- No change
- U.S. territory

Map 4B legend:
- Increase in power
- Decrease in power
- No change in power
- U.S. territory

1830 CENSUS APPORTIONMENT

Although no new states were added to the Union between the 1821 apportionment and the fifth census in 1830, westward expansion continued steadily, modifying the balance of power in the House of Representatives. The June 1830 census reported a total population of 12,866,020, an increase of 3,227,567 since the previous census. Population grew at the slightly increased growth rate of 33.5 percent compared with the period between 1810 and 1820. New York remained the most populous state with 1,918,608 inhabitants. Frontier states grew at three times the national rate, pushing Delaware back into the position of having the smallest population (76,748).[24] Immigration, mainly from England, was modest; 23,000 arrived during 1830, for example, so the population continued to increase principally by high natural fertility.[25]

When Congress passed the apportionment act of 1832 the ratio of representation was raised to 1:47,700, while the House increased from 213 to 240 members.[26] Irregularities in apportionment caused by the application of the fixed ratio with rejected fractions method stirred Daniel Webster to protest the resulting inequalities. Webster argued that the method of apportionment left large fractions in the small states of New England and in the contiguous states of the then Southwest (Alabama, Louisiana, and Mississippi). For example, New York had two more representatives than the New England states, although these states combined had a total population that was 40,000 greater than New York's. The malapportionment debate was to extend to future Congresses, culminating perhaps in the stalemate of the 1920s.[27] Although his revised formula was not adopted in 1832, Webster helped to bring about changes in the method of apportionment a decade later. The reapportionment resulted in a ratio of forty to one between the largest delegation (New York), and the smallest delegation (Delaware), a range of difference twice as large as in 1790.

A total of thirty-one seats were reapportioned, twenty-seven from the increase in the House size and four were reapportioned as a result of losses (see Table 2-13). States that had joined the Union since 1800 received twenty of the new seats created by the 1832 apportionment act. New York's allocation, increasing by six to forty representatives, accounted for one-sixth of the total House membership. Map 5A shows Ohio received five additional seats; Indiana and Tennessee each gained four seats. Alabama, Georgia, Illinois, and Pennsylvania each added two seats. Maryland, Massachusetts, New Hampshire, and Virginia each lost one representative.

Table 2-14 delineates the changes in states' power, showing that nine states gained relative power and that fourteen lost it. Two of the thirteen original Atlantic Coast states, Georgia and New York, showed modest relative gains in power, as shown in Map 5B. The remaining eleven original states lost relative strength, but most individual decreases were small. Virginia's position continued to weaken with a net loss of 1.5 percent. Two trans-Appalachian states, Kentucky and Louisiana, experienced a decrease in power. Although inconsequential in size, the existence of a relative decline in Kentucky serves to emphasize the inexorable westward movement, as states on the agricultural frontier gained in strength. Seven new states, led by Indiana, Ohio, and Tennessee, gained power. Table 2-14 shows the transfer of power westwards; trans-Appalachian states had a net increase of 5.8 percent and controlled 27.9 percent of the House of Representatives. As the Northwest increased in relative importance, the slave states continued to lag in relative power, as evidenced by Table 2-15.

The continuation of extensive settlement throughout the western states characterized population growth and change from 1820 to 1830. Population densities of more than forty-five people per square mile extended along the Atlantic coast from Maine to Maryland, up the Hudson-Mohawk valleys and along the shores of Lake Ontario.[28] Islands of similar population density were scattered through Ohio, Indiana, Kentucky, and Tennessee. Only the northern extremes of Ohio, Indiana, and western Illinois remained on the frontier. Settlement was almost continuous along the Missouri River, as abundant water transportation assisted migrants and trading.[29]

The age of steam had reached maturity on the major inland waterways, and the lure of inexpensive water transportation had encouraged widespread canal building. The Erie Canal became the most famous and the most successful of the numerous canals completed during a canal-building era lasting thirty years. With the opening of the Erie Canal it became possible for westward migrants to travel from New York to Buffalo in eight days or less, and on to Detroit in two more by Lake Erie steamboat.[30] Other canal companies strove to penetrate the interior from the East Coast and Great Lakes but none had the success of the Erie Canal. The combination of available, cheap land and more reliable means of movement reinforced and accelerated the western spread of the population and consequently the importance of the western section in the House of Representatives.

Assisted by the Erie Canal, the dominant position of New York City was confirmed among rival ports on the eastern seaboard. From 1820 to 1830 the city grew from 125,000 to 200,000 inhabitants.[31] As the United States entered the era of mass European immigration, New York City and its hinterland were preadapted to benefit through a combination of having the major port of arrival and the most accessible routes to the interior.

24. Bogue, *Population*, 65.
25. Ibid. Immigration estimates are unreliable until twentieth-century censuses.
26. The apportionment act was passed on May 22, 1832 (4 Stat. L. 516).
27. *Congressional Debates*, 22d Cong., 1st. sess., 488.
28. H. Gannett, *Statistical Atlas of the United States Based upon Results of the Eleventh Census* (Washington, D.C.: Government Printing Office, 1898).
29. See Brown, *Historical Geography*, 260–265.
30. Ibid.
31. In 1830 the population of New York City was 202,500.

Table 2-13. 1830 Apportionment Statistics

State	Change in Seats	Seats Apportioned	Percent of House	Percentage Change
Alabama	2	5	2.1	0.7
Connecticut	0	6	2.5	-0.3
Delaware	0	1	0.4	-0.1
Georgia	2	9	3.8	0.5
Illinois	2	3	1.3	0.8
Indiana	4	7	2.9	1.5
Kentucky	1	13	5.4	-0.2
Louisiana	0	3	1.3	-0.1
Maine	1	8	3.3	0.0
Maryland	-1	8	3.3	-0.9
Massachusetts	-1	12	5.0	-1.1
Mississippi	1	2	0.8	0.3
Missouri	1	2	0.8	0.3
New Hampshire	-1	5	2.1	-0.7
New Jersey	0	6	2.5	-0.3
New York	6	40	16.7	0.7
North Carolina	0	13	5.4	-0.7
Ohio	5	19	7.9	1.3
Pennsylvania	2	28	11.7	-0.5
Rhode Island	0	2	0.8	-0.1
South Carolina	0	9	3.8	-0.4
Tennessee	4	13	5.4	1.2
Vermont	0	5	2.1	-0.2
Virginia	-1	21	8.8	-1.5
Total	27	240		

Table 2-14. Percentage Change for Original and New States, 1830

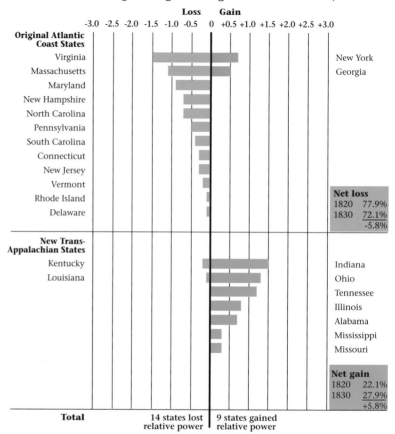

Maine remained the same.

Table 2-15. Percentage Change for Slave and Free States, 1830

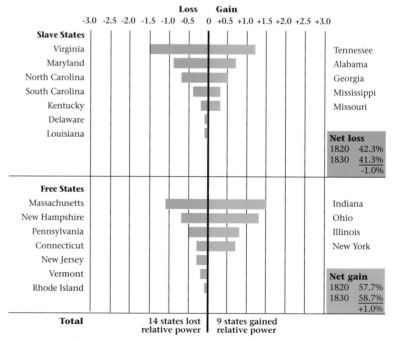

Maine remained the same.

Map 5A. Change in Seats–1830

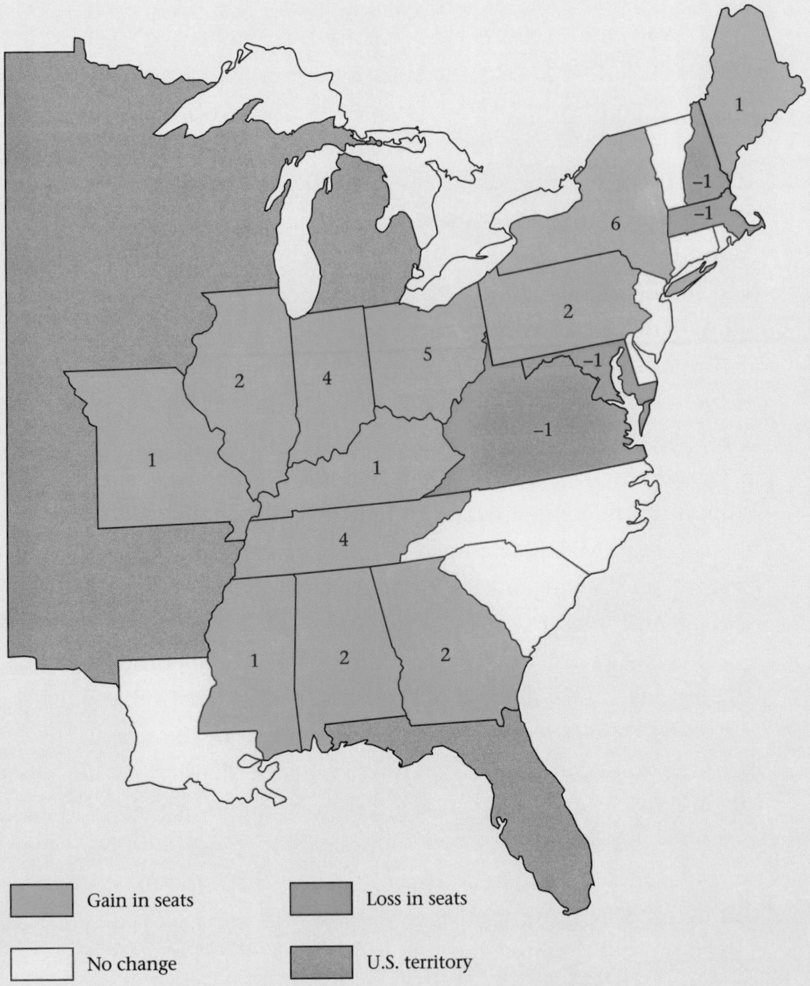
1
−1
−1
6
2
−1
5
4
2
1
−1
1
4
1
2
2
Gain in seats
Loss in seats
No change
U.S. territory

Map 5B. Percentage Change in Power–1830

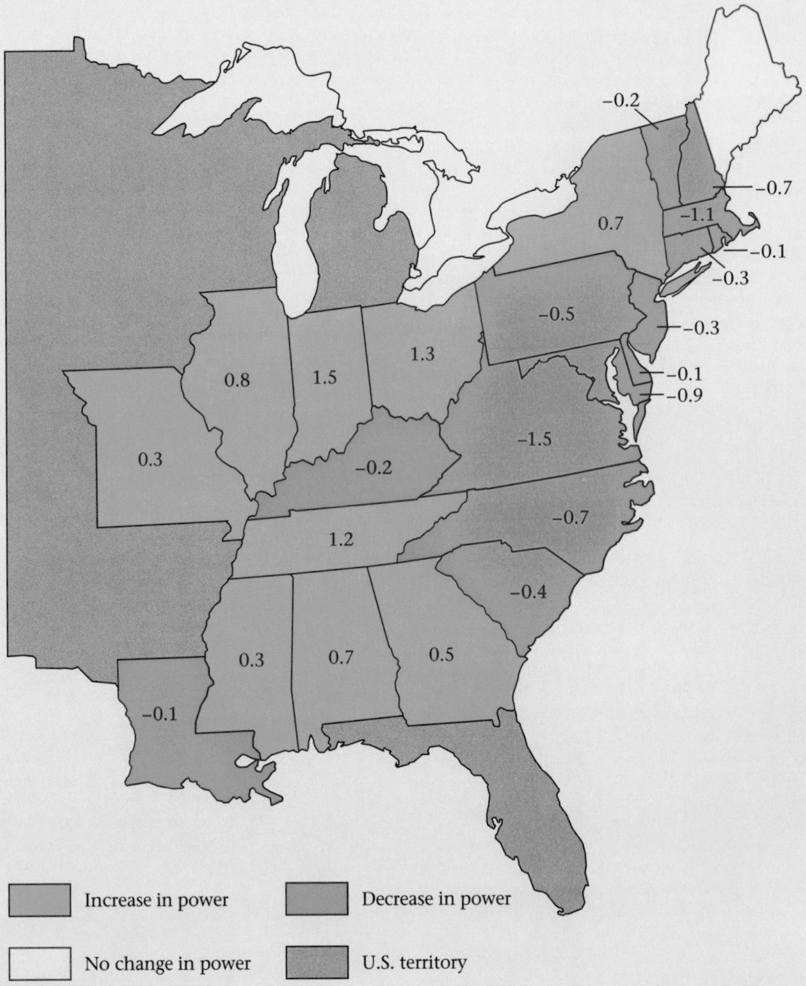
−0.2
−0.7
0.7
−1.1
−0.1
−0.3
−0.5
−0.3
1.3
1.5
0.8
−0.1
−0.9
0.3
−0.2
−1.5
1.2
−0.7
−0.4
0.3
0.7
0.5
−0.1
Increase in power
Decrease in power
No change in power
U.S. territory

1840 CENSUS APPORTIONMENT

In 1840 the sixth census reported a population increase of 4,203,433 (32.7 percent) to register a total U.S. population of 17,069,453 residents. Of individual states, New York's population remained the largest, increasing by half a million people to 2,428,921. At the other extreme, Delaware grew by less than 2,000 to reach 78,085. Three other states had populations greater than one million: Pennsylvania, Ohio, and Virginia. Ohio's population had almost doubled in the decade, Pennsylvania increased by more than 300,000, but Virginia increased by fewer than 30,000. While immigration in 1840 had more than doubled from the previous decade to average 84,000 per year, the number of immigrants was still small in comparison with the total increase.[32]

During the intercensal period Arkansas was admitted as a state in 1836. After the longest period of territorial development experienced by any state, Michigan joined the Union in 1837. On entry both Arkansas and Michigan were allotted a single representative until the next apportionment.

Following Webster's protests during the Senate apportionment debate of 1832, a new method of apportionment was introduced by the 1842 act. The new method partially accounted for the significant remainders, called fractions, resulting from the division of the ratio into the apportionment population in some states. A ratio of 76,680 people per representative was established with "one additional member for each state having a fraction greater than one moiety of the said ratio."[33] Significantly the new House was set at 223 members, a reduction of 17 seats from the 1832 total. As the new states of Arkansas and Michigan received a total of four members, the other states experienced a net loss of twenty-one seats.

The distribution of seat changes in Map 6A is characterized by the widespread loss of House membership among the original Atlantic Coast states, and the early trans-Appalachian states and the complementary westward transfer of power. The rapid growth in the frontier block contrasts strikingly with losses in the block of original states. The first-settled trans-Appalachian states are included in the eastern region that loses seats. Kentucky and Tennessee, losers of three and two seats, respectively, illustrate both the rate and degree of change of the distribution of American population, as these states had been recipients of seats in the four previous apportionments of the nineteenth century. Major losers in the number of representatives were New York and Virginia, which lost six seats each, followed by Pennsylvania and North Carolina, each relinquishing four seats (see Table 2-16). Atlantic Coast states having the largest populations bore the brunt of the reduction in House size. The small delegations of Delaware and Rhode Island alone remained unchanged.

Table 2-17 indicates that ten states gained relative power and fifteen lost it. Map 6B corroborates the tabular information and accentuates the East-West split. Of the thirteen original states, only Rhode Island achieved a statistical gain in power, albeit so small to be negligible. Twelve original states lost relative strength but many individual changes were significant, and collectively dramatic. Virginia's position continued to weaken with a net loss of 2.1 percent. For the first time New York experienced a net loss (1.5 percent). North Carolina lost 1.4 percent. Three new states—Vermont, Kentucky, and Tennessee—had measurable decreases in power and Map 6B emphasizes the continuing western extension of the frontier. Nine new trans-Appalachian states, led by Illinois, Indiana, Ohio, Missouri, Michigan, Alabama, and Mississippi, gained power. The net increase in congressional membership for new states was 9.3 percent. New trans-Appalachian states now controlled 37.2 percent of the House of Representatives (see Table 2-17).

Disputes over the ability of states to nullify federal legislation provided a potential platform for sectoral unification between the West and the South. During the Webster-Hayne debate over nullification of 1830, the growing sectional rivalry between the original Atlantic Coast states and the new western states was linked to the preexisting tensions between the slave states and the free states.[34] The nature and scope of state sovereignty was central to the issue of expansion. The West, insisting on the liberalization of land acquisition by lowering the minimum purchase price and affirming squatters' rights, was in conflict with conservative national land policies supported by northeastern states. In part, the Northeast wished to diminish the effects of regional labor shortages resulting from out-migration.[35] The South chafed under protectionist tariffs favoring the Northeast.[36] Since neither West nor South by itself was sufficiently large to outvote the Northeast, cooperation was essential.

The erosion of the power of the slave states was well recognized by the federal legislature and continued with the 1840 apportionment. Table 2-18 reveals a net transfer of power from slave to free states of 1.8 percent, which reduced the proportion of the House representing slave states to 39.5 percent. Under the Missouri Compromise the northern limit of new slave states that could be created from the Louisiana Purchase was 36°30' north latitude. As the proportion of U.S. territory extending north of that latitude far exceeded that to the south, the slave states could only continue to lose proportional power if the nation continued to expand under existing legislation.

The 1830s had been the last decade with significant portions of the frontier east of the Mississippi.[37] Among the Northwest states, Michigan and Illinois were still substantially uninhabited by pioneers. At seventeen times the national average, Michigan grew faster than any other state. Illinois, Arkansas, Missouri, and Mississippi all grew at about five times the national rate.[38] West of the Mississippi River, Missouri, Arkansas, and Louisiana also had extensive frontier areas. During the decade, growth began in territories that would become Wisconsin, Iowa, and Minnesota, where thousands of squatters established land claims in advance of the public land survey and treaties with Indian tribes.[39] Elsewhere settlement patterns reflected accessibility, particularly by water, good soils, and cultivable terrain. By 1840 the railroad was more than an experimental technology. The first lines spanned the eastern seaboard and were beginning to penetrate the interior from ports such as Charleston, Baltimore, New York, and Boston. Initially the railroad made contributions to trade, rooting well-placed settlements in the national economy. Within two decades the railroad companies were to play a direct and substantial role in the settlement process itself.

32. Ibid., 349–352.

33. The apportionment act of 1842 was adopted June 25, 1842. A second section of the act required election "by districts composed of contiguous territory equal in number to the number of Representatives to which said State may be entitled, no one district electing more than one Representative" (5 Stat. L. 491). The 1842 method of apportionment was a true method of major fractions (greater than 0.5). Schmeckebier, *Congressional Apportionment*, 113.

34. The debate between Senators Daniel Webster (Massachusetts) and Robert Hayne (South Carolina) pitted states' rights against federal laws over the issue of protective tariffs. See J. D. Hicks, G. E. Mowry, and R. E. Burke, *A History of American Democracy* (Boston: Houghton Mifflin Company, 1970), 205–211.

35. Ibid.

36. Ibid.

37. For maps of frontier and settled areas 1800–1840, see Davis, *Frontier America*, 29–33

38. See Bogue, *Population*, 65, for the index of relative differential growth in states, geographic divisions, and census regions: 1790 to 1957.

39. Hicks et al., *History of American Democracy*, 225.

Table 2-16. 1840 Apportionment Statistics

State	Change in Seats	Seats Apportioned	Percent of House	Percentage Change
Alabama	2	7	3.1	1.0
Arkansas	1	1	0.4	0.4
Connecticut	-2	4	1.8	-0.7
Delaware	0	1	0.4	0.0
Georgia	-1	8	3.6	-0.2
Illinois	4	7	3.1	1.8
Indiana	3	10	4.5	1.6
Kentucky	-3	10	4.5	-0.9
Louisiana	1	4	1.8	0.5
Maine	-1	7	3.1	-0.2
Maryland	-2	6	2.7	-0.6
Massachusetts	-2	10	4.5	-0.5
Michigan	3	3	1.3	1.3
Mississippi	2	4	1.8	1.0
Missouri	3	5	2.2	1.4
New Hampshire	-1	4	1.8	-0.3
New Jersey	-1	5	2.2	-0.3
New York	-6	34	15.2	-1.5
North Carolina	-4	9	4.0	-1.4
Ohio	2	21	9.4	1.5
Pennsylvania	-4	24	10.8	-0.9
Rhode Island	0	2	0.9	0.1
South Carolina	-2	7	3.1	-0.7
Tennessee	-2	11	4.9	-0.5
Vermont	-1	4	1.8	-0.3
Virginia	-6	15	6.7	-2.1
Total	-17	223		

Table 2-17. Percentage Change for Original and New States, 1840

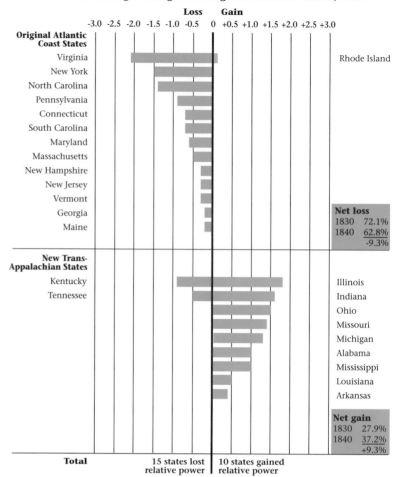

Delaware remained the same.

Table 2-18. Percentage Change for Slave and Free States, 1840

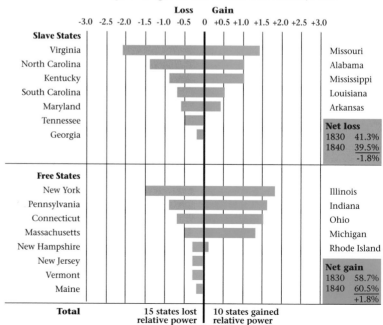

Delaware remained the same.

Map 6A. Change in Seats–1840

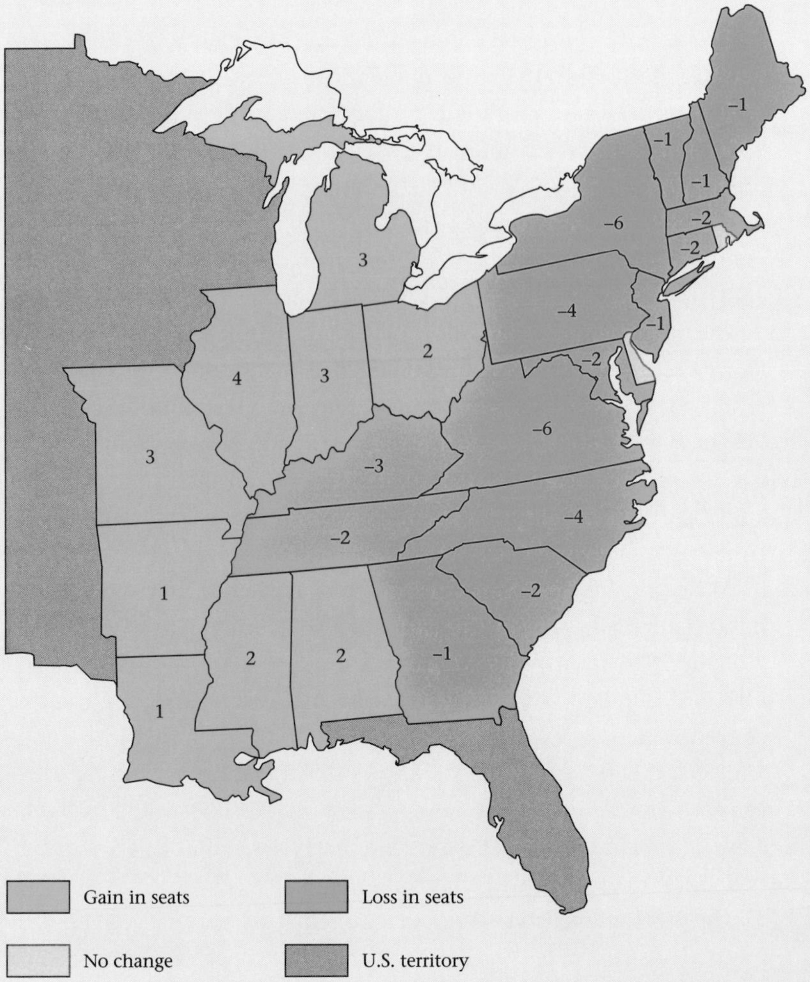

-1
-1
-1
-6
-2
-2
3
-4
-1
-2
2
4
3
-6
3
-3
-4
-2
1
-2
2
2
-1
1
Gain in seats
Loss in seats
No change
U.S. territory

Map 6B. Percentage Change in Power–1840

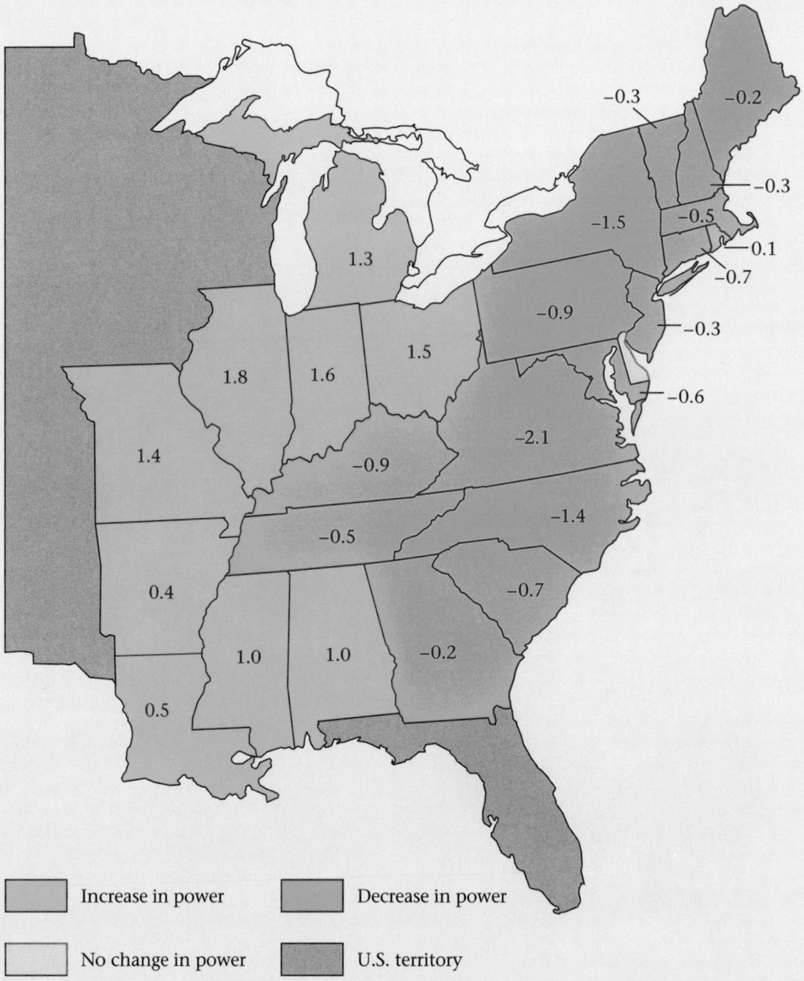

-0.3
-0.2
-0.3
-1.5
-0.5
0.1
-0.7
1.3
-0.9
-0.3
1.8
1.6
1.5
-0.6
-2.1
1.4
-0.9
-1.4
-0.5
0.4
-0.7
1.0
1.0
-0.2
0.5
Increase in power
Decrease in power
No change in power
U.S. territory

1850 CENSUS APPORTIONMENT

The seventh census recorded a total U.S. population of 23,191,876. Between 1840 and 1850 the population increased by 6,122,423 or 35.9 percent, a rate of growth only exceeded in the period between 1800 and 1810. Five states exceeded one million inhabitants. The population of New York, still the largest state, reached 3,097,408, with half a million residing in New York City. The population of Pennsylvania was 2,311,786, Ohio had 1,980,408, Virginia had 1,421,661, and Tennessee had 1,002,625 people.

Five states joined the Union between 1840 and 1850. Texas and Florida joined the Union in 1845 as slave states under provisions extending the Missouri Compromise to territories beyond the Louisiana Purchase. The admission of Iowa in 1846 and Wisconsin in 1848 as free states once again created a balance between the number of free and slave states. California's admission in 1850 necessitated further compromise between the political sections.[40]

Although the American government had demonstrated territorial interests in California in the early 1840s—gaining control of the region in 1846 during the Mexican-American War—the rise of California to statehood in 1850 was spectacularly accelerated by the discovery of gold in 1848. In 1845 it was estimated that, of a white population of 7,000, only 700 Americans lived in California.[41] By 1850 census, officials estimated a population of 165,000 residents, sufficient for the allocation of two representatives. California's entry to the Union made a total of thirty-one states.

The Vinton method of apportionment was adopted in 1850, a method that prevailed until 1900.[42] In 1850 Congress determined to set aside the contentious and time-consuming debates around the apportionment and to "fix the Number of Members of the House of Representatives, and provide for their future Apportionment among the several States."[43] Initially the size of the House was set at 233, increasing to 234 under an amendment in 1852.[44]

As a result of the apportionment, thirteen states gained seats, eight lost seats, and ten states had no change in the size of their delegations (see Map 7A). The five states admitted since the last apportionment accounted for ten seats. Although the population increase of New York (668,473) was larger than the total population of eighteen other states, the apportionment cost the state a seat in the House. Even in losing a seat, New York retained the largest delegation at thirty-three members (see Table 2-19). Of the original Atlantic Coast states, Massachusetts (eleven representatives) and Pennsylvania (twenty-five representatives) each gained a seat, whereas five original states each lost one. Virginia lost two members to drop to thirteen seats.

Table 2-20 indicates that of the twelve states that gained relative power and seventeen that lost it, the net result was a marked transfer of relative strength to the new trans-Appalachian states. Of the original states, only Massachusetts had a statistical gain in power but this was of negligible size. Reference to Map 7B indicates ten original states lost relative strength, and although individual changes were small for most, the collective pattern is marked. A Northeast to Southwest partition divides those states with settlement histories dating to the turn of the century from those more recently on the frontier. The relative strength of the gains increases in a westward direction. Five trans-Appalachian states had measurable decreases in power. Map 7B emphasizes the differences in the effect of the apportionment between the rapid western spread of the frontier and the infilling of the first trans-Appalachian states. Eleven new states, led by Wisconsin, gained power. The net increase in congressional membership for new states was 5.5 percent. New trans-Appalachian states now controlled 42.7 percent of the House of Representatives (see Table 2-20).

Within the region of relative decline, New York experienced a net loss of 1.1 percent. By virtue of their small size, Delaware and Rhode Island experienced no relative change. Virginia's position as the most powerful southern state continued to weaken with a further net loss of 1.1 percent. Table 2-21 shows that overall the fifteen slave states lost an additional percentage point to fall to 38.5 percent of the House.

Arguably the most important event of the middle decade of the nineteenth century was the establishment of the first state on the Pacific coast, fulfilling aspirations dating to colonial demarcations and reviving the contemporary sense of Manifest Destiny.[45] A new image emerged of the final form that the United States might take, one no longer petering out in the "Great American Desert" of the arid West, but a nation infilling all the territory between the Atlantic and the Pacific, subject to the power of the Mexicans and the British to constrain the nation to the South and North.

Population dynamics of the decade leading to 1850 had been marked by the initiation of railroads in the interior and revolutionized by the California gold rush. The railroads formed a network in the North and were reaching back from the Northwest to existing land and water transportation routes, providing accessibility to the markets of the East Coast. Yet the great inland waterways still dominated the human and commercial traffic of the frontier and many intermediate lands. The frontier itself was west of the Mississippi, everywhere but in the northern regions of Michigan, Wisconsin, and Minnesota. The Oregon and Santa Fe trails initiated significant migration streams to the Pacific Coast and arid Southwest. Primarily trading routes, they were overshadowed by the migration of Mormons from Iowa to the Salt Lake valley beginning in 1847, and the establishment of the Mormon Trail.

40. Two of the proposals by Henry Clay and others incorporated in the compromise of 1850 have some bearing on apportionment: (1) California was admitted as a free state; (2) New Mexico and Utah were designated as territories not covered by the Wilmot Proviso (which prohibited slavery in territories acquired from foreign powers) introduced in 1846. Oregon's status as a territory had been delayed two years until 1848 by debates relating to the Wilmot Proviso. Ibid., 272, 274.

41. Ibid., 265.

42. Samuel F. Vinton, a representative from Ohio, proposed a method wherein the apportionment population of the United States is divided by a predetermined number of members of the House to get a ratio. This fixed ratio—number of persons in each district—is divided into the apportionment population of each state to get each state's exact quota. One representative is awarded for each state with a quota less than one, and all other states receive representatives on the basis of the whole number in its exact quota. The remaining representatives are distributed on the basis of the highest fractions. Schmeckebier, *Congressional Apportionment,* 114–116.

43. The census act included language specifying the responsibility for census enumeration in 1850 and for future censuses, fixed the House composition at 233, and provided for apportionment using the Vinton method to be the responsibility of the secretary of interior (9 Stat. L. 428).

44. Amendments to the apportionment were adopted on July 30, 1852 (10 Stat. L. 25).

45. Connecticut, Virginia, and North Carolina claimed territory extending from the Atlantic to the Pacific. For examples of these grand belts or sea-to-sea claims, see Meinig, *Shaping of America,* 231–235.

Table 2-19. 1850 Apportionment Statistics

State	Change in Seats	Seats Apportioned	Percent of House	Percentage Change
Alabama	0	7	3.0	-0.1
Arkansas	1	2	0.9	0.5
California	2	2	0.9	0.9
Connecticut	0	4	1.7	-0.1
Delaware	0	1	0.4	0.0
Florida	1	1	0.4	0.4
Georgia	0	8	3.4	-0.2
Illinois	2	9	3.8	0.7
Indiana	1	11	4.7	0.2
Iowa	2	2	0.9	0.9
Kentucky	0	10	4.3	-0.2
Louisiana	0	4	1.7	-0.1
Maine	-1	6	2.6	-0.5
Maryland	0	6	2.6	-0.1
Massachusetts	1	11	4.7	0.2
Michigan	1	4	1.7	0.4
Mississippi	1	5	2.1	0.3
Missouri	2	7	3.0	0.8
New Hampshire	-1	3	1.3	-0.5
New Jersey	0	5	2.1	-0.1
New York	-1	33	14.1	-1.1
North Carolina	-1	8	3.4	-0.6
Ohio	0	21	9.0	-0.4
Pennsylvania	1	25	10.7	-0.1
Rhode Island	0	2	0.9	0.0
South Carolina	-1	6	2.6	-0.5
Tennessee	-1	10	4.3	-0.6
Texas	2	2	0.9	0.9
Vermont	-1	3	1.3	-0.5
Virginia	-2	13	5.6	-1.1
Wisconsin	3	3	1.3	1.3
Total	11	234		

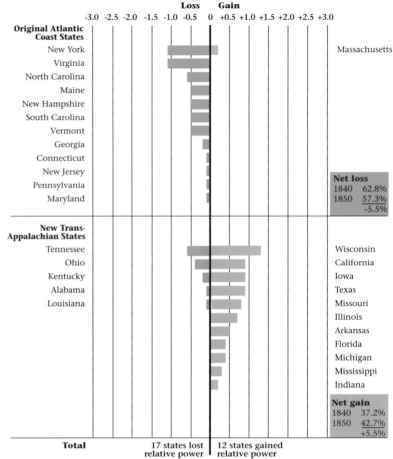

Table 2-20. Percentage Change for Original and New States, 1850

Rhode Island and Delaware remained the same.

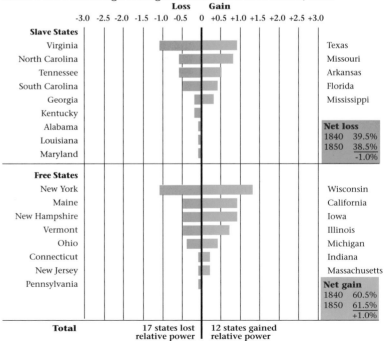

Table 2-21. Percentage Change for Slave and Free States, 1850

Rhode Island and Delaware remained the same.

Map 7A. Change in Seats–1850

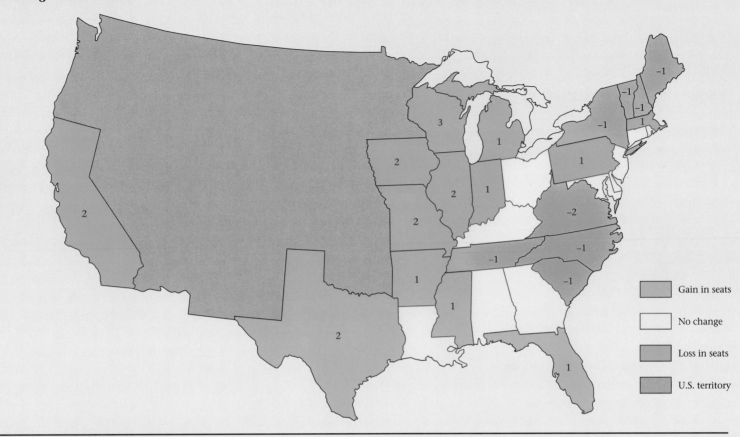

Gain in seats

No change

Loss in seats

U.S. territory

Map 7B. Percentage Change in Power–1850

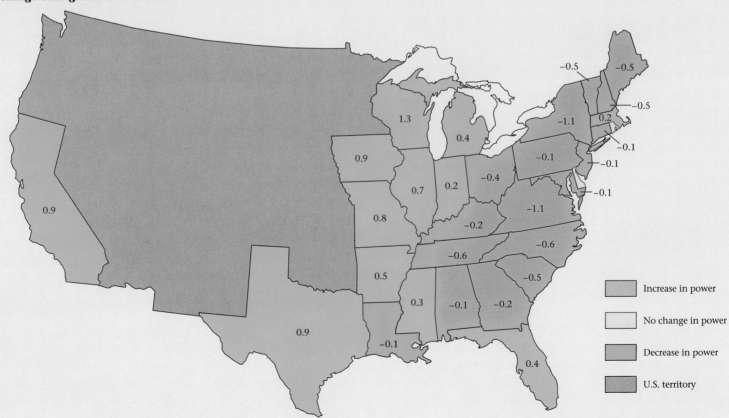

Increase in power

No change in power

Decrease in power

U.S. territory

1860 CENSUS APPORTIONMENT

In June 1860 the eighth census recorded a total population of 31,443,321. Between 1850 and 1860 the population increased by 8,251,445 (35.6 percent), almost twice the population increase between 1840 and 1850. New York (3,880,735) was the most populous state, followed by Pennsylvania (2,906,215), Ohio (2,339,511), and Illinois (1,711,951) with Virginia (1,596,318) dropping to fifth. Indiana, Massachusetts, and Missouri all surpassed the population of Tennessee, which had been fifth in size in 1850.

Immigration, estimated at 300,000 per year between 1845 and 1855, substantially increased particularly from Ireland and Germany. The Irish were being driven out by British oppression, very large rates of population growth, and the potato famine. Disproportionately these immigrants were attracted to the northern states, mainly because their labor was not required in the slave states. The Irish landed in large numbers in Boston and New York and frequently, though not invariably, took urban jobs and helped to energize metropolitan growth (note the accelerated growth of Massachusetts above, for example). On the other hand, the German immigrants preferred to settle in the Midwest, more often as farmers than factory workers.

Three free states were admitted to the Union before the apportionment was certified by the secretary of the interior in 1861: Minnesota (1858), Oregon (1859), and Kansas (1861), making a total of thirty-four states, fifteen of which were slave states. The territory of the United States increased slightly through the acquisition of the Gadsden Purchase from Mexico for $10 million in 1853. This land was added to New Mexico Territory.

The method of apportionment adopted under the census act of 1850 was applied to the apportionment populations derived from the 1860 census. Initially the size of the House was fixed at 233, but the number was increased to 241 under an amendment in 1862.[46]

Division between gains and losses of the 1860 apportionment was aligned North to South from Ohio to Mississippi. In having no actual change, Indiana and Mississippi appear to buffer the division, thereby accentuating it on Map 8A. Twelve western states gained representatives as a result of the apportionment, thirteen eastern states lost, and nine states, which appear to be situated peripherally to the core of losing states, had no change in the size of their delegations.[47] Of the gains, the new states of Minnesota, Oregon, and Kansas accounted for four seats.

Although the population of New York increased by three quarters of a million, a figure larger than the apportionment population of twenty-one states, the apportionment reduced the state delegation by two seats. New York remained the largest delegation at thirty-one members, and the ratio between largest and smallest delegations was somewhat reduced (see Table 2-22). Of the other original Atlantic Coast states, Massachusetts with ten representatives and Pennsylvania with twenty-four each lost a seat. Virginia and South Carolina lost two seats each. Maine, Massachusetts, Maryland, North Carolina, and Georgia lost one seat each. In the interior, Tennessee and Ohio each lost two seats and Kentucky and Alabama lost one. The focus of increased representation was in the central and upper Midwest as illustrated in Map 8A. A total of sixteen additional representatives—Illinois (five seats), Iowa (four seats), Wisconsin (three seats), and Michigan, Missouri, and Minnesota (two seats each)—were added to the fastest growing region of the nation.[48]

Map 8B indicates that twelve states gained relative power and seventeen lost it. East of the Mississippi only three states increased in strength: Wisconsin, Illinois, and Michigan. Ten of the original states lost relative strength, and although individual changes were small for most, the collective pattern is evident. States east of the Mississippi having population densities greater than forty-five people per square mile are divided from those to the west where densities were generally between six and eighteen per square mile.[49]

The strength of the gains reflects the additional midwestern representatives, and Map 8B emphasizes the contrast between the rapid western spread of the frontier and the relatively slow infilling of Indiana, Ohio, and Mississippi. Twelve new trans-Appalachian states, led by Illinois, gained relative strength in the House. The net increase in congressional membership for new states was 6.9 percent.

Within the region of relative decline, New York experienced a net loss of 1.2 percent and Ohio lost 1.1 percent. In the South, Virginia and Tennessee lost 1.0 percent each. Table 2-23 shows that the slave states lost by an additional 3.2 percent to decline to 35.3 percent of the House. Principally as a result of western expansion but in part due to the lower rates of population growth in the South, the power of the southern alliance had reached its nadir just as the final struggle to protect slavery and the southern economy began.

Development in the United States from 1850 to 1860 was largely of infrastructure improvements, especially of the railroad network, and of growing industrialization in the Northeast-Midwest corridor. Thirty thousand miles of railroad connected the Atlantic seaboard to

the Mississippi River and beyond, extending to the Kansas border and the heads of the western trails. In the North the network was dense with multiple east to west routes, whereas only two railroads linked the Mississippi River with the southeastern states. The density of the rail network indicated the importance of a growing manufacturing sector in the North and, significantly, the early development of an urban hierarchy. In 1860 nearly one-fifth of the population lived in urban territory.[50] A majority of the 392 "places in urban territory" were in the North and Midwest. The South had only one major city, New Orleans (168,000), which was seen to be critical to the health of many Midwestern cities that were upstream on the Mississippi and its tributaries. The urban population of the North was approaching six million, long-established cities such as New York, Boston, Baltimore, and Philadelphia recently joined by Detroit and Chicago were about to benefit enormously as lake shore terminals, and railroad and manufacturing centers.

If industrial capacity was going to be a deciding factor in the Civil War, so also was agricultural production, particularly of cereals and livestock. The Corn Belt states from Ohio to Illinois were well established and productive. The 2,100,000 people living in the emerging Grain Belt of Iowa, Missouri, Minnesota, Kansas, and Nebraska Territory caused a striking shift in representation as reflected in the maps of apportionment for 1860.[51]

46. On March 4, 1862, an act fixed the number of representatives at 241, assigning one additional representative each to Pennsylvania, Ohio, Kentucky, Illinois, Iowa, Minnesota, Vermont, and Rhode Island (12 Stat. L. 353). Schmeckebier describes this act as "confusing" since in part it supersedes the census act of 1850 (9 Stat. L. 432) when amending the size of the House, whereas in part it alters the apportionment of 1861 made pursuant to the act by the secretary of interior. See Schmeckebier, *Congressional Apportionment,* 117.

47. The apportionment of representatives describes the amended total membership of 241 seats (12 Stat. L. 533).

48. From 1850 to 1860 Minnesota experienced the highest index of relative population growth recorded by any state for any intercensal period in U.S. history. This index relates the rate of state growth to the national rate. A value of 7570 indicates that Minnesota was growing at more than 75 times the national rate of 36 percent. The extreme nature of this value is biased by the admission of the state during this intercensal period but comparable values for Washington State (1860) 2331, Arkansas (1820) 3658, North Dakota (1880) 4666 indicate the extraordinary magnitude of the relative growth of Minnesota in this decade. Figures from Bogue, *Population,* 65. The region of Iowa, Kansas, Minnesota, Missouri, and Nebraska grew at 146.7 percent from 1850 to 1860. Ibid., 64.

49. Population densities are drawn from Gannett, *Statistical Atlas.*

50. In 1860, 19.8 percent lived in urban territory, 5.2 percent in cities of 250,000 or more (all in the North), 4.6 percent in cities of 100,000 to 250,000 (all in the North except for New Orleans). U.S. Department of Commerce, Bureau of the Census, *U.S. Census of Population: 1950,* vol. 1, U.S. Summary (Washington, D.C.: Government Printing Office, 1955), Table 5b.

51. Carson and Weisberger, "Great Countdown," *American Heritage,* 10.

Table 2-22. 1860 Apportionment Statistics

State	Change in Seats	Seats Apportioned	Percent of House	Percentage Change
Alabama	-1	6	2.5	-0.5
Arkansas	1	3	1.2	0.3
California	1	3	1.2	0.3
Connecticut	0	4	1.7	0.0
Delaware	0	1	0.4	0.0
Florida	0	1	0.4	0.0
Georgia	-1	7	2.9	-0.5
Illinois	5	14	5.8	2.0
Indiana	0	11	4.6	-0.1
Iowa	4	6	2.5	1.6
Kansas	1	1	0.4	0.4
Kentucky	-1	9	3.7	-0.6
Louisiana	1	5	2.1	0.4
Maine	-1	5	2.1	-0.5
Maryland	-1	5	2.1	-0.5
Massachusetts	-1	10	4.1	-0.6
Michigan	2	6	2.5	0.8
Minnesota	2	2	0.8	0.8
Mississippi	0	5	2.1	0.0
Missouri	2	9	3.7	0.7
New Hampshire	0	3	1.2	-0.1
New Jersey	0	5	2.1	0.0
New York	-2	31	12.9	-1.2
North Carolina	-1	7	2.9	-0.5
Ohio	-2	19	7.9	-1.1
Oregon	1	1	0.4	0.4
Pennsylvania	-1	24	10.0	-0.7
Rhode Island	0	2	0.8	-0.1
South Carolina	-2	4	1.7	-0.9
Tennessee	-2	8	3.3	-1.0
Texas	2	4	1.7	0.8
Vermont	0	3	1.2	-0.1
Virginia	-2	11	4.6	-1.0
Wisconsin	3	6	2.5	1.2
Total	7	241		

Table 2-23. Percentage Change for Slave and Free States, 1860

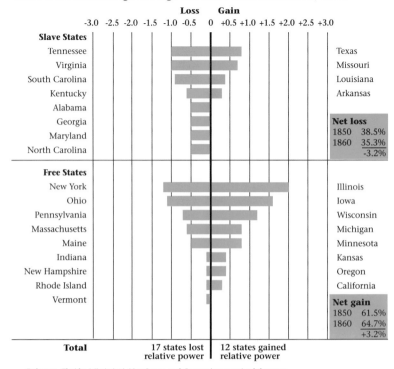

Delaware, Florida, Mississippi, New Jersey, and Connecticut remained the same.

Map 8A. Change in Seats–1860

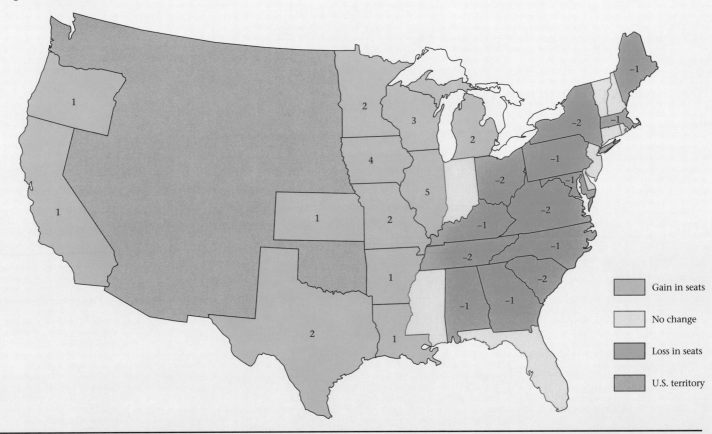

Gain in seats

No change

Loss in seats

U.S. territory

Map 8B. Percentage Change in Power–1860

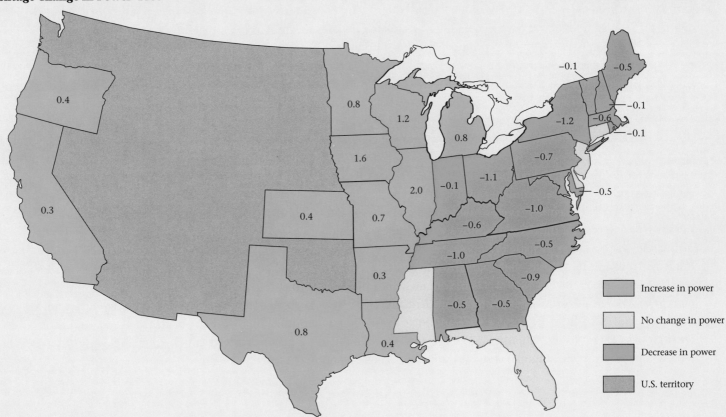

Increase in power

No change in power

Decrease in power

U.S. territory

1870 CENSUS APPORTIONMENT

Disorganized by the aftermath of the Civil War, the ninth census was subject to errors resulting from underenumeration of the population, especially in the South. Originally the superintendent of the census reported a U.S. population of 38,558,371; however, biases introduced by political patronage, the enumeration of blacks, and the still disabled government in the South necessitated a revised estimation.[52] After revision the adjusted total population was 39,818,449.[53] In spite of the size of the adjustment, the first major drop in the U.S. growth rate occurred between 1860 and 1870. The population grew at only 26.6 percent, and rates exceeding 30 percent have not been recorded since. While it is impossible to assess to what extent population growth rates might have declined by the end of the nineteenth century under the influences of other circumstances, it is evident that the Civil War precipitated an abrupt and persistent change in U.S. population geography that was to influence the composition of the House of Representatives for many decades.

With the passage of the Fourteenth Amendment to the Constitution, granting citizenship to all persons born or naturalized in the United States, the three-fifths rule was no longer in effect in the South. Provisions in Section 2 of the amendment mandated the apportionment of representatives by "counting the whole number of persons in each State, excluding Indians not taxed." The numbers of untaxed Indians had been so reduced by conflict and forced migration that even in Kansas, Nebraska, and California, which had the greatest number of Native Americans, the difference between total population and apportionment population was not much greater than ten thousand.

Civil War upheavals in the political and economic sphere placed a temporary curb on the rising number of immigrants in the second half of the nineteenth century. Even while immigration slowed during the first five years of the decade, positive net-migration made up nearly one quarter of the increase in population.[54] Only 707,234 immigrants landed from 1860 to 1864; but with the end of hostilities, arrivals leaped. From 1865 to 1869, 1,374,018 immigrants arrived, 80 percent of them from northwestern Europe and Germany.[55]

During the 1860s three new states were admitted: West Virginia (1863), Nevada (1864), and Nebraska (1867). Congress assigned three representatives to West Virginia and one each to Nebraska and Nevada. Nevada, with a population of 58,711, displaced Oregon (101,883) as the smallest state. Nevada's apportionment population was even smaller at 42,491. New York's total population remained the largest at 4,387,464. Virginia lost population by division: most of the three western Virginia congressional districts had become the state of West Virginia during the Civil War.

The apportionment act of 1872 set the House size to 283, an increase of forty-two seats over 1860.[56] The basis for apportionment was one member for every 131,425 persons, however this ratio was not specifically written into the act.[57] The original apportionment act of 1872 was eventually amended to add nine more representatives, which set the House size at 292.

Map 9A indicates that, in contrast to the apportionments since 1820, states either gained seats or remained the same. No state lost any seat because of the large increase in the size of the House.[58] New York remained the largest delegation with thirty-three representatives, accounting for 11.3 percent of House membership (Table 2-24).

Map 9B illustrates the widespread distribution of the seventeen states that gained relative power. They are dispersed from the West Coast and western frontier to the Midwest and, perhaps unexpectedly, the South. Missouri made the largest gain increasing by 0.8 percent to account for 4.5 percent of the House total. Illinois (0.7 percent), Iowa (0.6 percent), and Michigan (0.6 percent) also had big gains. On the Great Plains and southern frontier, Kansas (0.6 percent), Nebraska (0.3 percent), and Texas (0.4 percent) increased their power in the House. Nevada's increase of 0.3 percent is accounted for by its being a new state with its first representative—0.3 percent was its total proportion of the House.

Map 9B also illustrates an important geographical pattern of the loss of political power focused on the Northeast. Within this region of relative decline, New York experienced a net loss of 1.6 percent and Ohio lost 1.1 percent, as large state populations with lower relative population growth rates were vulnerable under the Vinton method of apportionment. Losses from individual New England states were negligible, but collectively the region declined 1.5 percent. The inclusion of Pennsylvania and Indiana, which both had small relative declines, forms an emphatic block of losses in the North.

In the South, Virginia and North Carolina lost 0.2 percent each (see Table 2-25). While Louisiana, Mississippi, and South Carolina showed no change, Texas, Florida, Alabama, Arkansas, Georgia, and Tennessee each increased in relative power. The enumeration of African-Americans as whole people in the census accounts for the increases. The southern states that showed loss or no gain in power were probably affected by the disorganization and malfeasance surrounding the ninth census. For example, the total population of South Carolina in 1860 was 703,708; its apportionment population was 542,745, indicating a slave population of 402,406.[59] In 1870 South Carolina's total population was enumerated as 705,606, far below reasonable estimates even after consideration of the disruptive effects of war on South Carolina's people. Similar observations may be made in other southern states.

The need for war material had accelerated the Industrial Revolution in the North. Given the region's political domination after 1865, the North was able to hold onto this advantage for industrial development over the next century. Restrictive trade tariffs protected American industry, the federal government granted railroads extensive lands towards their transcontinental expansion, and national banking and currency policies favored the spread of business dominated by the commercial interests of the Northeast. The former alliance between the two leading agricultural sections of the country, the South and the Northwest, had been weakened in the antebellum period and was finally destroyed by the Northwest's assistance to the Northeast during the war. In the future, the Northwest would have to mount its own opposition to northeastern interests that clashed with its own.

In 1865 the socioeconomic structure of the South was ruined. Hunger was rampant after the scorched earth policies followed by Sherman in Georgia and South Carolina, and by Sheridan in the Shenandoah, and by sweeping warfare in Tennessee and southern Virginia. There was no currency or organized system of commerce and industry. Some 250,000 Confederate soldiers had died along with uncounted numbers of civilians. On the other hand, because land prices were decimated, many who had been unable to afford land were now able to become farmers. The 1870 census revealed major increases in the number of farms in South Carolina, Mississippi, and Louisiana since the previous census. Other physical structures were also rebuilt rapidly—for example, railroads by 1870 exceeded their prewar extent in the South by 2,500 miles. The railroad network connected a rapidly growing number of industries that were being reconstructed in the southern cities.

With respect to population shifts, the completion of the transcontinental railroad in 1869 was only symbolic, yet other forces had acted in the West that shaped the composition of the House of Representatives in 1870 and afterward. Mineral ore discoveries in Colorado and Nevada in 1859 and Idaho in 1860 drew thousands westward. Because of political consideration, Nevada was granted statehood precipitously only three years after being declared a territory in 1861. The territories of Colorado (1861), Idaho (1863), Arizona (1863), and Montana (1864) were all created as the result of mining booms. In most cases the populations dwindled as rapidly as they had formed, but the process of political organization had been initiated and would be influential on the structure of the House in the upcoming decades.

52. " . . . the U.S. marshals looked upon the census as an opportunity to distribute the offices [census assistants] to deserving henchmen. . . . The entire force of enumerators was taken from the Republican party and included some who could not read or write." Ibid.

53. U.S. Department of Commerce, Bureau of the Census, *Statistical Abstract of the United States* (Washington, D.C.: Government Printing Office, 1956), 5.

54. From 1860 to 1870 immigration totaled 2,081,252 (24 percent) of the 8,375,128 increase in population. Of the immigrants 1,374,018 landed after the Civil War had ended, the majority was from Germany, followed by Great Britain and Ireland. See Bogue, *Population,* Table 14.1, 350.

55. *Historical Statistics of the United States* (Washington, D.C.: Government Printing Office, 1975), Table B-304.

56. The act of apportionment was passed on February 2, 1872. The language of the act specified the number of members from each state on the basis of the Vinton method (17 Stat. L. 28). New states admitted after the apportionment were to be given additional seats. Under the 1872 act, 283 seats were allotted. A supplemental act passed in May of that year added representatives to Alabama, Florida, Indiana, Louisiana, New Hampshire, New York, Pennsylvania, Tennessee, and Vermont (17 Stat. L. 192), bringing the House total to 292 representatives.

57. Schmeckebier, *Congressional Apportionment,* 118. Schmeckebier also draws attention to three other provisions of the act of 1872: (1) requiring each member have one district composed of contiguous territory, and approximately equal numbers of inhabitants, (2) prohibiting the admission of new states thereafter "without having the necessary population to entitle it to at least one representative according to the ratio of representation fixed by this bill," and (3) requiring reduction of representation if the right of male citizens to vote was abridged. Provision (2) of the act did not specify the ratio, nor could the provision be enforced as no Congress can bind a succeeding Congress. Schmeckebier also presents contemporary statements on the difficulties involved in enforcing the Fourteenth Amendment. Ibid., 94–97.

58. See footnote 10 for the method of calculation.

59. Schmeckebier, *Congressional Apportionment,* Appendix C, 230.

Table 2-24. 1870 Apportionment Statistics

State	Change in Seats	Seats Apportioned	Percent of House	Percentage Change
Alabama	2	8	2.7	0.2
Arkansas	1	4	1.4	0.2
California	1	4	1.4	0.2
Connecticut	0	4	1.4	-0.3
Delaware	0	1	0.3	-0.1
Florida	1	2	0.7	0.3
Georgia	2	9	3.1	0.2
Illinois	5	19	6.5	0.7
Indiana	2	13	4.5	-0.1
Iowa	3	9	3.1	0.6
Kansas	2	3	1.0	0.6
Kentucky	1	10	3.4	-0.3
Louisiana	1	6	2.1	0.0
Maine	0	5	1.7	-0.4
Maryland	1	6	2.1	0.0
Massachusetts	1	11	3.8	-0.3
Michigan	3	9	3.1	0.6
Minnesota	1	3	1.0	0.2
Mississippi	1	6	2.1	0.0
Missouri	4	13	4.5	0.8
Nebraska	1	1	0.3	0.3
Nevada	1	1	0.3	0.3
New Hampshire	0	3	1.0	-0.2
New Jersey	2	7	2.4	0.3
New York	2	33	11.3	-1.6
North Carolina	1	8	2.7	-0.2
Ohio	1	20	6.8	-1.1
Oregon	0	1	0.3	-0.1
Pennsylvania	3	27	9.2	-0.8
Rhode Island	0	2	0.7	-0.1
South Carolina	1	5	1.7	0.0
Tennessee	2	10	3.4	0.1
Texas	2	6	2.1	0.4
Vermont	0	3	1.0	-0.2
Virginia	1[a]	9	3.1	-0.2
West Virginia	0[a]	3	1.0	-0.3
Wisconsin	2	8	2.7	0.2
Total	51	292		

[a]West Virginia was a part of Virginia until June 1863. In the 1860 apportionment Virginia was allotted eleven representatives. In the 1850s and through the 1860 congressional election, three of these representatives were given districts in the northwestern portion of the state. In the 1870 apportionment Virginia received nine representatives and West Virginia three for a total of twelve. Virginia is assigned a seat change of plus one, because of the increased count of African-Americans in this area, and West Virginia is assigned a seat change of zero because of the past allocation.

Table 2-25. Percentage Change by Region, 1870

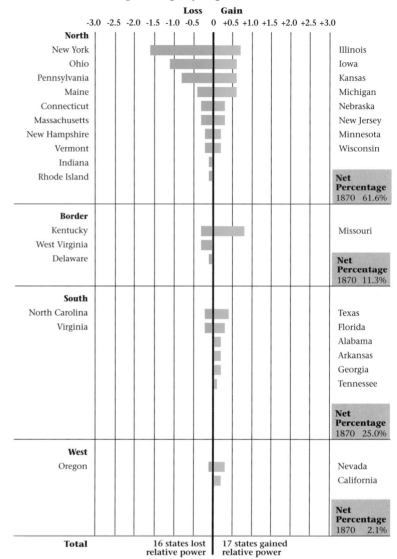

Louisiana, Maryland, Mississippi, and South Carolina remained the same.

Map 9A. Change in Seats–1870

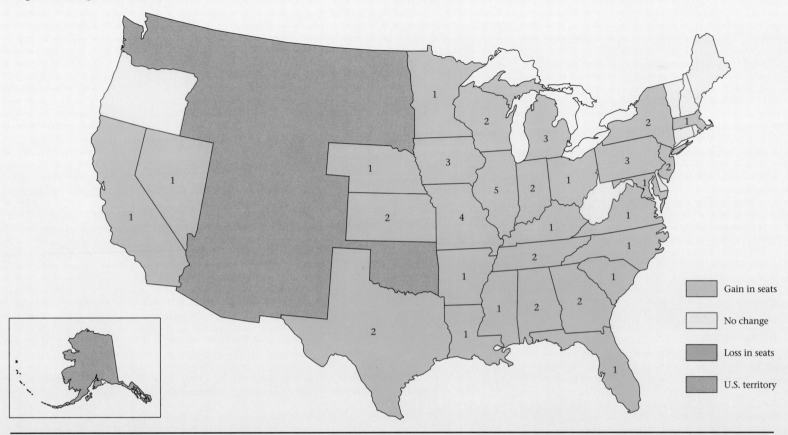

Gain in seats

No change

Loss in seats

U.S. territory

Map 9B. Percentage Change in Power–1870

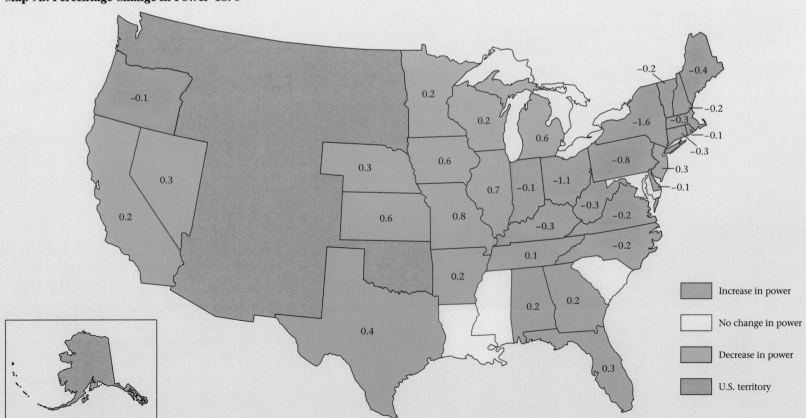

Increase in power

No change in power

Decrease in power

U.S. territory

1880 CENSUS APPORTIONMENT

As the national economy developed, so did the demand for information. Consequently, the tenth census exceeded all previous enumerations in the detail of information sought.[60] The total population in 1880 was 50,155,783, an increase of 10,337,334 or 26 percent since 1870. Of this increase, nearly two and three-quarter million were immigrants, signaling a growing shift in American population growth away from natural reproduction.[61] Corrections to the populations of several southern states were apparent, but new forces of segregation and disenfranchisement started to become significant in the differential undercounting of the black population. Although Colorado was recently admitted to the Union in 1876, Nevada's population remained the smallest (62,265). New York still had the largest population with 5,083,810 residents.

The apportionment act of 1882 provided for 325 House representatives, an increase of thirty-three seats over 1870.[62] The basis for apportionment was not written into the act.[63] New York remained the largest delegation at thirty-four members, accounting for 10.5 percent of House membership. Colorado, Delaware, Nevada, and Oregon each had one member under the constitutional requirement that every state have at least one representative.

The patterns illustrated on Map 10A express clearly the several factors that influenced the change of seats in the House. In the West, California's population continued to grow long after the infusion of Americans during the gold rush had subsided because of its wide range of economic opportunities. In contrast, Nevada was unable to capitalize on its mining boom, as there were too few alternative economic resources and a lack of irrigation water to attract farmers. Similarly Oregon, despite considerable agricultural and forest resources, failed to capitalize on its early development because of its distance from markets. Oregon was completely isolated from the East until the completion of a connection to the Northern Pacific Railroad in 1883. California continued to grow in part because it was able to meet the agricultural, forestry, and mineral needs of its own market, and in part because of the transcontinental railroad link to the growing U.S. market. As a result of its increasing population, California gained two seats whereas Nevada and Oregon remained static with one each. With six members, California's delegation had already outstripped that of thirteen other states (see Table 2-26).

The states with the largest gains in House seats were part of the westward-moving frontier. Texas received five additional seats; Kansas had four new members; Minnesota, Nebraska, and Iowa received two each; and Colorado and Arkansas had one seat each. If California's gains are included, a total of nineteen new members were added to states that were still considered to have frontier areas.

The additional members in the southern states reflected both the rejuvenating influence of reconstruction on population growth and the more accurate enumeration of the tenth census, especially with respect to African-Americans. Here natural increase and internal migration rather than immigration was the stimulus for population growth. The South was not a major destination of the renewed wave of immigrants from northwestern Europe. In spite of the large increase in the size of the House, four southern states had no change from the size of their 1870 membership: Alabama, Florida, Louisiana, and Tennessee.

The contribution of immigrants is evident in gains made in the Northeast (for example, Massachusetts, New York, and Pennsylvania) and the central midwestern states (for example, Ohio, Michigan, Illinois) where urban growth had begun to surpass the still considerable increase of the farming population. Only a small geographic concentration in the New England states failed to expand sufficiently to maintain the size of their previous delegations. Maine, New Hampshire, and Vermont each lost one member. Additionally five others, all small Atlantic Coast states, experienced limited population growth imposed by their restricted territories and did not increase their delegations even though the House increased by thirty-three members in all.

Map 10A also highlights the growth and form of the frontier but exaggerates the extent of the settled area. To the north the settled area ran diagonally across Minnesota, then reached hundreds of miles westward across the Great Plains in Nebraska and Kansas. The contiguity of Colorado with Nebraska and Kansas exaggerates this penetration of white settlers—several hundred miles of lands without permanent settlers separated the western agricultural frontier from the mining-induced populations around Denver. Plains Indians, already displaced west several times, were now between the hammer of frontier expansion and the anvil of the Rockies. Reentrants in the frontier, to the north in the Dakotas and to the south in Indian Territory, mark the much reduced domain of Native Americans.

Separated from Kansas by Indian Territory, Texas with five new seats benefited from agricultural expansion, particularly of cotton, in the eastern part of the state and the short-lived explosion of Texas open-range cattle raising. From 1870 to 1880 more than one million cattle were driven annually over the Fort Worth and Fort Griffin trails.[64]

In contrast to the widespread actual gains of seats across the nation, Map 10B indicates the irregular distribution of the fourteen states that gained relative power. Texas and Kansas had the largest individual gains, increasing by 1.3 and 1.2 percent, respectively, followed by Nebraska with a 0.6 percent increase (see Table 2-27 for the percentage change by region for the 1880 apportionment). When the relative increases of Colorado, Iowa, and Minnesota are included, the dominant change of this period can be seen to accrue to the frontier. California had a positive change in power. Elsewhere, South Carolina's 0.5 percent gain and increases in Arkansas, Mississippi, and North Carolina probably reflect a correction from the 1870 census undercount of freed slaves.

Relative losses should be interpreted with care since geographic contiguity tends to overstate the region of decline in the South, where individual losses were small. Extending from Maine to Missouri, the swath of northern and midwestern states that lost relative strength is apparently separated from those in the South by a wedge of unchanging and increasing strength including the Virginias, the Carolinas, Kentucky, and Georgia. The overriding explanation for the losses demonstrated by all eighteen states is the continued transfer of political strength westward.

Certain anomalies resulted from local changes in population distribution. Note, for example, that New York (-0.8 percent) lost a slightly greater proportion of power than Maine (-0.5 percent), yet the population of New York increased by nearly seven hundred thousand and that of Maine by only twenty-two thousand.[65] New York actually gained a representative, Maine lost one. However, these interstate changes are leveled by the greater national events. By 1880 the states west of the Mississippi amounted to 20 percent of the House.

60. Two hundred schedules (census forms) "asked an almost unbelievable total of thirteen thousand questions" on every aspect of life, Carson and Weisberger, "The Great Countdown," 11.

61. Bogue, *Population,* Table 14.1, "Number of Immigrants to the United States, by continent, region and nation of origin, 1820 to 1957," 350.

62. The act of apportionment was passed on February 25, 1882, and specified the number of members from each state on the basis of the Vinton method (18 Stat. L. 474). Additional provisions required that state districts be compact and of approximately equal population.

63. Schmeckebier, *Congressional Apportionment,* 119. However, if as prescribed by Vinton, the total population of the states, 49,369,595 (p. 230), is divided by the size of the House, 325, the ratio is estimated as 151,906. As the population total of the 1880 census has been adjusted several times, it is not certain that this is the actual figure used by the secretary of interior.

64. The destination and magnitude of drives revealed that their purpose was largely for the stocking of the northern plains for breeding and to the Indian Agencies, rather than for the slaughterhouses of Kansas City and places east. The extent of such data illustrates the scope of the 1880 census. C. Gordon, "Report on Cattle, Sheep, and Swine, Supplementary to the Enumeration of Livestock on Farms in 1880," *Tenth Census,* 1880, vol. 3, 951–1110.

65. The population of New York (5,083,810) increased by more than the population of Maine (648,945) between 1870 and 1880.

Table 2-26. 1880 Apportionment Statistics

State	Change in Seats	Seats Apportioned	Percent of House	Percentage Change
Alabama	0	8	2.5	-0.2
Arkansas	1	5	1.5	0.1
California	2	6	1.8	0.4
Colorado	1	1	0.3	0.3
Connecticut	0	4	1.2	-0.2
Delaware	0	1	0.3	0.0
Florida	0	2	0.6	-0.1
Georgia	1	10	3.1	0.0
Illinois	1	20	6.2	-0.3
Indiana	0	13	4.0	-0.5
Iowa	2	11	3.4	0.3
Kansas	4	7	2.2	1.2
Kentucky	1	11	3.4	0.0
Louisiana	0	6	1.8	-0.3
Maine	-1	4	1.2	-0.5
Maryland	0	6	1.8	-0.3
Massachusetts	1	12	3.7	-0.1
Michigan	2	11	3.4	0.3
Minnesota	2	5	1.5	0.5
Mississippi	1	7	2.2	0.1
Missouri	1	14	4.3	-0.2
Nebraska	2	3	0.9	0.6
Nevada	0	1	0.3	0.0
New Hampshire	-1	2	0.6	-0.4
New Jersey	0	7	2.2	-0.2
New York	1	34	10.5	-0.8
North Carolina	1	9	2.8	0.1
Ohio	1	21	6.5	-0.3
Oregon	0	1	0.3	0.0
Pennsylvania	1	28	8.6	-0.6
Rhode Island	0	2	0.6	-0.1
South Carolina	2	7	2.2	0.5
Tennessee	0	10	3.1	-0.3
Texas	5	11	3.4	1.3
Vermont	-1	2	0.6	-0.4
Virginia	1	10	3.1	0.0
West Virginia	1	4	1.2	0.2
Wisconsin	1	9	2.8	0.1
Total	33	325		

Table 2-27. Percentage Change by Region, 1880

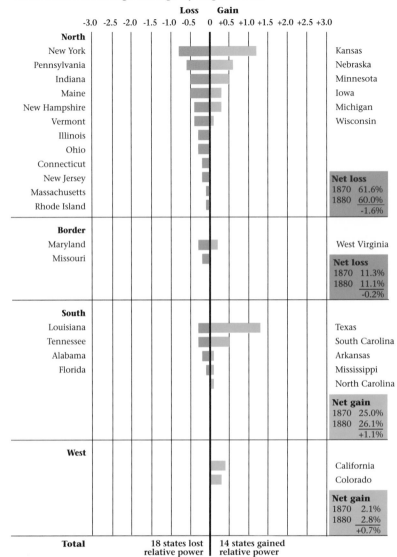

Delaware, Kentucky, Nevada, Oregon, Virginia, and Georgia remained the same.

Map 10A. Change in Seats–1880

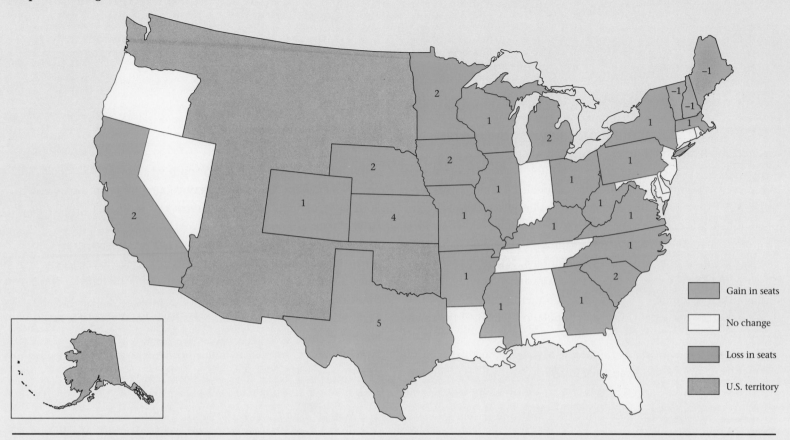

Gain in seats

No change

Loss in seats

U.S. territory

Map 10B. Percentage Change in Power–1880

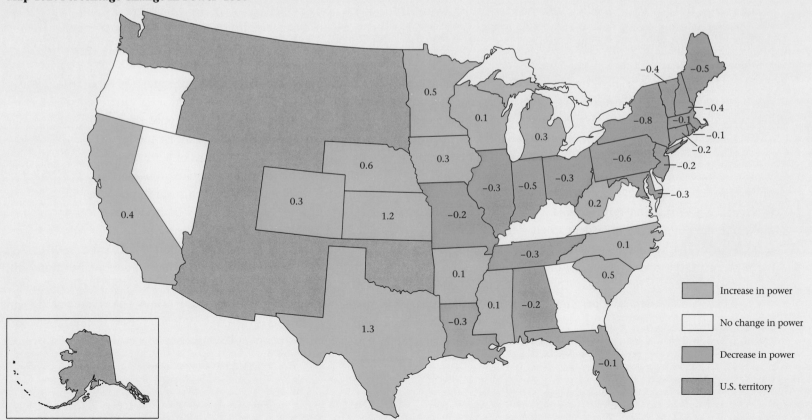

Increase in power

No change in power

Decrease in power

U.S. territory

1890 CENSUS APPORTIONMENT

One hundred years after the first census, the eleventh census reported a total population of 62,947,714, an increase of 12,791,931 or 25.5 percent over the decade, and a sixteenfold increase over the century. From 1880 to 1890, immigration exceeded five million, almost twice that of the preceding decade, rebounding from the prolonged economic depression that began in 1878.[66] Again New York had the largest population with 5,997,853 inhabitants. Six states were admitted to the Union from 1880 to 1890: Montana, North Dakota, South Dakota, and Washington in 1889; and Idaho and Wyoming in 1890. Even with the addition of Idaho and Montana, western states that had mining as their origin, Nevada's population remained the smallest with only 62,265 inhabitants.

The apportionment act of 1891 provided for 356 members, an increase of 31 from 1880.[67] As in 1880, the ratio with which apportionment quotas were determined was not written into the act.[68] Table 2-28 lists the changes resulting from the allocation of the 356 representatives among the states. New York remained the largest delegation with thirty-four members, accounting for 9.6 percent of House membership, while Pennsylvania reduced the gap with thirty members and 8.4 percent. Six states—Delaware, Idaho, Montana, Nevada, North Dakota, and Wyoming—each were allotted one member in accordance with the constitutional requirement.

Map 11A shows that twenty-three states added congressional districts following the census. No states lost seats in the apportionment but twenty-one states had no change in the size of their delegation even though the size of the House of Representatives increased. The pattern of change in Map 11A depicts an allocation of new seats primarily to states west of the Mississippi whereas most of the states to the east had no change. The exceptions in the Northeast were Massachusetts, New Jersey, and Pennsylvania. Growing urbanization and industrial development were evident in all three states. Pennsylvania's industrial growth was literally fueled by indigenous resources of coal and oil, coupled with the extraordinary entrepreneurial abilities of Andrew Carnegie and J. Edgar Thompson, among others. Although the state's growth of 22 percent was slower than the 25.5 percent national rate of increase, Pennsylvania gained two districts. In gaining one additional seat, Massachusetts grew at the national rate,

and New Jersey grew somewhat faster, as did Michigan and Wisconsin in the Midwest.[69]

While the growth rate in the South was slower than the national rate, Alabama and Georgia still gained an additional member each.[70] Both were undergoing strong urban and industrial growth on the basis of natural resources. Of the central states the population of the northern region grew most rapidly, led by the Dakotas. Nebraska gained three seats; Minnesota and South Dakota each gained two seats. Although the western states registered growth from two to ten times the national rate, Oregon and California gained just one seat each because of relatively small base populations. Washington with an exceptional growth rate fourteen times that of the nation was awarded two members on admission to the Union. The block of other new states in the West—Idaho, Montana, and Wyoming—were each allotted one member. Nevada lost population but retained the single member allotted under the Constitution.

Differences between Map 11A of seat change and Map 11B of percentage change in power appear to be due predominantly to the addition of six new states in the Great Plains, Rocky Mountain, and Pacific regions of the country. The six newly admitted states accounted for half (2.4 percent) of the net gain of states increasing their percentage in the House.

Discounting the effect of the new states, the acceleration of forces active in the 1880s account for the greatest variation in 1890. Demographic changes in the West outstripped the fast pace of economic growth in the industrializing Northeast and lower Great Lakes states, which still suffered a relative loss of 0.5 percent of the House membership (see Table 2-29). Border states from Maryland to Missouri lost relative power, along with their adjacent southern neighbors Virginia and Tennessee. Relative losses were widespread across the Deep South, including the Carolinas, Mississippi, and Louisiana.

Neither were large numbers of immigrants contributing to the urban populations of the New England, Middle Atlantic, and Midwest regions able to outweigh the westward shift of relative political strength as the frontier era neared its close. The volume of immigration was causing resistance, particularly to those not of Anglo-Saxon heritage. Immigrant populations to California and the West were impacted by the Chinese Exclusion Act of 1882. Other disincentives to immigration were enacted as a growing demand to set quotas found political expression.

It should be noted that Map 11B is inversely related to the population density of 1890, the greatest relative declines occur in the areas that exceed ninety people per square mile, the greatest relative gains being associated with regions having two to six persons per square mile.[71] As the economic power of the East was increasing through manufacturing and commerce, a transition of the vast agricultural lands from subsistence to commercial farming contributed to the patterns observed on the 1890 maps. The productive "New West" now included Kansas, Nebraska, the Dakotas, and the Great Plains sections of Colorado, Wyoming, and Montana. Economically the region was dominated by the railroad companies. Land was granted to the railroads for every mile of track laid, and in turn the companies encouraged settlers with cheap land and easy payment schemes, combined with discount fares to the destination. Additionally, the Homestead Act of 1862 made the acquisition of public land virtually free. As Native Americans were pushed out, more such rail-accessible land became available. Other acts enabled farmers to increase their 160-acre homestead land holding through special provisions for woodlot development, or as veteran's preferences. The population of the "New West" doubled from one and one-half million in 1880 to three million in 1890.

By way of contrast, agriculture in the "New South" was very similar in location, practice, and outcome to the agriculture of the old South. Cotton cultivation had spread west but southern patterns of tobacco, sugar cane, corn, and livestock remained basically the same. By 1890 total production had increased with more than a doubling of the cotton crop. Unlike the spread of "New West" homesteads, although the southern farm population had increased, tenant farming was predominant with very low rates of land ownership prevailing. Credit and land being scarce there was little incentive for migration southward, and the vast majority of the rural population, black and white, looked forward only to continued poverty and modified serfdom. With the modest exceptions of Georgia, Alabama, and Arkansas, the agricultural South experienced a decline in the proportion of political representation.

66. Immigration totaled 5,248,568 between 1880 and 1889, a majority, 3,037,594 landed in the first five years of the decade. The immigrants were overwhelmingly European.

67. The act of apportionment was passed on February 7, 1891, and specified the number of members from each state using the Vinton method (26 Stat. L. 735). Additional provisions were again included to require states meriting several representatives to create contiguous districts and of approximately equal population.

68. Schmeckebier, *Congressional Apportionment,* 119. The apportionment population (which was the same as the total population of states in 1890—61,908,906) divided by the size of the House, 356, provides an estimated ratio of 173,901.

69. See Bogue, *Population,* Table 4.4, "Index of Relative Differential Growth in States, 1790–1957."

70. Ibid.

71. Paullin, *Atlas of Historical Geography.*

Table 2-28. 1890 Apportionment Statistics

State	Change in Seats	Seats Apportioned	Percent of House	Percentage Change
Alabama	1	9	2.5	0.0
Arkansas	1	6	1.7	0.2
California	1	7	2.0	0.2
Colorado	1	2	0.6	0.3
Connecticut	0	4	1.1	-0.1
Delaware	0	1	0.3	0.0
Florida	0	2	0.6	0.0
Georgia	1	11	3.1	0.0
Idaho	1	1	0.3	0.3
Illinois	2	22	6.2	0.0
Indiana	0	13	3.7	-0.3
Iowa	0	11	3.1	-0.3
Kansas	1	8	2.2	0.0
Kentucky	0	11	3.1	-0.3
Louisiana	0	6	1.7	-0.1
Maine	0	4	1.1	-0.1
Maryland	0	6	1.7	-0.1
Massachusetts	1	13	3.7	0.0
Michigan	1	12	3.4	0.0
Minnesota	2	7	2.0	0.5
Mississippi	0	7	2.0	-0.2
Missouri	1	15	4.2	-0.1
Montana	1	1	0.3	0.3
Nebraska	3	6	1.7	0.8
Nevada	0	1	0.3	0.0
New Hampshire	0	2	0.6	0.0
New Jersey	1	8	2.2	0.0
New York	0	34	9.6	-0.9
North Carolina	0	9	2.5	-0.3
North Dakota	1	1	0.3	0.3
Ohio	0	21	5.9	-0.6
Oregon	1	2	0.6	0.3
Pennsylvania	2	30	8.4	-0.2
Rhode Island	0	2	0.6	0.0
South Carolina	0	7	2.0	-0.2
South Dakota	2	2	0.6	0.6
Tennessee	0	10	2.8	-0.3
Texas	2	13	3.7	0.3
Vermont	0	2	0.6	0.0
Virginia	0	10	2.8	-0.3
Washington	2	2	0.6	0.6
West Virginia	0	4	1.1	-0.1
Wisconsin	1	10	2.8	0.0
Wyoming	1	1	0.3	0.3
Total	31	356		

Table 2-29. Percentage Change by Region, 1890

Map 11A. Change in Seats–1890

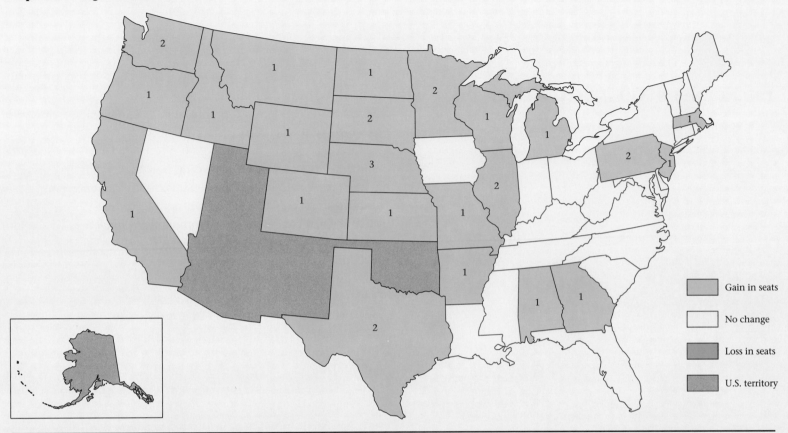

Gain in seats

No change

Loss in seats

U.S. territory

Map 11B. Percentage Change in Power–1890

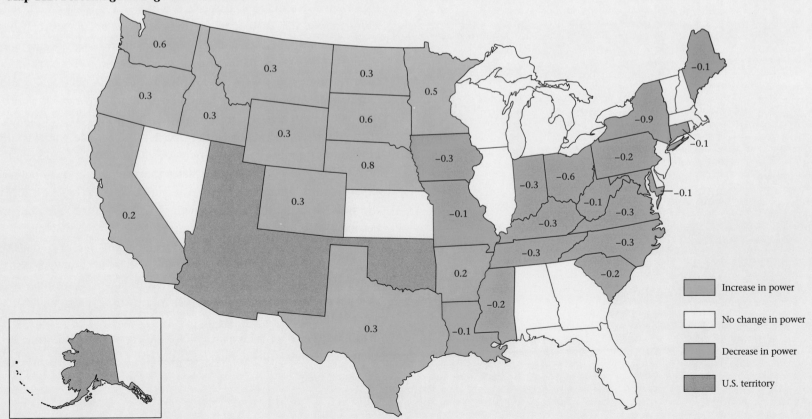

Increase in power

No change in power

Decrease in power

U.S. territory

1900 CENSUS APPORTIONMENT

In 1900 the twelfth census enumerated a total population in the United States of 75,994,575 inhabitants. Immigration contributed 3,694,294 of the net increase in population of 13,046,861 from 1890 to 1900.[72] Between 1890 and 1900, the overall rate of population growth fell from 25.5 to 20.7 percent. New York, again the most populous state, had 7,268,894 inhabitants. Nevada's population further declined from 1890, reaching its historical low of 42,335 people, of whom 40,670 comprised the apportionment population. At the turn of the century, twenty-seven states had populations greater than one million and 33 percent of the population lived in urban places. Utah (1896) was admitted to the Union between the eleventh and twelfth censuses. Utah's population of 276,749 was larger than most states recently added in the arid West, on account of its delay in admission and the agricultural improvements of the Mormon settlers.

The apportionment act of 1901 provided for a House of Representatives of 386 members, an increase of 30 seats over 1890.[73] As before in 1872, 1882, and 1892, the ratio with which apportionment quotas were determined was not written into the act.[74] Table 2-30 lists the states' actual distribution of seats. As through most of the nineteenth century, New York remained the largest delegation at thirty-seven members, accounting for 9.6 percent of the House. Delaware, Idaho, Montana, Nevada, Utah, and Wyoming each had one member.

No state lost any seat in the apportionment although twenty-four states had no change in the size of their delegations (see Map 12A). Many of these states were in the "New West" and Rocky Mountains and had recently entered the Union but had not experienced significant population growth. For those states that gained seats in this region—Colorado, Minnesota, and North Dakota—the impetus for growth was from the continued homesteading in railroad land grants.

With the exception of Texas, states that had strong metropolitan expansion made multiseat gains. The outstanding example of this is the veritable explosion of the growth of Chicago and its environs to become the second most populous city in the nation, providing three new seats to Illinois. In 1900 Chicago had a population of 1,700,000, an increase of 500,000 from 1880. In the Northeast, New York (three seats), New Jersey (two seats) and Pennsylvania (two seats) increased as a direct consequence of metropolitan growth. Even in agriculturally based Minnesota, the driving force of population growth was primarily the metropolitan expansion of Minneapolis–St. Paul, which by 1900 had 200,000 inhabitants, twice the size of Los Angeles, and five times that of Birmingham, Alabama. The vital force of many of the largest cities were recent immigrants, creating cities within cities, sustaining the urban growth with their ill-rewarded labor.

The growth of Texas, which gained three seats, was anomalous in this context, since it had neither railroad land grants from the federal government nor unusually large urban growth. Texas, however, benefited from major streams of migrants from the Deep and upper South and the development of its diverse agricultural base free from the worse problems of sharecropping and tenancy that plagued other southern states.

Map 12B of percentage change in power shows the general decline in the Northeast, except for Connecticut and New Jersey, which were caught up in the urbanization of New York City. Overall changes were slight however as the region, which was rapidly becoming the Manufacturing Belt, declined 1 percent.[75] By any measure the regional concentration of congressional power was associated with the North. Industrializing northern states controlled 52.3 percent of the House.[76] The most marked regional change was in the South—Texas grouping with Arkansas, Louisiana, and Mississippi to form a zone of relative increase. Western states showed a marginal

net gain of 0.6 percent to represent 5.4 percent of the House. Table 2-31 illustrates the decreasing significance of changes of one or two seats as the House size increased during the latter part of the nineteenth century. Regional differences became progressively less important and care is required in the interpretation of shifts in relative power.

72. The immigrants were overwhelmingly European although a greater proportion was coming from central and eastern Europe than previously. See Bogue, *Population,* 350.

73. The apportionment act was passed on January 16, 1901, and specified the number of members from each state using the Vinton method (31 Stat. L. 733). Additional provisions again required states meriting several representatives to create contiguous districts and of approximately equal population.

74. The apportionment population of 1901, 74,562,608 (which is not the same as the total population of states in 1901—74,607,225), divided by the size of the House, 386, provides an estimated ratio of 193,167. Schmeckebier, *Congressional Apportionment,* 231.

75. While not a fixed or sharply defined geographic region, the Manufacturing Belt usually comprises, in whole or in part, Massachusetts, Rhode Island, Connecticut, New York, New Jersey, Delaware, Pennsylvania, Maryland, West Virginia, Ohio, Kentucky, Indiana, Illinois, Michigan, and Wisconsin. See, for example, J. Patterson, *North America* (Oxford: Oxford University Press, 1984), 141–144.

76. Included are Vermont, Maine, New Hampshire, plus the Manufacturing Belt, see list in footnote 75, less Kentucky.

Table 2-30. 1900 Apportionment Statistics

State	Change in Seats	Seats Apportioned	Percent of House	Percentage Change
Alabama	0	9	2.3	-0.2
Arkansas	1	7	1.8	0.1
California	1	8	2.1	0.1
Colorado	1	3	0.8	0.2
Connecticut	1	5	1.3	0.2
Delaware	0	1	0.3	0.0
Florida	1	3	0.8	0.2
Georgia	0	11	2.8	-0.3
Idaho	0	1	0.3	0.0
Illinois	3	25	6.5	0.3
Indiana	0	13	3.4	-0.3
Iowa	0	11	2.8	-0.3
Kansas	0	8	2.1	-0.1
Kentucky	0	11	2.8	-0.3
Louisiana	1	7	1.8	0.1
Maine	0	4	1.0	-0.1
Maryland	0	6	1.6	-0.1
Massachusetts	1	14	3.6	-0.1
Michigan	0	12	3.1	-0.3
Minnesota	2	9	2.3	0.3
Mississippi	1	8	2.1	0.1
Missouri	1	16	4.1	-0.1
Montana	0	1	0.3	0.0
Nebraska	0	6	1.6	-0.1
Nevada	0	1	0.3	0.0
New Hampshire	0	2	0.5	-0.1
New Jersey	2	10	2.6	0.4
New York	3	37	9.6	0.0
North Carolina	1	10	2.6	0.1
North Dakota	1	2	0.5	0.2
Ohio	0	21	5.4	-0.5
Oregon	0	2	0.5	-0.1
Pennsylvania	2	32	8.3	-0.1
Rhode Island	0	2	0.5	-0.1
South Carolina	0	7	1.8	-0.2
South Dakota	0	2	0.5	-0.1
Tennessee	0	10	2.6	-0.2
Texas	3	16	4.1	0.4
Utah	1	1	0.3	0.3
Vermont	0	2	0.5	-0.1
Virginia	0	10	2.6	-0.2
Washington	1	3	0.8	0.2
West Virginia	1	5	1.3	0.2
Wisconsin	1	11	2.8	0.0
Wyoming	0	1	0.3	0.0
Total	30	386		

Table 2-31. Percentage Change by Region, 1900

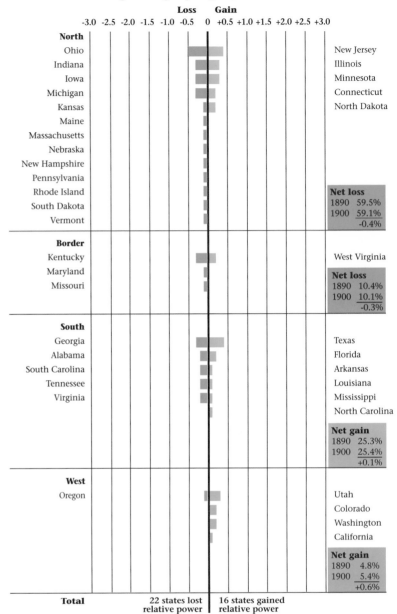

7 states remained the same.

Map 12A. Change in Seats–1900

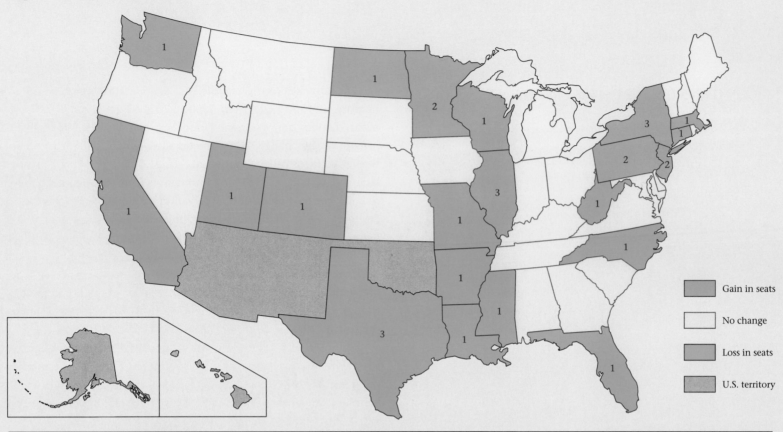

■	Gain in seats
□	No change
■	Loss in seats
■	U.S. territory

Map 12B. Percentage Change in Power–1900

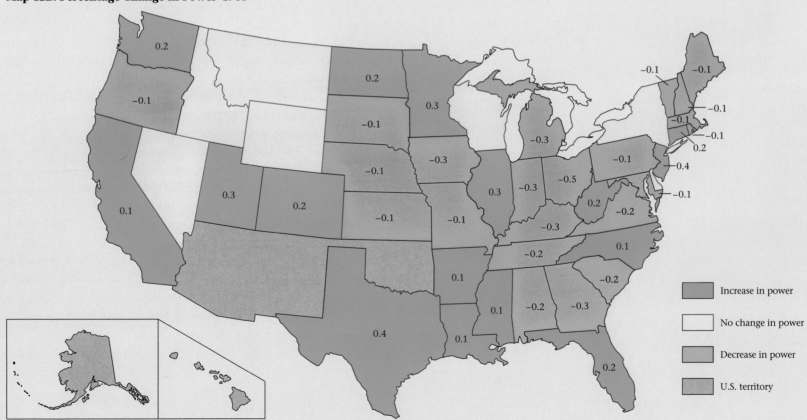

■	Increase in power
□	No change in power
■	Decrease in power
■	U.S. territory

1910 CENSUS APPORTIONMENT

The thirteenth census recorded a U.S. population of 91,972,266, an increase of 15,977,691 from 1900. 8,202,388 immigrants, predominantly eastern and southern Europeans, composed a remarkable 51 percent of the change.[77] Over the decade the national rate of population growth rose slightly from 20.7 to 21.0 percent. An increasingly large and visible proportion of immigrants from new sources renewed popular concern about the preservation of "American" values in the face of a large pool of cheap labor, linguistic enclaves, and diverse religious beliefs.[78] New York continued as the most populous state with 9,108,934 inhabitants; Pennsylvania had over seven million; Illinois had over five million; and Ohio had nearly five million people. These four largest states accounted for 30 percent of the national total. Although its population almost doubled to 81,875, Nevada remained the smallest state.

Oklahoma was admitted to the Union in 1907 and was granted five representatives until the apportionment of 1911. The apportionment act of 1911 provided for a House of Representatives of 433 members, an increase of 47 over 1901 (see Map 13A for change in seats). Provisions in the act allowed New Mexico or Arizona to have one seat each if they became states before the next apportionment. Accordingly the House would be increased to 435, its current membership. The 1911 act repeated provisions from previous apportionment law to require states deserving several representatives to create contiguous districts and of approximately equal population.[79] Table 2-32 lists the allocation of the 435 seats among the states, after Arizona and New Mexico had both been granted statehood in 1912. In receiving six new seats, New York continued to be the largest delegation at forty-three members, accounting for 9.9 percent of House membership. Five states—Arizona, Delaware, Nevada, New Mexico, and Wyoming—each had a single representative.

As in the three previous apportionments, no state lost seats because of the continued increase in the size of the House. In 1910 twenty-seven states gained representatives; twenty-one states had no change in the size of their delegations. Again, increases of more than one seat continued to be allocated in states that had a high proportion of urban growth. In the Northeast, New York (six seats), Pennsylvania (four seats), New Jersey (two seats), and Massachusetts (two seats) all increased as a direct consequence of metropolitan growth. The expansion of Chicago also continued to spur the increase in the Illinois delegation. Urban growth was no less important on the West

Coast, as Los Angeles, San Francisco, and Seattle developed rapidly.

In relative terms, western states gained appreciably. Map 13B shows that of the eighteen states that gained in relative power, half were located in the West and Rocky Mountain states. Population growth in this region was faster than the national rate and, with the exception of Utah, was considerably more than twice the national average.[80] California and Washington had the greatest proportion (0.4 and 0.3 percent, respectively) of the 2.2 percent net total gain of representative strength in the West (see Table 2-33).

A northern tier extending westward from Minnesota to Washington increased in House strength and was complemented by net gains in the arid Southwest. The new states of Oklahoma, New Mexico, and Arizona contributed significantly to the appearance of western strength. An increase of two seats in Texas was sufficient only to maintain its relative position. No change in seats in Kansas, Nebraska, Nevada, and Wyoming resulted in small losses of relative power in these states. Additional population growth in Kansas and Nebraska, in particular, was checked by a series of drought years at the end of the nineteenth century. Fear of drought did little to curb the grab for the last spacious tracts of homesteading land in Oklahoma.

The continued expansion in the West was balanced by broad relative declines from states in the Mississippi River valley eastward, even where there was considerable economic and demographic growth. Gains of population above the national average in New Jersey, New York, West Virginia, and Florida were the result of underlying forces of change as diverse as urban expansion, immigration, industrial raw materials, and agricultural expansion. New Jersey grew two-thirds faster than the national rate, and Florida's population expanded twice as fast.

The integration and diversification of the national economy, which accelerated during this period, necessitates deeper and more subtle explanations of variations in population than are permitted by the scope of this work. From 1890 onward the interplay of different factors was shaped less by the relations of settlers and available land, than those of capital and labor, the characteristics of the environment, the drive of the United States to acquire its own empire, and the consequent impact of global affairs. Because the U.S. House of Representatives has remained fixed at 435 since the 1910 apportionment, Map 13B is the last of the relative apportionment maps in this atlas. These relative change maps detect even the slightest variation in relative strength (as in Maps 1B–13B) and permit comparisons to be made as the size of the House constantly altered from 1790 to 1910. However, as has been stressed in the decennial descriptions above, states can have had high economic and demographic growth yet lag in relative political growth because of the dominating effect of the expansion of the Republic. Any relative changes must be interpreted with care and consideration of the computational rules used in this work.[81] After 1910 the House size remained fixed, even with the admission of Alaska and Hawaii midway through the twentieth century, and apportionment is illustrated on a single map of gains and losses.

77. Of an estimated 1,200,000 immigrants in 1907, the proportion coming from "new" sources in southern and eastern Europe reached 80 percent as opposed to the traditional or "old" sources in Great Britain and Germany. Of the more than eight million immigrants arriving between 1900 and 1910, only 256,650 were from Asia, Africa, or Australasia. An additional 277,800 arrived from the Americas, the majority from Canada. Figures from Bogue, *Population*, Table 14-1, 350–352.

78. The paradoxical history of an immigrant nation's attempts to restrict immigration, whether from China, southern and eastern Europe, or Latin America is long and convoluted. Effective exclusion of the Chinese laborers began in 1879 and was completed in 1882; in 1891 an immigration bureaucracy was created that could enforce restrictions; attempts to discriminate against "new" immigrants and Asians began with a literacy bill first introduced in 1896; and repeatedly thereafter until it was successfully enacted in 1917. The "Golden Door" of the inscription on the Statue of Liberty, erected in 1886 was selectively closed by 1920. Hicks et al., *History of American Democracy,* 440.

79. The apportionment act was passed on August 8, 1911. The act specified the number of members from each state using the method of major fractions. Schmeckebier, *Congressional Apportionment,* 119–120.

80. Bogue, *Population,* Table 4-4, 65.

81. See footnote 7 in Part 1.

Table 2-32. 1910 Apportionment Statistics

State	Change in Seats	Seats Apportioned	Percent of House	Percentage Change
Alabama	1	10	2.3	0.0
Arizona	1	1	0.2	0.2
Arkansas	0	7	1.6	-0.2
California	3	11	2.5	0.4
Colorado	1	4	0.9	0.1
Connecticut	0	5	1.1	-0.2
Delaware	0	1	0.2	-0.1
Florida	1	4	0.9	0.1
Georgia	1	12	2.8	0.0
Idaho	1	2	0.5	0.2
Illinois	2	27	6.2	-0.3
Indiana	0	13	3.0	-0.4
Iowa	0	11	2.5	-0.3
Kansas	0	8	1.8	-0.3
Kentucky	0	11	2.5	-0.3
Louisiana	1	8	1.8	0.0
Maine	0	4	0.9	-0.1
Maryland	0	6	1.4	-0.2
Massachusetts	2	16	3.7	0.1
Michigan	1	13	3.0	-0.1
Minnesota	1	10	2.3	0.0
Mississippi	0	8	1.8	-0.3
Missouri	0	16	3.7	-0.4
Montana	1	2	0.5	0.2
Nebraska	0	6	1.4	-0.2
Nevada	0	1	0.2	-0.1
New Hampshire	0	2	0.5	0.0
New Jersey	2	12	2.8	0.2
New Mexico	1	1	0.2	0.2
New York	6	43	9.9	0.3
North Carolina	0	10	2.3	-0.3
North Dakota	1	3	0.7	0.2
Ohio	1	22	5.1	-0.3
Oklahoma	8	8	1.8	1.8
Oregon	1	3	0.7	0.2
Pennsylvania	4	36	8.3	0.0
Rhode Island	1	3	0.7	0.2
South Carolina	0	7	1.6	-0.2
South Dakota	1	3	0.7	0.2
Tennessee	0	10	2.3	-0.3
Texas	2	18	4.1	0.0
Utah	1	2	0.5	0.2
Vermont	0	2	0.5	0.0
Virginia	0	10	2.3	-0.3
Washington	2	5	1.1	0.3
West Virginia	1	6	1.4	0.1
Wisconsin	0	11	2.5	-0.3
Wyoming	0	1	0.2	-0.1
Total	49	435		

Table 2-33. Percentage Change by Region, 1910

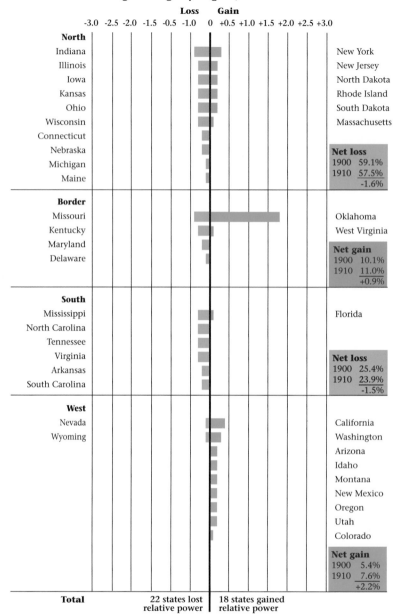

8 states remained the same.

Map 13A. Change in Seats–1910

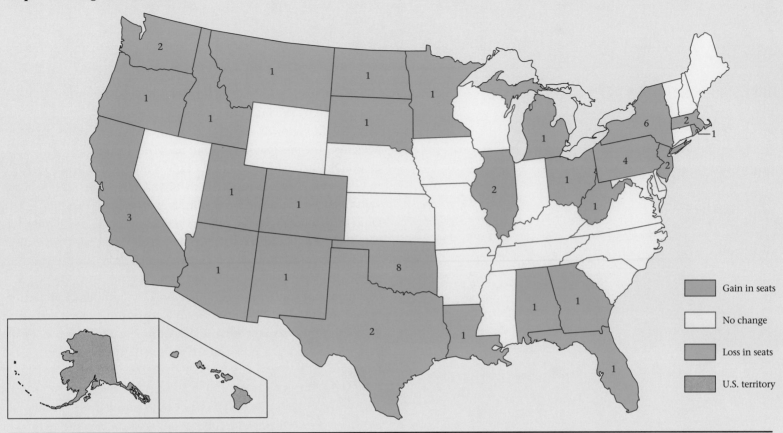

Gain in seats

No change

Loss in seats

U.S. territory

Map 13B. Percentage Change in Power–1910

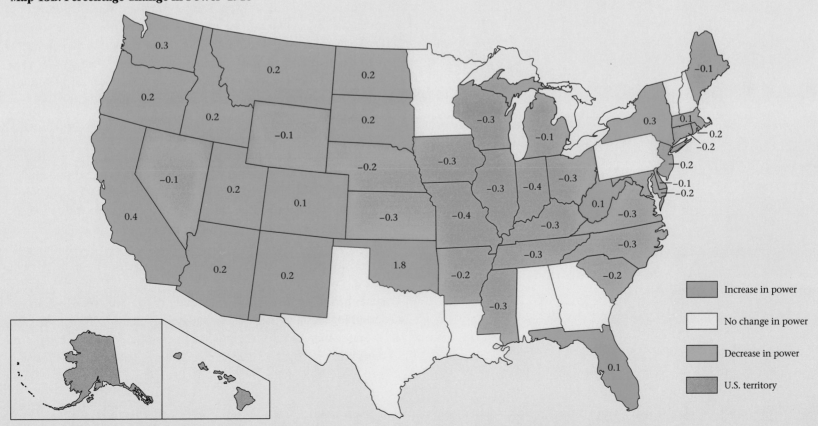

Increase in power

No change in power

Decrease in power

U.S. territory

1930 CENSUS APPORTIONMENT

The population of the United States increased to 122,775,046 as enumerated by the fifteenth census in 1930. In 1930 the overall rate of population growth was 16.1 percent, a slight increase from 14.9 percent of the previous decade, but markedly reduced from the immigration boosted rates of the turn of the century. New York continued to be the most populous state with 12,587,967 inhabitants. Pennsylvania had over nine million, Illinois had over seven million, and Ohio had more than six million residents. Texas and California, climbing to fifth and sixth in population size, had over five million inhabitants each. Nevada's population of 91,058 was the smallest among the states.

Following many unsuccessful attempts to agree on an apportionment based on the 1920 census (see the case study on rural and urban places and the 1920 nonapportionment in Part 3), section 22 of the act of June 18, 1929, provided for automatic apportionment of 435 members of the House of Representatives, the same size as in 1910.[82] Table 2-34 lists the allocation of the gains and losses of House seats among the states.[83] The statement of the apportionments submitted to Congress in 1930 included allocations calculated by the method of major fractions and by the method of equal proportions. As the numbers of seats allocated by the different methods were the same, Congress took no action and the method used after the 1910 census became the basis for apportionment under provisions made in the 1929 act.[84] Because of their small populations, Arizona, Delaware, Nevada, New Mexico, Vermont, and Wyoming did not appear on the priority list for the method of major fractions. In accordance with the Constitution these states were allotted one member each.

Patterns of change of the apportionment of 1930 had very pronounced geographical groupings as indicated in Map 14. Eleven states gained and twenty-one states lost seats in the reapportionment. Of the losing states, five lost multiple seats, the effect of reduction in power being intensified by the political stalemate of the Sixty-sixth through Seventy-first Congresses on the question of apportionment. The failure of successive Congresses to agree on reapportionment in the 1920s meant that newly emerging characteristics of population change were unrepresented. Conversely, Map 14 indicates sixteen states had no change in the size of their delegation, whereas representation for six states increased by more than one seat.

States that had the highest urban growth primarily had the increases in seats. As befitted the magnitude of its economic expansion,

California led the increases with nine new seats. In the Midwest Michigan gained four and Ohio gained two seats. While New Jersey and New York both gained two representatives and Connecticut added one, all three states increased as a direct consequence of the metropolitan growth of New York City. Conversely, growth in Chicago failed to compensate for rural losses, and the Illinois delegation remained unchanged.

In receiving two new seats, New York continued to have the largest delegation at forty-five members, accounting for 10.3 percent of the House (Table 2-34). Despite its loss of two seats, Pennsylvania had the second largest delegation (thirty-four) accounting for 7.8 percent of the House. The unchanging Illinois delegation of twenty-seven accounted for 6.2 percent of the House. These three largest delegations controlled 24.3 percent of the House, a share consistent with their proportion of nearly one-fourth the U.S. population total (24 percent). Table 2-35 illustrates the change in House seats by region.

Since the last apportionment in 1910, the United States had been through a series of unprecedented changes in its population structure and economy, changes that above all seemed to benefit California. The migration from rural to urban places begun at the end of the nineteenth century was confirmed by the 1920 census, which reported that half the national population lived in urban areas. Consumer products rose in relative importance in value of output against such traditional strengths of the economy as infrastructure and construction, producer products, and heavy manufactures. The striking rise of automobile manufacture and sales typified the role of consumer-oriented economic growth of a new urban America for which California was the model.

The diversity of reasons for relative population change can only be hinted at in this section. In Texas and Oklahoma petroleum discoveries energized the regional economy drawing large numbers of migrants and immigrants to rapidly expanding cities of the South-west. Michigan and Ohio benefited from the establishment of the automobile industry and the industrial linkage engendered by automobile manufacture. New York City consolidated its position as a world trade capital, accumulating at the same time a dominant industrial hinterland. North Carolina grew as textile and chemical industries sought to expand and relocate from established New England sites in search of cheaper, nonunion labor. Florida demonstrated effects of the initial migration from the Northeast for recreation, second homes, and retirement, primarily of the newly wealthy.

The Midwest and Great Plains lost blocks of seats due to the extended agricultural depression following World War I. The depression induced out-migration from agricultural regions. Agricultural areas encountered massive problems as overproduction of staples and cash crops was exacerbated by technological change, such as the introduction of tractors and chemical fertilizers. Production far exceeded market demand as European agriculture recovered from wartime conditions and other suppliers entered the world market. In the South these fundamental agricultural problems occurred on top of entrenched problems of land ownership and tenancy. Tenant farmers driven off the land by debt migrated to industrial jobs in northern cities.

82. The main provisions of the act of June 18, 1929, fixed the size of the House at 435, provided for the apportionment in advance of the census, prescribed the method of apportionment, and delegated the calculation of the apportionment to an officer of the executive branch (46 Stat. L. 26). Both automatic apportionment and the freezing of the number of members had been elements of the apportionment act of 1850 (9 Stat. L. 428). Schmeckebier, *Congressional Apportionment*, 122.

83. During the apportionment hiatus of the 1920s alternative methods of apportionment were debated at length. Committees of the National Academy of Sciences and the American Statistical Society had recommended the method of equal proportions. The act of 1929 required the reporting of the apportionment by: the method used in the preceding apportionment; the method of major fractions; and the method of equal proportions. If Congress failed to pass a new apportionment act, the method of the last preceding census was to prevail for the second succeeding Congress and each subsequent Congress. Ibid., 122.

84. U.S. Department of Commerce, Bureau of Census, H. Doc 664, 71st Cong., 3d sess., 1930.

Table 2-34. 1930 Apportionment Statistics

State	Change in Seats	Seats Apportioned	Percent of House	Percentage Change
Alabama	-1	9	2.1	-0.2
Arizona	0	1	0.2	0.0
Arkansas	0	7	1.6	0.0
California	9	20	4.6	2.1
Colorado	0	4	0.9	0.0
Connecticut	1	6	1.4	0.3
Delaware	0	1	0.2	0.0
Florida	1	5	1.1	0.2
Georgia	-2	10	2.3	-0.5
Idaho	0	2	0.5	0.0
Illinois	0	27	6.2	0.0
Indiana	-1	12	2.8	-0.2
Iowa	-2	9	2.1	-0.4
Kansas	-1	7	1.6	-0.2
Kentucky	-2	9	2.1	-0.4
Louisiana	0	8	1.8	0.0
Maine	-1	3	0.7	-0.2
Maryland	0	6	1.4	0.0
Massachusetts	-1	15	3.4	-0.3
Michigan	4	17	3.9	0.9
Minnesota	-1	9	2.1	-0.2
Mississippi	-1	7	1.6	-0.2
Missouri	-3	13	3.0	-0.7
Montana	0	2	0.5	0.0
Nebraska	-1	5	1.1	-0.3
Nevada	0	1	0.2	0.0
New Hampshire	0	2	0.5	0.0
New Jersey	2	14	3.2	0.4
New Mexico	0	1	0.2	0.0
New York	2	45	10.3	0.4
North Carolina	1	11	2.5	0.2
North Dakota	-1	2	0.5	-0.2
Ohio	2	24	5.5	0.4
Oklahoma	1	9	2.1	0.3
Oregon	0	3	0.7	0.0
Pennsylvania	-2	34	7.8	-0.5
Rhode Island	-1	2	0.5	-0.2
South Carolina	-1	6	1.4	-0.2
South Dakota	-1	2	0.5	-0.2
Tennessee	-1	9	2.1	-0.2
Texas	3	21	4.8	0.7
Utah	0	2	0.5	0.0
Vermont	-1	1	0.2	-0.3
Virginia	-1	9	2.1	-0.2
Washington	1	6	1.4	0.3
West Virginia	0	6	1.4	0.0
Wisconsin	-1	10	2.3	-0.2
Wyoming	0	1	0.2	0.0
Total	0	435		

Table 2-35. Seat Change by Region, 1930[a]

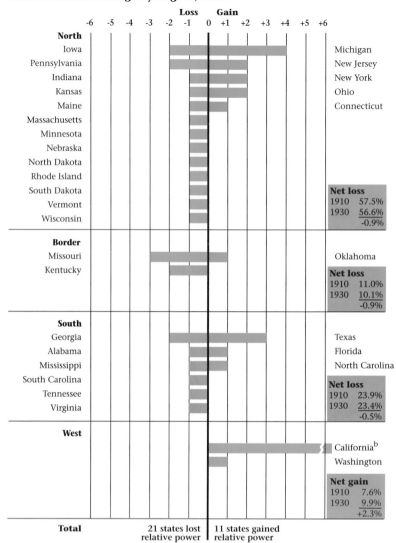

16 states remained the same.
[a]*From 1930 on, absolute change in seats is reported as the House size is fixed at 435.*
[b]*California gained 9 seats.*

Map 14. Change in Seats–1930

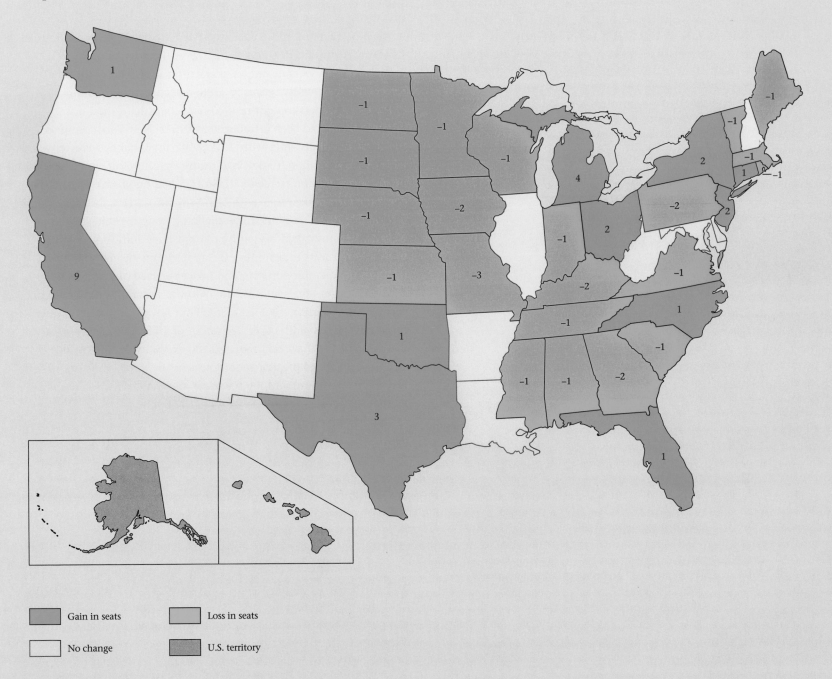

Gain in seats

Loss in seats

No change

U.S. territory

1940 CENSUS APPORTIONMENT

In 1940 the sixteenth census reported a total U.S. population of 131,669,275, an increase of 8,894,229 over the population of 1930. At 7.2 percent, the overall rate of population growth was the smallest recorded since the first census in 1790, reflecting the combined effects of the Great Depression of the 1930s and the strict restrictions on immigration that had been introduced in 1927.[85] New York continued as the most populous state with 13,479,142 inhabitants. Pennsylvania had over nine million, Illinois had nearly eight million, and Ohio had nearly seven million residents. California had outgrown Texas to become the fifth-ranked state with 6,907,387 inhabitants. Nevada's population of 110,247 remained the smallest among the states. Delaware, Nevada, Vermont, and Wyoming did not have sufficient population to be allotted seats under either the apportionment method of major fractions or equal proportions, and hence received one seat each.

Allocation of representatives in 1940 was accomplished under the permanent apportionment act of 1929 but not without certain political ramifications and other technical problems requiring amendments.[86] The 1929 act had required the executive branch of the federal government to prepare apportionments by the method of the last preceding apportionment, by the method of major fractions, and the method of equal proportions. In 1930 the methods produced identical apportionments of the 435 seats among the states, but in 1940 the method of major fractions assigned Michigan the 435th seat, whereas the method of equal proportions assigned the last seat to Arkansas. Under the method of equal proportions neither Democratic Arkansas nor Republican Michigan stood to lose a seat and, given a Democratic House majority, the method of equal proportions, which favored the Democratic numbers, was selected.[87]

In sharp contrast to the major reshaping of the House in 1930, Map 15 shows that no change in representation was the predominant pattern of the reapportionment of seats in 1940. Thirty-two states held the same number of seats that were assigned under the 1930 reapportionment. Table 2-36 shows 1940 as having the smallest reassignment of House seats in modern American history. The suppression of change is in part due to the freezing of the total number of seats to 435 by the act of 1929, combined with the limiting effect of the Great Depression on demographic processes. Meager economic opportunities stifled reproduction and hindered migration leading to the small net changes in the population of the states. Against the backdrop of no change the effects on reapportionment of a few demographic changes stand out clearly. Table 2-37 illustrates the change in House seats by region.

States of the Manufacturing Belt stretching from Illinois to Massachusetts consistently experienced population growth only one-half to two-thirds of the already anemic national average as demand slumped for the staple industrial products of the region—for example, producer goods, machine tools, and consumer goods. Illinois, Indiana, Ohio, and Pennsylvania each lost one seat, as did Massachusetts. On the Great Plains the massive exodus of family farmers in the face of the dust bowl is reflected in losses of seats in Nebraska, Kansas, and Oklahoma. Net out-migration in the Great Plains states of the Dakotas, Nebraska, Kansas, and Oklahoma resulted in an absolute population decline of a quarter of a million between 1930 and 1940.[88]

California was the destination of many laborers forced from their homes on the Great Plains and elsewhere. The population of California grew by 1,230,000 inhabitants, three times the national rate of growth, primarily due to in-migration from the dust bowl states and the Northeast. New Mexico and Arizona both grew at more than twice the national rate (New Mexico's rate exceeded even that of California) as westward-bound migrants found opportunities, or merely respite, before they reached the Pacific coast. Oregon and Washington were also recipients of eastern immigrants though only Oregon was able to convert the increase into an additional seat in the House.

In the Southeast, Florida had the fastest rate of growth of any state in the nation, predominantly the result of net in-migration from the Northeast, and gained one seat. North Carolina also experienced sufficient, albeit moderate, growth to add a seat to its 1930 apportionment of eleven members. If the additional seat in North Carolina can be argued to be in part due to the New Deal policies of the Roosevelt administration, then the additional seat in Tennessee almost certainly was the result of federal programs. Draining seven states in the

Southeast, the Tennessee River valley was selected as the location of one of the few far-reaching efforts at direct regional development policy implemented by any U.S. government. Authorized in 1933, the Tennessee Valley Authority (TVA) by 1940 had constructed four hydroelectric schemes, serving over 300,000 consumers. But its demographic effect, as recorded in Map 15, in an era of stagnation, was in large part due to the wide range of social benefits and contributions to the general welfare provided under TVA.

Given the dramatic events of the thirties, the map of subsequent reapportionment is remarkable as a mirror of the geography of those circumstances. Of the sixteen states experiencing any change, only one, California, changed by more than a single seat. It is tempting to focus on the widespread nature of the Great Depression and a view of California as the ultimate hope for displaced workers. Perhaps the more accurate reflection of the times is found in the general lack of change on Map 15.

85. Under the Emergency Immigration Act of 1921, the total number of immigrants was limited to 150,000 per year after July 1, 1927, with quotas set on national origins to be determined from the fourteenth census of 1920.

86. Ratification on January 23, 1933, of the Twentieth Amendment to the Constitution modified the dates of the convening of Congress causing the second regular session to be advanced by eleven months to begin on January 3 in each even-numbered year. The permanent apportionment act (46 Stat. L. 26) required the apportionment report to be submitted at the beginning of the second session of the Seventy-sixth Congress, January 3, 1940, before the census had been taken. An amendment to the act of 1929 was passed in April 1940 (54 Stat. L. 162) to permit the apportionment report to be submitted "on the first day, or within one week thereafter, of the first regular session of the Seventy-seventh Congress, and of each fifth Congress thereafter" (54 Stat. L. 162: Sec. 22a).

87. The method of equal proportions has been used in every apportionment since 1941 as provided by the act of November 15, 1941 (55 L. Stat. 761). Differences occur between the states allotted the last seat(s) awarded under the two contemporary systems of apportionment. However, since the act of 1929 provides for use of the method of the last preceding census in the lack of congressional action, the method of equal proportions has prevailed without challenge.

88. U.S. Department of Commerce, Bureau of Census, *Historical Statistics of the United States, Colonial Times to 1970* (Washington, D.C.: Government Printing Office, 1975), Series A 195–209, 24–37.

Table 2-36. 1940 Apportionment Statistics

State	Change in Seats	Seats Apportioned	Percent of House	Percentage Change
Alabama	0	9	2.1	0.0
Arizona	1	2	0.5	0.3
Arkansas	0	7	1.6	0.0
California	3	23	5.3	0.7
Colorado	0	4	0.9	0.0
Connecticut	0	6	1.4	0.0
Delaware	0	1	0.2	0.0
Florida	1	6	1.4	0.3
Georgia	0	10	2.3	0.0
Idaho	0	2	0.5	0.0
Illinois	-1	26	6.0	-0.2
Indiana	-1	11	2.5	-0.3
Iowa	-1	8	1.8	-0.3
Kansas	-1	6	1.4	-0.2
Kentucky	0	9	2.1	0.0
Louisiana	0	8	1.8	0.0
Maine	0	3	0.7	0.0
Maryland	0	6	1.4	0.0
Massachusetts	-1	14	3.2	-0.2
Michigan	0	17	3.9	0.0
Minnesota	0	9	2.1	0.0
Mississippi	0	7	1.6	0.0
Missouri	0	13	3.0	0.0
Montana	0	2	0.5	0.0
Nebraska	-1	4	0.9	-0.2
Nevada	0	1	0.2	0.0
New Hampshire	0	2	0.5	0.0
New Jersey	0	14	3.2	0.0
New Mexico	1	2	0.5	0.3
New York	0	45	10.3	0.0
North Carolina	1	12	2.8	0.3
North Dakota	0	2	0.5	0.0
Ohio	-1	23	5.3	-0.2
Oklahoma	-1	8	1.8	-0.3
Oregon	1	4	0.9	0.2
Pennsylvania	-1	33	7.6	-0.2
Rhode Island	0	2	0.5	0.0
South Carolina	0	6	1.4	0.0
South Dakota	0	2	0.5	0.0
Tennessee	1	10	2.3	0.2
Texas	0	21	4.8	0.0
Utah	0	2	0.5	0.0
Vermont	0	1	0.2	0.0
Virginia	0	9	2.1	0.0
Washington	0	6	1.4	0.0
West Virginia	0	6	1.4	0.0
Wisconsin	0	10	2.3	0.0
Wyoming	0	1	0.2	0.0
Total	0	435		

Table 2-37. Seat Change by Region, 1940

Map 15. Change in Seats–1940

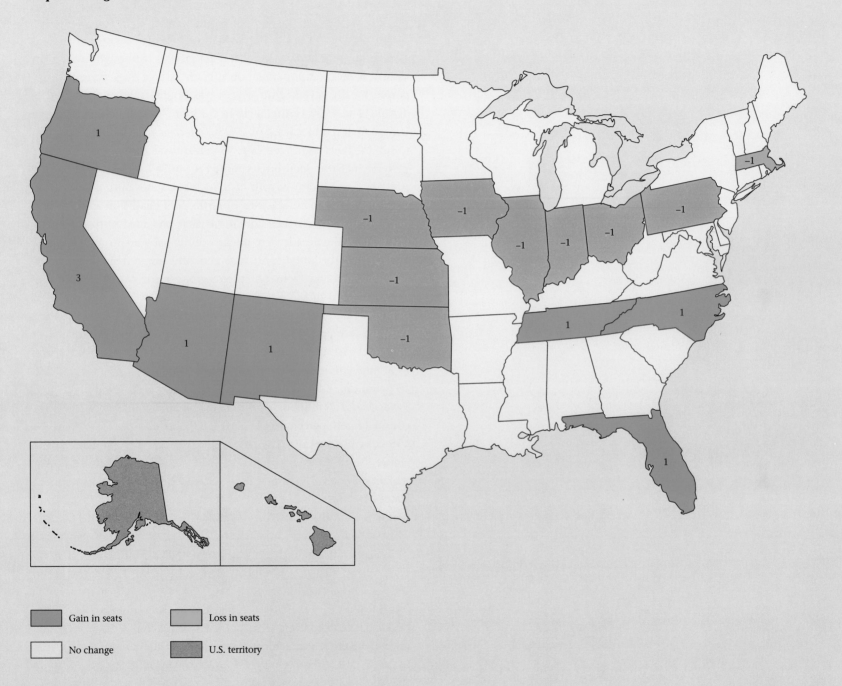

Gain in seats

Loss in seats

No change

U.S. territory

1950 CENSUS APPORTIONMENT

The population of the United States rebounded between 1940 and 1950 from its stagnant depression-era growth. Although lower than historical levels, the population growth rate of 14.5 percent as reported by the seventeenth census was double that of the previous decade. The 1950 census registered 150,697,361 inhabitants in the United States, an increase of 19,028,086 over the 1940 total population.[89] Of the total net increase, 93 percent was through reproductive increase, net immigration accounted for only 1.4 million additional people.[90] The vibrant growth of the United States during this period was caused by a natural excess of births over deaths, in spite, or perhaps because of, wartime conditions that prevailed until 1945. The last years of the decade were the first of the baby boom.

Together the Middle Atlantic and Midwest remained the most populous and most densely settled regions of the nation. Accounting for 9.4 percent of the total U.S. population, New York was the most populous state in 1950 with 14.8 million inhabitants. Growth in the West was a countervailing force against the traditional dominance of the Northeast. California had risen from fifth rank to second with a total population of 10.6 million. Pennsylvania fell to third rank with 10.5 million. Illinois had 8.7 million, Ohio had 7.9 million, and Texas had 7.7 million inhabitants. The six largest states thus accounted for 40 percent of the total U.S. population and for 173 of the 435 congressional districts, 40 percent of the representatives in the House. Nevada's total population remained the smallest at 160,000, which was half the size of the next smallest state, Delaware. Four states—Delaware, Nevada, Vermont, and Wyoming—had insufficient populations to be allotted seats under the equal proportions method of apportionment and were allotted one seat each under the constitutional requirement. The six smallest states accounted for just 1.5 percent of the total U.S. population and 1.8 percent of the House of Representatives.

Allocation of representatives in 1950 was accomplished under the provisions of the permanent apportionment act of 1929 as amended in 1941. Map 16 and Table 2-38 show that while the number of seats in most states did not change in 1950, the distribution of those states that did have change has regional regularities. Thirty-two states held the same number of seats in the Eighty-third Congress as they had had under the 1940 apportionment. Seven states gained and nine states lost representatives.

One cluster of seven contiguous states centered on the Mississippi valley transcends the usual geographical and political divisions by including portions of the South, Border, and Midwest regions. In 1950 Tennessee relinquished its one seat gain of 1940, while Illinois and Oklahoma compounded earlier decline with further losses of one and two seats, respectively. Arkansas, Mississippi, Missouri, and Kentucky also lost one seat each.

In the Middle Atlantic region, New York and Pennsylvania combined to lose five seats, more than 1 percent of the total House membership. Pennsylvania had lost a total of six seats in three successive apportionments and would continue to lose power in the second half of the century. Although the loss for New York was the first in the twentieth century, the decline marked a significant turning point, as New York would continue to lose power thereafter. (See Table 1-3 for a comparison of the trajectory of New York with other shifts in state power through time.)

The wide geographical scatter of gains suggests the action of multiple influences on positive change in states' populations. On the Pacific Coast, gains in Washington and California increased regional power. In adding seven seats, California grew in power equal to all seat gains in the other six expanding states. In the South, Texas, Florida, and Virginia increased. Michigan added a seat in the Midwest and Maryland added one on the Atlantic Coast. Table 2-39 illustrates the change in House seats, emphasizing gains in the South and West.

Economic recovery, industrial location policy of World War II, and the growth of federal government from the 1930s onward contributed variously to the redistribution of representational power. During and following World War II, California, the center of war industry for the Pacific theater, strengthened its economic foundations in oil, manufacturing, and agriculture; in basic steel and petroleum products; in marine and aviation industries, and in a host of related industries. California's population increase of 53.3 percent from 1940 to 1950 was the largest among the states, virtually all the result of in-migration. Seattle, a second West Coast wartime manufacturing center, was aided by cheap hydroelectricity from the fruition of New Deal projects along the Columbia River to become the major generator of population growth in Washington.

Along with California and Washington, Texas and Florida had benefited from strategic dispersal of war industries but the growth of the southern states was more substantial after 1945. Postwar needs for housing and consumer durable goods became acute as one half the total increase of the U.S. resident population was added in just eighteen months following July 1945.[91] The economic boom that fol-

lowed the war favored diverse economies in states with space available for rapid expansion. The addition of a seat in Michigan may be considered as one deferred from the previous apportionment through the change in method from major fractions to equal proportions. Michigan's gain was the result of long-term industrial growth centered on automobile manufacture and its more recent expanded wartime production, drawing a major influx of migrants from Appalachia and the South.

The influence of the federal government had been omnipresent during World War II, consequently Washington, D.C., had continued to build on its metropolitan growth of the New Deal era. Given the physical restrictions of the federal district, it was inevitable that the adjacent states, Maryland and Virginia, would accommodate most of the new residents. Each gained a seat from suburbanization around the capital city.

The reasons for declining strength, particularly in the Northeast, appear to be partially explained by the decentralization of industry and the continuing relative growth of Florida, Texas, and the West at rates in excess of the national average. Of the cluster in the interior, Illinois, Kentucky, and Mississippi reported losing population in more than half their counties.[92] Arkansas, Missouri, and Oklahoma lost population from three-fourths of their counties. The large agriculturally based African-American population of the Mississippi River valley and adjoining states had experienced great out-migration since World War I. This existing condition was exacerbated by employment needs of World War II and agricultural mechanization. While industrial and urban growth in Texas more than sufficiently counterbalanced a major exodus from rural counties of the state, apparently such forces were insufficient in the extensive, central region of seven states depicted on Map 16.

89. In 1950, 449,000 armed forces were reported as living overseas, yet to be demobilized following World War II. See Bogue, *Population*, 9. Armed forces overseas were not included in the population of the United States for apportionment purposes. Had that been the case in 1950, the apportionment would have been altered to the extent that the priority numbers would have reflected disproportionate sizes of military contingents between states. Note that the overseas population was not considered for apportionment until 1990, when 922,000 overseas Americans, many of whom were civilians, were included for the first time.

90. Figures from Bogue, *Population*, 8. Bogue points out that as World War II deaths were accounted as emigration by the Census Bureau, net immigration was artificially low. Had war losses not been charged against immigration, the net inflow would have been about 10 percent of the population change between 1940 and 1950, or about 1.9 million.

91. Ibid., 5.

92. See Taeuber and Taeuber, *Changing Population*, 17.

Table 2-38. 1950 Apportionment Statistics

State	Change in Seats	Seats Apportioned	Percent of House	Percentage Change
Alabama	0	9	2.1	0.0
Arizona	0	2	0.5	0.0
Arkansas	-1	6	1.4	-0.2
California	7	30	6.9	1.6
Colorado	0	4	0.9	0.0
Connecticut	0	6	1.4	0.0
Delaware	0	1	0.2	0.0
Florida	2	8	1.8	0.4
Georgia	0	10	2.3	0.0
Idaho	0	2	0.5	0.0
Illinois	-1	25	5.7	-0.3
Indiana	0	11	2.5	0.0
Iowa	0	8	1.8	0.0
Kansas	0	6	1.4	0.0
Kentucky	-1	8	1.8	-0.3
Louisiana	0	8	1.8	0.0
Maine	0	3	0.7	0.0
Maryland	1	7	1.6	0.2
Massachusetts	0	14	3.2	0.0
Michigan	1	18	4.1	0.2
Minnesota	0	9	2.1	0.0
Mississippi	-1	6	1.4	-0.2
Missouri	-2	11	2.5	-0.5
Montana	0	2	0.5	0.0
Nebraska	0	4	0.9	0.0
Nevada	0	1	0.2	0.0
New Hampshire	0	2	0.5	0.0
New Jersey	0	14	3.2	0.0
New Mexico	0	2	0.5	0.0
New York	-2	43	9.9	-0.4
North Carolina	0	12	2.8	0.0
North Dakota	0	2	0.5	0.0
Ohio	0	23	5.3	0.0
Oklahoma	-2	6	1.4	-0.4
Oregon	0	4	0.9	0.0
Pennsylvania	-3	30	6.9	-0.7
Rhode Island	0	2	0.5	0.0
South Carolina	0	6	1.4	0.0
South Dakota	0	2	0.5	0.0
Tennessee	-1	9	2.1	-0.2
Texas	1	22	5.1	0.3
Utah	0	2	0.5	0.0
Vermont	0	1	0.2	0.0
Virginia	1	10	2.3	0.2
Washington	1	7	1.6	0.2
West Virginia	0	6	1.4	0.0
Wisconsin	0	10	2.3	0.0
Wyoming	0	1	0.2	0.0
Total	0	435		

Table 2-39. Seat Change by Region, 1950

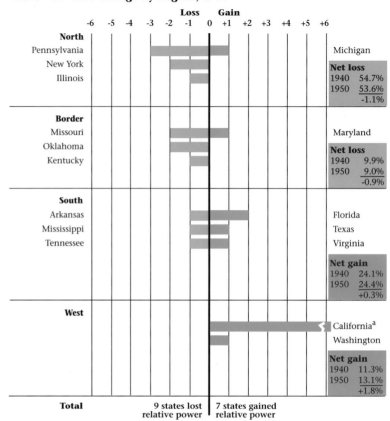

32 states remained the same.
[a] California gained 7 seats.

Map 16. Change in Seats–1950

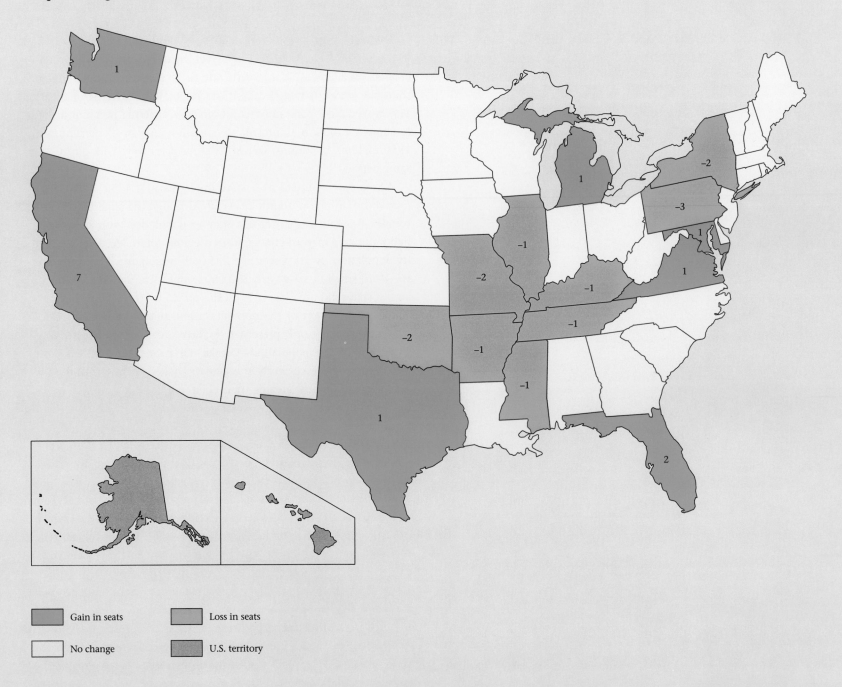

Gain in seats   Loss in seats

No change   U.S. territory

1960 CENSUS APPORTIONMENT

The eighteenth census revealed a total population of 179,323,175 in the United States in April 1960. Over the decade the population increased by 27,997,377, a growth rate of 18.5 percent, much greater than the previous two decades. The population difference between first-ranked New York and second-ranked California had diminished to about 1.4 million. California's population grew by 49 percent from 1950 to 1960, in contrast to just 13 percent for New York during the same period.

Alaska was admitted as a state on January 3, 1959, and Hawaii joined the Union on August 21, 1959. Although the largest state territorially, Alaska was the smallest state in population with 226,000 inhabitants. In a marked change from previous totals, Nevada increased its population by 78 percent to 285,000 inhabitants. Wyoming was the third smallest state with 330,000 people. The ranking of the six largest states did not change from the previous census, and they contained 40.8 percent of the population and held 40.6 percent of the seats in the House of Representatives. Five states composing less than 1 percent of the population—Alaska, Delaware, Nevada, Vermont, and Wyoming— each received one seat. Their share of the House was 1.1 percent, slightly greater than their population numbers would have dictated under theoretical apportionment of equal representation.

Comparison of Tables 2-36, 2-38, and 2-40 shows that more transfers of seats occurred in 1960 than in the two previous apportionments. Map 17 illustrates that ten states gained seats under the 1960 apportionment.[93] California gained eight while Florida gained four new districts; the two states accounted for more than half the twenty-one seats transferred (Table 2-40). Sixteen states lost members, reinforcing a concentration of power begun in the 1930s, as fewer states gained seats than lost them, in a zero-sum transfer of seats in the House. Twenty-four states had no change under the automatic apportionment that applied the method of equal proportions, following the precedent of the last apportionment.

Of the sixteen states that lost power, twelve were located in the northern tier (see Table 2-41) accounting for a 3.7 percent decline in the representational strength compared with 1950. Five northern states—Alaska, Maryland, Michigan, New Jersey, and Ohio—gained 1.1 percent, resulting in a net northern-tier loss of 2.6 percent. The transfer of power is distinctly to the South and West. Four states in the South—Alabama, Arkansas, Mississippi, and North Carolina—lost a total of 1.1 percent of House representation, but five southern/West Coast states gained 3.7 percent. Although the northern tier lost 2.6 percent, it still controlled 59.8 percent of the House.

Although immigration numbers were severely restricted by a strict quota system, under an exploding birth rate and much reduced mortality rate the relative growth rate was again in the same order of magnitude as in the first decade of the twentieth century. The postwar increase in fertility, the baby boom, was most prominent in the fifties and the absolute increase in numbers from 1950 to 1960 far outweighed earlier increments. The geographic mobility of the American population was unequaled, enabling population movements to develop at unprecedented rates. A major element was the accelerated transition from rural to urban places of residence. The 1960 census recorded one-third of the population as living in rural areas, the inverse of the distribution at the turn of the century. Changes in apportionment in the House of Representatives reflected these changes in population, although the power of urban voters continued to lag behind that of rural voters in both houses of Congress and in state houses across the nation.

In the Manufacturing Belt, Michigan and Ohio each gained seats. The post–World War II economic boom demanded very high production levels of the consumer goods, especially automobiles, in which these two states excelled. Similar production of consumer goods, coupled with massive suburban growth around New York City, fostered population growth in New Jersey, which received an additional seat. Metropolitan growth of Baltimore and Washington, D.C., encouraged corresponding suburban development in Maryland, which also gained a representative. By 1960 more than one-sixth of the U.S. population lived in suburban areas.[94] In the eighteenth census, seven of the ten largest cities reported loss or minimal change in population. Migration from the central city to suburbs across state boundaries had major implications for the state of New York, which lost two seats. New York had a delegation of forty-one representatives, 9.4 percent of the House. Pennsylvania lost three seats, the greatest loss of any state. Multiple factors in Pennsylvania, including a less favorable mix of industries than in other midwestern states, combined to create a much slower growth rate than the national average.

Both in the North and in the South, agricultural states continued to lose population. A core region of states that lost congressional districts is visible in Map 17. Predominantly rural, these states extend from Minnesota through the agricultural heartland of Illinois and Iowa to Missouri, Arkansas, and the Gulf Coast states of Mississippi and Alabama. Plains states such as Iowa, Minnesota, Nebraska, and Kansas suffered out-migration as the character of farming was transformed by mechanization and corporations (see the case study on rural and urban places and the 1920 nonapportionment in Part 3). Mechanization continued to hasten rural out-migration from Alabama, Arkansas, Mississippi, and North Carolina. The Appalachian states of West Virginia and Kentucky were similarly affected as coal production and small-scale agriculture were unable to provide the necessary economic opportunities.

Population shifts on a large scale were responsible for widespread shifts in political power during the sixth decade of the twentieth century. The Southwest and Pacific Coast, including the newly admitted states of Alaska and Hawaii, gained twelve seats. The intensity of gains illustrated in the 1960 reapportionment augments those of 1950, as population growth concentrated in California, Florida, and Texas. The rise of the Sunbelt was ensured as the net transfer of seats consistently favored the southern tier. But within the southern tier, growth was uneven. In 1960 the gains of the Southwest and Pacific Coast were offset by losses of six seats elsewhere in the South (see Table 2-41).

93. To be consistent with the methods used in this atlas, Alaska and Hawaii are each credited with gains as they are apportioned for the first time in 1960.

94. Bogue, *Population,* 784.

Table 2-40. 1960 Apportionment Statistics

State	Change in Seats	Seats Apportioned	Percent of House	Percentage Change
Alabama	-1	8	1.8	-0.3
Alaska	1	1	0.2	0.2
Arizona	1	3	0.7	0.2
Arkansas	-2	4	0.9	-0.5
California	8	38	8.7	1.8
Colorado	0	4	0.9	0.0
Connecticut	0	6	1.4	0.0
Delaware	0	1	0.2	0.0
Florida	4	12	2.8	1.0
Georgia	0	10	2.3	0.0
Hawaii	2	2	0.5	0.5
Idaho	0	2	0.5	0.0
Illinois	-1	24	5.5	-0.2
Indiana	0	11	2.5	0.0
Iowa	-1	7	1.6	-0.2
Kansas	-1	5	1.1	-0.3
Kentucky	-1	7	1.6	-0.2
Louisiana	0	8	1.8	0.0
Maine	-1	2	0.5	-0.2
Maryland	1	8	1.8	0.2
Massachusetts	-2	12	2.8	-0.4
Michigan	1	19	4.4	0.3
Minnesota	-1	8	1.8	-0.3
Mississippi	-1	5	1.1	-0.3
Missouri	-1	10	2.3	-0.2
Montana	0	2	0.5	0.0
Nebraska	-1	3	0.7	-0.2
Nevada	0	1	0.2	0.0
New Hampshire	0	2	0.5	0.0
New Jersey	1	15	3.4	0.2
New Mexico	0	2	0.5	0.0
New York	-2	41	9.4	-0.5
North Carolina	-1	11	2.5	-0.3
North Dakota	0	2	0.5	0.0
Ohio	1	24	5.5	0.2
Oklahoma	0	6	1.4	0.0
Oregon	0	4	0.9	0.0
Pennsylvania	-3	27	6.2	-0.7
Rhode Island	0	2	0.5	0.0
South Carolina	0	6	1.4	0.0
South Dakota	0	2	0.5	0.0
Tennessee	0	9	2.1	0.0
Texas	1	23	5.3	0.2
Utah	0	2	0.5	0.0
Vermont	0	1	0.2	0.0
Virginia	0	10	2.3	0.0
Washington	0	7	1.6	0.0
West Virginia	-1	5	1.1	-0.3
Wisconsin	0	10	2.3	0.0
Wyoming	0	1	0.2	0.0
Total	0	435		

Table 2-41. Seat Change for Snowbelt and Sunbelt States, 1960

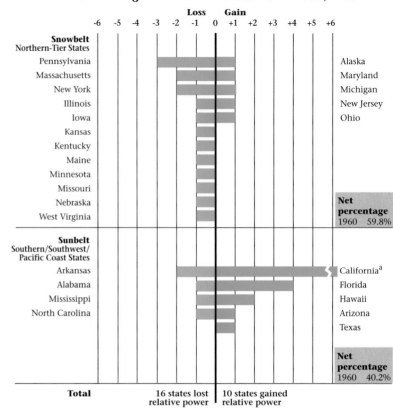

24 states remained the same.
[a]California gained 8 seats.

Map 17. Change in Seats–1960

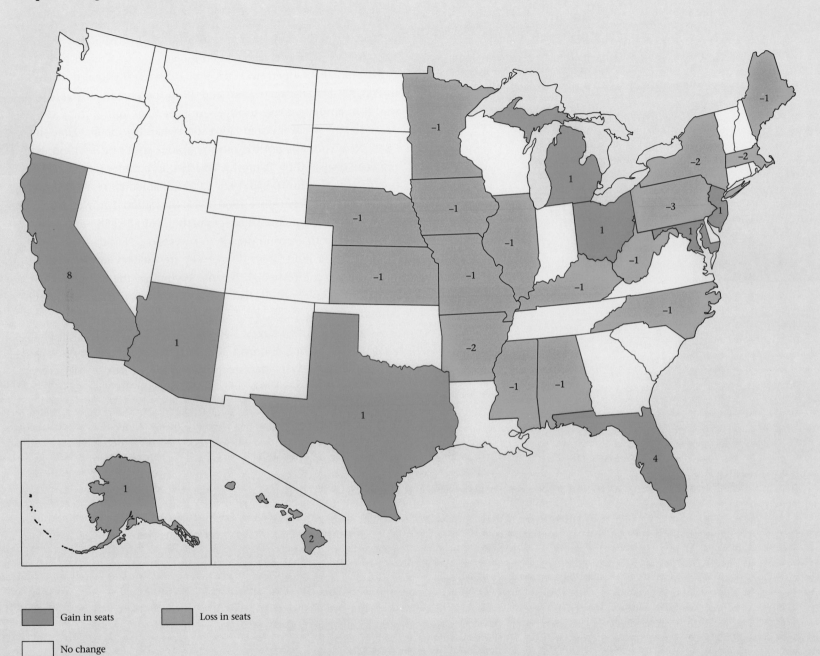

Gain in seats   Loss in seats

No change

1970 CENSUS APPORTIONMENT

More than 200 million people lived in the United States in 1970. The nineteenth census recorded an increase of 23,978,856 people, a growth rate of 13.4 percent since 1960, to bring the total population to 203,302,175. Between 1960 and 1970 the growth of population was both absolutely and relatively smaller than during the previous decade as the postwar boom faded somewhat. For the first time since 1810, New York was not the most populous state in the Union, having been displaced by California in 1964. In becoming the largest in population, California had 19,971,069 inhabitants, representing an increase of 27 percent since 1960, twice the national growth rate.

Alaska had the smallest state population with 302,583 inhabitants. Moreover, for the second decade in succession, Nevada increased its population by more than 70 percent to 488,000 inhabitants and moved up to the forty-eighth rank. Wyoming, the second smallest state with 332,000 people, had a virtually negligible increase in population from 1960.

As in 1960, the six largest states accounted for 40.8 percent of the total U.S. population and held 40.9 percent of the seats in the House of Representatives. Six states composing 1.3 percent of the population—Alaska, Delaware, Nevada, North Dakota, Vermont, and Wyoming—each received only one seat and shared 1.4 percent of the political power in the House. As in every reapportionment since 1941, the method of equal proportions was used without additional congressional action.

Although continuing and reinforcing many of the same trends, the redistribution of political power was far less dramatic in 1970 than in 1960. Just fourteen states were involved in the transition and, as documented in Table 2-42, nine states lost members and five gained members, continuing to strengthen the concentration of power in the leading growth states of California, Florida, and Texas. Map 18 of the 1970 apportionment is dominated by the thirty-six states for which no change occurred. Of the nine states that lost power, seven are located in the northern tier (see Table 2-43).

Of the seven northern states experiencing decline, four were in the Manufacturing Belt—Ohio, Pennsylvania, New York, and West Virginia—and three were predominantly rural agricultural states—Iowa, North Dakota, and Wisconsin. In the Great Plains region, North Dakota was reduced to a single member. Just two states in the South, Alabama and Tennessee, lost seats (totaling 0.5 percent of the House representation). Pennsylvania and New York lost two congressional districts each; the other seven states each lost a single district. On the other hand, southern-tier states gained all eleven seats lost by the northern tier (see Table 2-43). With a net gain of 2.1 percent, the southern and western states controlled 42.3 percent of the House. The North had a net loss of 2.1 percent, and after reapportionment controlled 57.7 percent of the House.

By 1970 the shift to the Sunbelt became well established on the strengths of the economic expansion that had developed during the fifties and sixties. Several components contributed to the redistribution of population from which were emerging different patterns of political power. From the perspective of migration, the Sunbelt is composed of at least two distinct destination regions, and subregions within these two may be easily distinguished.[95] The two regions attracting the majority of migrants are made apparent in Map 18 by the addition of six seats in the arid Southwest and three seats in Florida. As the pattern of Sunbelt growth has developed through time, the southwestern states of California, Arizona, New Mexico, and Nevada have attracted greater total numbers than the Southeast, but Florida recorded the greatest population rate increase, 81 percent from 1960 to 1970.[96] Although the meteoric growth rates of some Sunbelt states (such as Arizona and New Mexico) overstate the absolute numbers of people involved because of low base populations, California and Florida each added more than four million to their 1960 populations.

Throughout U.S. history employment opportunities have predominated as the force behind population movements. Beginning in the 1970s, however, migrants also cited retirement, health, environmental amenities, leisure, and recreational opportunities among their reasons for relocating away from the population centers of the Northeast and Midwest.[97] Elderly northeasterners preferentially move to the Southeast, preeminently to Florida.[98] Although many retired people from the Midwest relocated to the Southwest, their numbers were assimilated by the movement of the significantly larger cohort of the baby boom generation as it reached adulthood and sought employment. Well documented by demographers, sociologists, and journalists, the beginning of a third great national regime of population redistribution was identified by the nineteenth census and reflected in the deconcentration of political power from the Northeast and Midwest.[99]

95. George A. Schnell and Mark S. Monmonier, *The Study of Population; Elements, Patterns, Processes* (Columbus, Ohio: Charles E. Merrill, 1988), 152.

96. The three leading destinations of migration to the Sunbelt between 1965 and 1970 are identified as California, Arizona, and Florida in Jeanne C. Biggar, "The Sunning of America: Migration to the Sunbelt," *Population Bulletin* 34, no. 1 (Population Reference Bureau, 1979): 22. Biggar also characterizes different source regions for migrants to the Southwest as opposed to those moving to the Southeast.

97. See, for example, David Vining, R. Pallone, and D. A. Plane, "Recent migration patterns in the developed world: A clarification of some differences between our and IIASA's findings," *Environment and Planning A* 13 (1981): 243–250.

98. For descriptions of preferential movements of the elderly, see S. K. Smith and H. H. Fiskind, "Elderly Migration into Rapidly Growing Areas," *The Review of Regional Studies* 15, no. 2 (1985): 11–20; A. Rogers and J. Watkins, "General versus elderly interstate migration and population redistribution in the United States," *Research on Aging* 9 (1987): 483–529.

99. David A. Plane, "Age-composition change and the geographical dynamics of Interregional migration in the U.S.," *Annals of the Association of American Geographers* 82, no. 1 (1992): 64–85.

Table 2-42. 1970 Apportionment Statistics

State	Change in Seats	Seats Apportioned	Percent of House	Percentage Change
Alabama	-1	7	1.6	-0.2
Alaska	0	1	0.2	0.0
Arizona	1	4	0.9	0.2
Arkansas	0	4	0.9	0.0
California	5	43	9.9	1.2
Colorado	1	5	1.1	0.2
Connecticut	0	6	1.4	0.0
Delaware	0	1	0.2	0.0
Florida	3	15	3.4	0.6
Georgia	0	10	2.3	0.0
Hawaii	0	2	0.5	0.0
Idaho	0	2	0.5	0.0
Illinois	0	24	5.5	0.0
Indiana	0	11	2.5	0.0
Iowa	-1	6	1.4	-0.2
Kansas	0	5	1.1	0.0
Kentucky	0	7	1.6	0.0
Louisiana	0	8	1.8	0.0
Maine	0	2	0.5	0.0
Maryland	0	8	1.8	0.0
Massachusetts	0	12	2.8	0.0
Michigan	0	19	4.4	0.0
Minnesota	0	8	1.8	0.0
Mississippi	0	5	1.1	0.0
Missouri	0	10	2.3	0.0
Montana	0	2	0.5	0.0
Nebraska	0	3	0.7	0.0
Nevada	0	1	0.2	0.0
New Hampshire	0	2	0.5	0.0
New Jersey	0	15	3.4	0.0
New Mexico	0	2	0.5	0.0
New York	-2	39	9.0	-0.4
North Carolina	0	11	2.5	0.0
North Dakota	-1	1	0.2	-0.3
Ohio	-1	23	5.3	-0.2
Oklahoma	0	6	1.4	0.0
Oregon	0	4	0.9	0.0
Pennsylvania	-2	25	5.7	-0.5
Rhode Island	0	2	0.5	0.0
South Carolina	0	6	1.4	0.0
South Dakota	0	2	0.5	0.0
Tennessee	-1	8	1.8	-0.3
Texas	1	24	5.5	0.2
Utah	0	2	0.5	0.0
Vermont	0	1	0.2	0.0
Virginia	0	10	2.3	0.0
Washington	0	7	1.6	0.0
West Virginia	-1	4	0.9	-0.2
Wisconsin	-1	9	2.1	-0.2
Wyoming	0	1	0.2	0.0
Total	0	435		

Table 2-43. Seat Change for Snowbelt and Sunbelt States, 1970

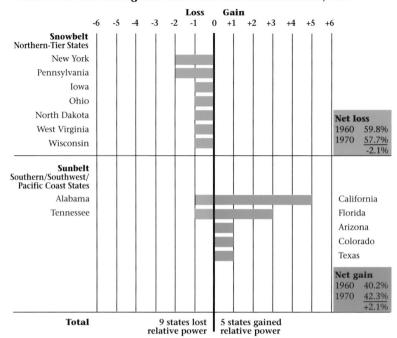

36 states remained the same.

Map 18. Change in Seats–1970

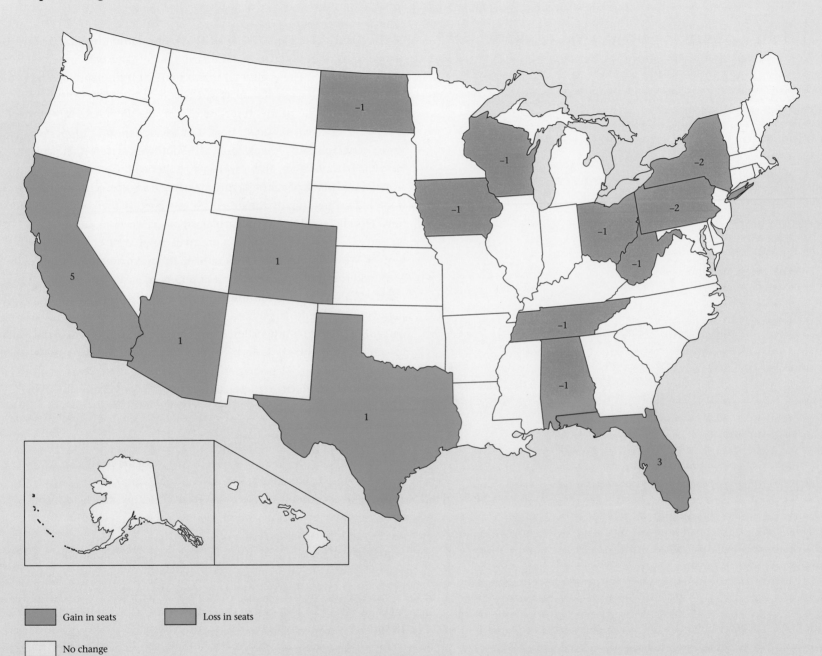

Gain in seats   Loss in seats

No change

1980 CENSUS APPORTIONMENT

The twentieth census of 1980 recorded the addition of 23,240,172 people to the U.S. population, an increase of 11.4 percent, for a total of 226,505,000.[100] The decline observed in 1970 in the absolute and relative increase of population was repeated in the 1980 census figures. In aggregate nearly three-fourths of the population of the United States lived in urban areas, but the urban-rural proportion varied geographically. For example, the Southwest states—California, Nevada, Arizona, Utah, and Arizona—together with Colorado formed a distinctive block of states having greater than 80 percent urbanization.[101] Elsewhere highly urbanized states were dispersed widely; Illinois, Florida, and the Northeast had urbanization rates greater than 80 percent. By way of contrast more than 60 percent of the inhabitants of West Virginia and Vermont lived in rural places.

In addition the urban-rural classification concealed more than it revealed. Along with a continuing decline in the proportion of the population living in large cites, 12.5 percent in 1980 down from 16 percent in 1960, the proportion living in central cities was declining in comparison with those in the urban fringe. In 1980 seventy-two million Americans, 32 percent of the total population, lived in the urban fringe. More than 10 percent of the U.S. population lived in rural sections of metropolitan regions.[102]

California consolidated its first ranking in terms of population size with 23.6 million people, more than 6 million greater than second-ranked New York. By 1980 one in ten U.S. residents lived in California. Texas rose to third with 14.2 million inhabitants. Pennsylvania's growth was inconsequential (0.05 percent) but the state held fourth rank, followed by Illinois and Ohio. Florida rose precipitously into seventh rank with a population of 9,746,961.

Alaska, Wyoming, and Vermont had the smallest populations. Alaska reported more than 400,000 inhabitants in the 1980 census. In continuing its explosive growth through the seventies, Nevada again increased its population by 71 percent to 799,000 inhabitants, advancing to the forty-third rank, up from last in 1940.

In 1980 the six largest states accounted for 39.5 percent of the total U.S. population and held an equivalent proportion of the seats in the House of Representatives. Six states, composing 1.5 percent of the population—Alaska, Delaware, South Dakota, North Dakota, Vermont, and Wyoming—each received one seat and shared 1.4 percent of the political power in the House. Once again the method of equal proportions was used to reallocate seats.

Table 2-44 summarizes the transfer of political power in the 1980 apportionment in which seventeen seats were relocated. Map 19 illustrates the most striking geographical redistribution of power from the Northeast and Midwest to the South and West of any decade in the twentieth century. The net transfer of power, 3.9 percent of the House, while less than the shift in 1960 (4.8 percent), was entirely the result of losses in the northern tier and gains in the Sunbelt (see Table 2-45); moreover, eleven states in the southern/Pacific Coast tier gained districts while ten northern states lost power.

The major losers were the states ranked second, fourth, fifth, and sixth in population size. New York lost five congressional districts, Pennsylvania, Illinois, and Ohio each lost two. These losses were at the core of a population agglomeration that had been initiated during the colonization of North America, then had grown in the formative years of the nation in the early nineteenth century. Development of the concentration of the U.S. population in the Northeast and the Midwest was most pronounced during industrialization and the associated urbanization from the mid-nineteenth to the mid-twentieth century.[103]

Two vigorous demographic processes, the mass immigration of the turn of the century and the out-migration of excess rural populations, that had been formative in the concentration of population had been replaced in 1980 by two other forces with diametrically opposed geographical outcomes. These new forces were the shift of the destination of immigrants to the Southwest, especially those from Latin America and Asia, compounded by the search for economic opportunity by the large post–World War II generation. During the 1970s the stream of out-migration from the Northeast and Midwest became a torrent, the flow to the South and West reaching 600,000 per year.[104]

Again the growth-pole states are California, Florida, and Texas. Florida gained four House districts on the basis of migration from the Northeast, Central America, and the Caribbean, showing an increase of 1 percent to 4.4 percent of the total representation in the House. Texas added three new districts to build a delegation of twenty-seven members, 6.2 percent of the House. California gained two seats for a total delegation of forty-five, 10.3 percent of the House. These three states in total added nine of the seventeen seats that were transferred and represented 20.9 percent of the House in 1980.

100. U.S. Department of Commerce, Bureau of the Census, *1980 Census of Population*, vol. 1, *Characteristics of the Population* (Washington, D.C.: Government Printing Office, 1984). The Census Bureau released a revised U.S. total of 226,542,203 in April 1989.

101. The figures from the 1980 census are well illustrated in M. W. Dempsey, *Daily Telegraph Atlas of the United States of America* (London: Nomad Publishers, 1986), 44–47.

102. Ibid., 46.

103. The definitive description of forces of population development in the industrial, metropolitan agglomerations of the American Manufacturing Belt is found in Edward Ullman, "Regional development and the geography of concentration," *Papers and Proceedings of the Regional Science Association* 4 (1958): 179–198.

104. See Vining et al., "Recent migration patterns," 234–235.

Table 2-44. 1980 Apportionment Statistics

State	Change in Seats	Seats Apportioned	Percent of House	Percentage Change
Alabama	0	7	1.6	0.0
Alaska	0	1	0.2	0.0
Arizona	1	5	1.1	0.2
Arkansas	0	4	0.9	0.0
California	2	45	10.3	0.4
Colorado	1	6	1.4	0.3
Connecticut	0	6	1.4	0.0
Delaware	0	1	0.2	0.0
Florida	4	19	4.4	1.0
Georgia	0	10	2.3	0.0
Hawaii	0	2	0.5	0.0
Idaho	0	2	0.5	0.0
Illinois	-2	22	5.1	-0.4
Indiana	-1	10	2.3	-0.2
Iowa	0	6	1.4	0.0
Kansas	0	5	1.1	0.0
Kentucky	0	7	1.6	0.0
Louisiana	0	8	1.8	0.0
Maine	0	2	0.5	0.0
Maryland	0	8	1.8	0.0
Massachusetts	-1	11	2.5	-0.3
Michigan	-1	18	4.1	-0.3
Minnesota	0	8	1.8	0.0
Mississippi	0	5	1.1	0.0
Missouri	-1	9	2.1	-0.2
Montana	0	2	0.5	0.0
Nebraska	0	3	0.7	0.0
Nevada	1	2	0.5	0.3
New Hampshire	0	2	0.5	0.0
New Jersey	-1	14	3.2	-0.2
New Mexico	1	3	0.7	0.2
New York	-5	34	7.8	-1.2
North Carolina	0	11	2.5	0.0
North Dakota	0	1	0.2	0.0
Ohio	-2	21	4.8	-0.5
Oklahoma	0	6	1.4	0.0
Oregon	1	5	1.1	0.2
Pennsylvania	-2	23	5.3	-0.4
Rhode Island	0	2	0.5	0.0
South Carolina	0	6	1.4	0.0
South Dakota	-1	1	0.2	-0.3
Tennessee	1	9	2.1	0.3
Texas	3	27	6.2	0.7
Utah	1	3	0.7	0.2
Vermont	0	1	0.2	0.0
Virginia	0	10	2.3	0.0
Washington	1	8	1.8	0.2
West Virginia	0	4	0.9	0.0
Wisconsin	0	9	2.1	0.0
Wyoming	0	1	0.2	0.0
Total	0	435		

Table 2-45. Seat Change for Snowbelt and Sunbelt States, 1980

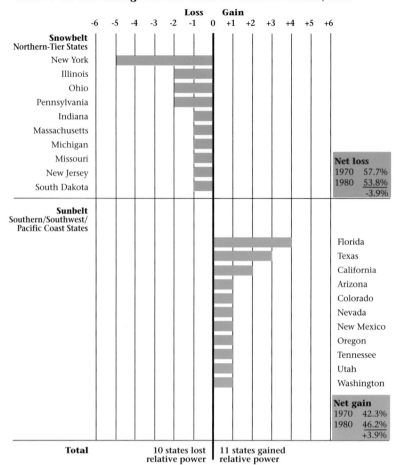

29 states remained the same.

Map 19. Change in Seats–1980

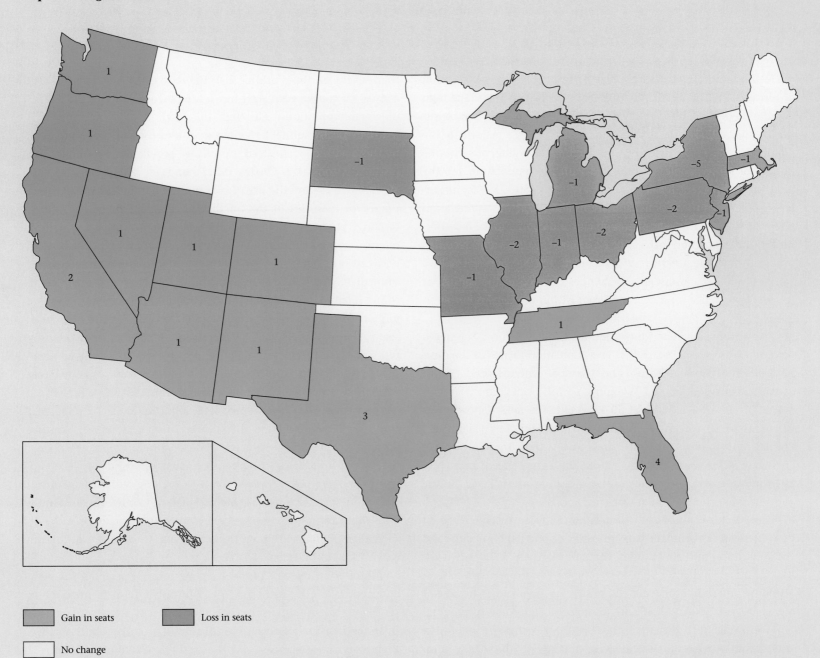

Gain in seats   Loss in seats

No change

1990 CENSUS APPORTIONMENT

Geographical changes in population resulted in the reallocation of nineteen seats in the House of Representatives in 1990. The total population of the United States as recorded by the April 1990 census was 249,632,692. For the first time in census history a majority of the population was recorded as living in large metropolitan areas of one million or more people.[105] Compared with precensus estimates, the total was 0.6 percent lower than the expected 250,172,000 and differences between the various estimations and the actual enumeration instigated dissent from state through city and county to local authorities.[106] The population increase of 22,205,000 (10.2 percent) recorded during the decade 1980 to 1990 included 922,000 overseas federal workers, military personnel, and families counted in the census for the first time, reflecting a decision taken within the Census Bureau in 1989.[107]

Discounting federal personnel stationed overseas, the U.S. residential population was 248,709,873. The population increased the most in California, Florida, Texas, and Georgia, whereas Iowa, North Dakota, West Virginia, and Wyoming all lost population. Nevada's rate of increase was notable at 50.4 percent. The rate of growth was greater than 20 percent in Alaska, Arizona, and New Hampshire. Overall more states (thirty-one) grew at less than the U.S. average change of 9.8 percent than grew more rapidly (nineteen states) and as in previous reapportionments the allocation of seats was in line with the gross changes of population (Table 2-46).

Map 20 clearly illustrates the reapportionment of congressional power reflecting the underlying processes of population change and the application of the method of equal proportions. In keeping with its continued and intensified development as the seventh largest economy on earth, California had the largest population increase of any state, 6,092,000 (25 percent), an increase equivalent to the total population of the thirteenth largest state, Massachusetts. California is typical of other southwestern states that have both net migration and natural increase above the national average.[108] The southern and Pacific Coast showed a net gain of nineteen seats (see Table 2-47). Of this total, California gained seven House seats to increase its total to fifty-two, the largest state delegation ever to be seated in the House of Representatives.

In 1992 the average ratio of representation was 1:573,848, more than seventeen times greater than the ratio established after the first census. Of course, each state has a different value under the method of equal proportions. Although the method of apportionment is mathematically equitable, serious questions for democracy are raised by those with concerns that the average population of congressional districts is too large. On the other hand, current popular opinion about Congress and the size of government hardly lends itself to proposals for increases in the number of representatives. The priority rankings produced by the apportionment are sensitive to small differences in population. Table 2-48 demonstrates that the relationship between population change and the apportionment of seats is not immediately obvious. For example, note that New Jersey with an absolute increase in population of 366,000 (5.0 percent) and West Virginia with an absolute decrease of 156,000 (-8.0 percent) both lose a seat, whereas Illinois with an increase of 12,000 (0.1 percent) loses two seats. Further to the counterintuitive effects of the method, Pennsylvania with an increase of 15,000 (0.1 percent) loses two seats while New York increasing by 433,000 (2.5 percent) loses three.

Antecedents for the trend of reapportionment of seats exist through the entire history of Southwest and Pacific Coast states. Defense industries linked with electronics, software, and similar high-technology industries, in conjunction with postindustrial employment opportunities continued to act as a strong pull for migrants. In the eighties, a fundamental change occurred in the cause of California's population increase. By the 1990 census 75 percent of the net increase in California's population was due to immigration, mostly from Asia and Mexico.[109] Together California, Florida, and Texas account for an increase of 14 seats, representing 74 percent of the total change in apportionment for 1990, but only 54.3 percent of the total U.S. population increase. The apportionment formula again acted to strengthen the relative power of these states disproportionally to their population increase. With the single exception of Texas in 1940, these three growth-oriented states have increased their proportional power in Congress every decade during this century.

The gain of a seat by the state of Washington may be attributed to growth resulting from interregional migration from the Southwest to the Pacific Northwest. The exodus of middle-class, well-educated Californians has been documented as being stimulated by increased demands on struggling public services, increased crime, deterioration in the environment through crowding and pollution, and perhaps racial tensions.[110] On the other hand, Washington was the last state to be allocated a seat under the apportionment formula and it benefited from the large number of overseas federal personnel claiming Washington as their home state.

Similar pushes in environmental values, housing, and "white flight" from California may account for the addition of a seat in Arizona, as the explosive growth of the Phoenix and Tucson metropolitan regions continued into the eighties. Additionally in-migration from the northern states, particularly of retired people, and immigration from Latin America contributed to the growth of Arizona.

In the Southeast a different set of forces appeared to be active. The apparent anomaly of a loss of a Sunbelt seat in Louisiana is related to severe declines in the traditional petrochemical industrial base coupled with a persistent low ebb of the energy production sector. On the positive side, Florida continues to lead in economic growth and, like California, is much influenced by immigration, particularly from Latin America. However, Florida, Georgia, North Carolina, and Virginia each gained seats on the strength of economic growth in the South that continues to draw major interstate migration flows from Northeast states ranging from Indiana to Massachusetts.

Partly as a result of out-migration, the northern tier had a net loss of eighteen seats (see Table 2-47). In losing twelve seats, the industrial heartland states of Massachusetts, New York, New Jersey, Pennsylvania, Ohio, Michigan, and Illinois epitomize deep and enduring economic decline in the rust belt. Losses of manufacturing jobs continued throughout the decade and spawned job losses in many sectors of the economy. Loss of family farm populations in Iowa, Illinois, and Kansas exacerbated job losses in the industrial sector of those states. Kentucky and West Virginia exhibited continued hardcore Appalachian economic decline, West Virginia having lost a seat in three of the last four reapportionments (1960, 1970, and 1990).

105. Carl Haub, "The Top 10 Findings from the 1990 Census (So Far...)," *Population Today* 19, no. 7 (Population Reference Bureau, July/August 1991): 3.

106. Carl Haub, "Census: 248,709,873 U.S. Residents," *Population Today* 19, no. 2 (Population Reference Bureau, February 1991): 4.

107. Felicity Barringer, "Census Count of People Abroad Gives Massachusetts' Seat in Congress to Washington," *New York Times,* January 5, 1991.

108. Immigration from Asia to the United States, mostly to the West Coast, has exceeded that from Europe since 1950. Latin American immigrants outnumber Asians. As illegal immigration is impossible to estimate accurately, the contribution of "undocumented aliens" is unknown. California, Arizona, and New Mexico are the most affected based on numbers of illegal immigrants apprehended. Estimates of net illegal immigration range from 80,000 to 250,000 per year. Schnell and Monmonier, *Study of Population,* 153–156.

109. Haub, "Census: 248,709,873 U.S. Residents," 3.

110. The factors contributing to the out-migration from California may well be exacerbated by the urban disturbances of May 1992.

Table 2-46. 1990 Apportionment Statistics

State	Change in Seats	Seats Apportioned	Percent of House	Percentage Change
Alabama	0	7	1.6	0.0
Alaska	0	1	0.2	0.0
Arizona	1	6	1.4	0.3
Arkansas	0	4	0.9	0.0
California	7	52	12.0	1.7
Colorado	0	6	1.4	0.0
Connecticut	0	6	1.4	0.0
Delaware	0	1	0.2	0.0
Florida	4	23	5.3	0.9
Georgia	1	11	2.5	0.2
Hawaii	0	2	0.5	0.0
Idaho	0	2	0.5	0.0
Illinois	-2	20	4.6	-0.5
Indiana	0	10	2.3	0.0
Iowa	-1	5	1.1	-0.3
Kansas	-1	4	0.9	-0.2
Kentucky	-1	6	1.4	-0.2
Louisiana	-1	7	1.6	-0.2
Maine	0	2	0.5	0.0
Maryland	0	8	1.8	0.0
Massachusetts	-1	10	2.3	-0.2
Michigan	-2	16	3.7	-0.4
Minnesota	0	8	1.8	0.0
Mississippi	0	5	1.1	0.0
Missouri	0	9	2.1	0.0
Montana	-1	1	0.2	-0.3
Nebraska	0	3	0.7	0.0
Nevada	0	2	0.5	0.0
New Hampshire	0	2	0.5	0.0
New Jersey	-1	13	3.0	-0.2
New Mexico	0	3	0.7	0.0
New York	-3	31	7.1	-0.7
North Carolina	1	12	2.8	0.3
North Dakota	0	1	0.2	0.0
Ohio	-2	19	4.4	-0.4
Oklahoma	0	6	1.4	0.0
Oregon	0	5	1.1	0.0
Pennsylvania	-2	21	4.8	-0.5
Rhode Island	0	2	0.5	0.0
South Carolina	0	6	1.4	0.0
South Dakota	0	1	0.2	0.0
Tennessee	0	9	2.1	0.0
Texas	3	30	6.9	0.7
Utah	0	3	0.7	0.0
Vermont	0	1	0.2	0.0
Virginia	1	11	2.5	0.2
Washington	1	9	2.1	0.3
West Virginia	-1	3	0.7	-0.2
Wisconsin	0	9	2.1	0.0
Wyoming	0	1	0.2	0.0
Total	0	435		

Table 2-47. Seat Change for Snowbelt and Sunbelt States, 1990

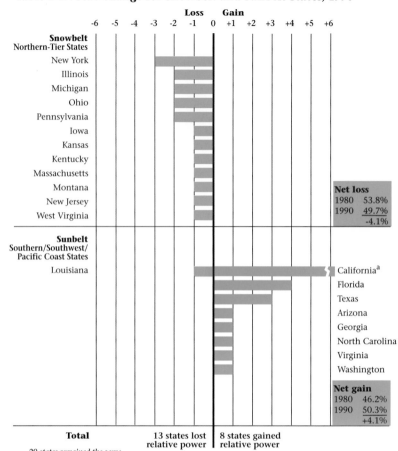

29 states remained the same.
[a]California gained 7 seats.

Map 20. Change in Seats–1990

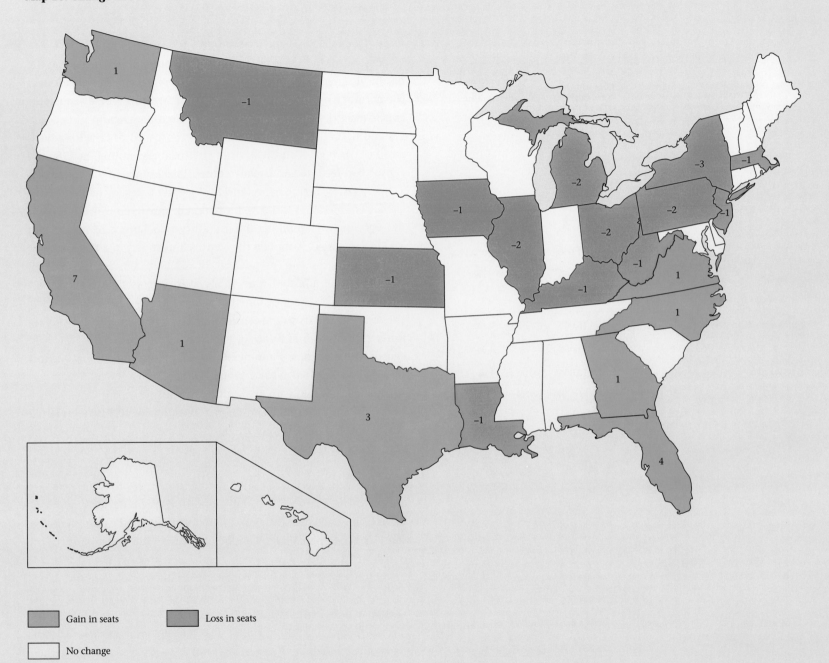

Gain in seats   Loss in seats

No change

Table 2-48. Apportionment and Population Changes by State, 1990.

	Change in Seats	Resident Population Change, 1980–1990	Percentage Change in Population
Losses			
New York	-3	433,000	2.5
Pennsylvania	-2	15,000	0.1
Illinois	-2	12,000	0.1
Michigan	-2	37,000	0.4
Ohio	-2	50,000	0.5
Iowa	-1	-137,000	-4.7
Kansas	-1	114,000	4.8
Kentucky	-1	24,000	0.7
Louisiana	-1	16,000	0.4
Massachusetts	-1	279,000	4.9
Montana	-1	12,000	1.6
New Jersey	-1	366,000	5.0
West Virginia	-1	-156,000	-8.0
Gains			
California	7	6,091,000	25.7
Florida	4	3,198,000	32.8
Texas	3	2,758,000	19.4
Arizona	1	947,000	34.9
Georgia	1	1,014,000	18.6
North Carolina	1	754,000	12.8
Virginia	1	841,000	15.7
Washington	1	737,000	17.8
Total United States		22,205,000	9.8

Source: The United States Population Date Sheet, *9th ed. (Washington, D.C.: Population Reference Bureau, Inc., 1991).*

Effects of 1990 Census Errors

Because of the stakes resting on apportionment, taxation, and the disbursal of federal funds to the states, there have been debates over the accuracy of the census since the first in 1790. The considerable controversy that accompanied the estimated undercount of between 4.3 and 6.3 million people in the 1990 census led to calls for adjustment of the figures on the basis of statistical resampling. In 1980 the census had recorded an equally contentious estimated undercount of 1.2 percent, initiating expectations of greater accuracy in 1990. Postcensus enumeration estimated a national undercount of 2.1 percent in 1990, mainly among ethnic minority populations of inner cities and in rural areas. Although the Census Bureau released a revised estimate of the resident population of 253,978,000, a difference of 5,268,127, the adjusted state totals were not used in reapportionment. The secretary of commerce ruled on July 16, 1991, that no statistical adjustments to the census were to be implemented. Although inner cities and rural areas suffered the greatest differences between census and postcensus enumeration, counterintuitive consequences would have resulted from a revised apportionment. California and Arizona each would gain an additional seat. Wisconsin would lose a seat and Pennsylvania would lose an additional seat. These potential changes would have further strengthened the increasing power of the Sunbelt in Congress.

As far as apportionment is concerned, census adjustment is a zero-sum game, for every seat gained by one state there must be a loss by another. The method of equal proportions formula for apportionment is very sensitive to small differences that could easily occur as a result of geographical and demographic variations in sampling.[111] Undercounts of 4.4 to 6.2 percent for blacks compared with 1.2 to 2.0 for nonblacks; 4.2 to 7.3 percent for Hispanic population and 2.5 to 7.3 for Native Americans are compounded by geographical variations within regions and states. California, New Mexico, Virginia, North Carolina, South Carolina, and Florida had undercount rates substantially greater than the national average.[112] Disputes and legal challenges initiated by the 1990 census in all probability will influence the census in the year 2000.

111. J. S. Passel, "What Census Adjustment Would Mean," *Population Today* 19, no. 6 (Population Reference Bureau, June 1991): 6–7.
112. Felicity Barringer, "Census Revisions Would Widen Political Gains of 3 Big States," *New York Times*, June 14, 1991, 7.

FUTURE TRENDS OF CONGRESSIONAL APPORTIONMENT

Strange things are going to happen halfway into the 1990s that we can't predict now. They always do. This is the most unpredictable area of law and politics.

Jeffrey Wice, *USA Today*[113]

A research report on population change and congressional representation published in 1972 confidently asserted that "the census will be an exact guide to the distribution of congressional districts within and between states," as contemporary U.S. Supreme Court decisions had ruled that the population among congressional districts within a state must be "as nearly equal as possible."[114] On the strength of those rulings, the author projected the apportionment of congressional districts among states for each decade until the year 2000 using population projections under Census Series B and E.[115] Comparison of these projections with the 1990 actual reapportionments reveals the dangers inherent in forecasting (see Table 2-49).

Using the 1970 projected populations, the growth of California in 1990 was overestimated by the equivalent of two districts, while that of Florida was underestimated by three seats. Actual growth in the large industrial states was slower than estimated resulting in underprediction of the decline in their delegations. New York lost four seats more than projected; Illinois, Michigan, and Ohio lost three more than the estimated number of districts for 1990.

Estimates over a short-time period will be more accurate as the mechanisms of demographic change tend to be persistent with long lead times. Using population forecasts from the 1990 census it is feasible to predict the composition of the House in 2000. Major changes in the demographic composition of the House have been set in motion by the 1992 reapportionment that will have significance for the next one in 2002. Changes were made in the enumeration method in 1989 to include overseas Americans in the apportionment population of the states. The determination of home states and congressional districts of overseas Americans adds a further complication to the difficulties in estimating the components of state population change. In addition, amendments to the Voting Rights Act in 1982 mandating the creation of minority group districts where feasible will substantially affect the political and demographic composition of the House in 1992. Under the 1980 apportionment blacks held 5 congressional seats out of 116 in eleven southern states. With the 1992 election blacks gained membership of the delegations from Alabama, Florida, North Carolina, South Carolina, and Virginia for the first time since

Table 2-49. Predicted Apportionment of Congressional Districts, 1990

State	Predicted 1990 Series B	Predicted 1990 Series E	Actual 1990	Difference: Actual- Series B
Alabama	6	6	7	1
Alaska	1	1	1	0
Arizona	5	6	6	1
Arkansas	3	3	4	1
California	54	59	52	-2
Colorado	6	6	6	0
Connecticut	7	7	6	-1
Delaware	1	1	1	0
Florida	20	23	23	3
Georgia	10	10	11	1
Hawaii	2	2	2	0
Idaho	1	1	2	1
Illinois	23	22	20	-3
Indiana	11	11	10	-1
Iowa	5	4	5	0
Kansas	4	4	4	0
Kentucky	6	5	6	0
Louisiana	7	7	7	0
Maine	2	2	2	0
Maryland	10	10	8	-2
Massachusetts	11	11	10	-1
Michigan	19	19	16	-3
Minnesota	8	7	8	0
Mississippi	4	3	5	1
Missouri	9	8	9	0
Montana	1	1	1	0
Nebraska	3	2	3	0
Nevada	2	2	2	0
New Hampshire	2	2	2	0
New Jersey	16	16	13	-3
New Mexico	2	2	3	1
New York	35	33	31	-4
North Carolina	10	10	12	2
North Dakota	1	1	1	0
Ohio	22	22	19	-3
Oklahoma	5	5	6	1
Oregon	5	5	5	0
Pennsylvania	21	21	21	0
Rhode Island	2	2	2	0
South Carolina	5	5	6	1
South Dakota	1	1	1	0
Tennessee	7	7	9	2
Texas	25	26	30	5
Utah	3	3	3	0
Vermont	1	1	1	0
Virginia	10	11	11	1
Washington	8	8	9	1
West Virginia	3	2	3	0
Wisconsin	9	9	9	0
Wyoming	1	1	1	0
Total	435	435	435	+23/-23

Source: R. Lehne, "Population Change and Congresssional Representation," in A. E. Nash, Commission on Population Growth and the American Future, vol. IV (Washington, D.C.: Government Printing Office, 1972), 87.

Reconstruction. Creation of specific majority-black districts increased the number of black-held seats to fifteen. Because of these redistricting measures the ethnic composition of the House after the 1992 elections more closely represents the ethnic composition of the U.S. population. Blacks make up 12 percent of the U.S. population and 9 percent of the 103d Congress. Hispanics are 9 percent of the population but make up only 4 percent of House membership.[116]

While some attempts at establishing statehood may be merely frivolous, for example, the Northern California separatist movement, others such as statehood for Washington, D.C., and for Puerto Rico are long established and, if successful, will call into debate issues that have been dormant since the 1920s. Would the membership of the House be increased to accommodate new states? If not, the reapportionment of 435 representatives over a larger number of states will reduce the strength of the others in an uneven fashion. The method of apportionment may again be called into question. At some point the large ratio of population per representative will also be questioned.

The census of 2000 will be examined more critically than any other, both in advance and after the fact. Massive changes in apportionment will not be evident but the distribution of the legislators will reflect a changing constituency as existing demographic forces work themselves out and other forces start afresh. The House of 2000 will be more urban and suburban in character than its predecessors; in consequence rural and urban policy issues will face more opposition. Sectional issues of the West and South will find stronger support than those affecting the North and Midwest more directly. Of course, the greatest demographic effects on the House will, in all probability, not be limited to the geographical distribution of population size but will include the representation of the composition of that population, in issues of gender and race. Regional differences of these matters, while difficult to predict, are emerging and will shape the House of Representatives in the twenty-first century.

113. Jeffrey Wice, quoted in *USA Today,* June 8, 1992, 8A.

114. R. Lehne, "Population Change and Congressional Representation," in A. E. Kier Nash, ed., *Governance and Population: The Governmental Implications of Population Change,* vol. IV, Research Reports, The Commission on Population Growth and the American Future (Washington, D.C.: Government Printing Office, 1972), 85.

115. Series B and Series E are Census Bureau population projections under different average family sizes. See U.S. Department of Commerce, Bureau of Census, *Projections of the Population of the United States by Age and Sex: 1970 to 2000,* Current Population Reports, Series P-25, no. 470 (Washington, D.C.: Government Printing Office, 1973).

116. John R. Cranford, "The New Class: More Diverse, Less Lawyerly, Younger," *Congressional Quarterly,* Supplement to No. 44, November 7, 1992, 7–8.

Part 3

Major Geographical Trends of Congressional Apportionment

Introduction

Shifts in State, Regional, and Sectional Political Power

The history of European settlement in what is now the United States began in the late sixteenth and early seventeenth centuries on the Atlantic coast and spread inexorably westward. British colonial policies inhibited settlement of Americans beyond the Appalachian Mountains; therefore, with the 1783 recognition of U.S. independence, the population was still mostly clustered along the Atlantic coast from New England south to Georgia. With the formation of the U.S. government in 1789, the thirteen original states both welcomed and feared the expansion of the American state. One of the conditions of the small coastal states to final ratification of the Constitution was the ceding of western trans-Appalachian lands to the federal government. These lands were to be sold by the federal government for revenue and settled by an ever-expanding population. The original states understood that new states would be formed and admitted into the Union and recognized the political consequences of an expansive republic.[1]

Independence opened the floodgates of westward migration. Vermont was the fourteenth state admitted into the Union in 1791. Within a year the first "frontier" trans-Appalachian state, Kentucky, also gained admission. After the 1796 admission of Tennessee, the pace of frontier state admission slowed for a period. Ohio was admitted in 1803 and noncontiguous Louisiana in 1812. However, throughout the nineteenth century the frontier of American settlement relentlessly moved westward. The last of the forty-eight contiguous United States, New Mexico and Ari-

1. Rosemarie Zagarri, *The Politics of Size* (Ithaca, N.Y.: Cornell University Press, 1987).

zona, were admitted in 1912. Westward expansion moved beyond the contiguous states with the admission of Alaska and Hawaii in 1959.

Although each of the U.S. decennial censuses has shown the center of population moving westward, this is not the only demographic trend that has had apportionment and political consequences. This part of the atlas discusses the major trends in population geography in U.S. history and the state, regional, sectional, and national consequences as manifested in the decennial apportionments to the House of Representatives and illustrated on the apportionment maps. In Part 2, the census and apportionment for each decade were discussed individually. Part 3 presents four case studies to highlight major trends in congressional representation and discuss the primary interstate shifts of political power. These historical case studies contain tables that highlight the major apportionment trends in American history. Similar to the decade analyses, the case studies also refer to, discuss, and analyze in detail the apportionment maps in Part 2, which are the heart of this work.

Patterns of Population Geography

Since political representation in the House of Representatives and in the presidential electoral college is based on a decennial census of population, demographic theories and geographic population trends are central to understanding the basis of shifting congressional and electoral college power. Five major internal demographic trends have characterized the population geography of the first two hundred years of American history: (1) westward expansion (1790s–1890s, and continuing to the present); (2) South to North migration (1914–1960s); (3) rural to urban migration (1890s–1920s, 1940s–1960s, and continuing to the present); (4) Sunbelt migration (1960s to the present); and (5) urban to suburban movement (post–World War II to the present).[2] Table 3-1 outlines the effects of the above five major American demographic trends on the apportionment of House seats. Since the United States is one of the largest countries in the world in both population and size, numerous other demographic trends, both historical and present, have obviously occurred.[3] However, the apportionment maps in this atlas are designed to illustrate the large national political power shifts for the first two hundred years of American history. Therefore, only the first four large sectional, regional, and interstate population shifts that have apportionment consequences are extensively discussed.[4]

Table 3-1. Effects of Demographic Trends on Apportionment

| | Apportionment Consequences | | |
Demographic Trend	Sectional/Regional	Intraregional	Intrastate
Westward expansion	great	short-term	little
South to North	great	little	little
Rural to urban	some	great	some
Snowbelt to Sunbelt	great	little	little
Urban to suburban	little	little	great

Obviously, intrastate movements of population, such as suburbanization or even movement from rural to urban areas, have substantial impacts on decennial redistricting *within* states, but do not have great consequences with respect to the national shifts illustrated in this atlas. There are, however, several major exceptions to this rule, two of which are large interstate metropolitan population concentrations that are reflected on the apportionment maps.[5] The first is the growth of New York City as the prime city of the United States and its spread, across the Hudson River into northeastern New Jersey and then its suburbanization into southwestern Connecticut. Second is the growth of Washington beyond the District of Columbia boundaries into Virginia and Maryland, especially beginning with the expansion of the federal government in the 1930s and World War II through the 1960s and 1970s. These and several other interstate suburbanization examples are discussed in the appropriate decade analyses.

2. The enumerated demographic trends are based on a number of sources (see footnote 4), especially Bernard L. Weinstein and Robert E. Firestine, *Regional Growth and Decline in the United States: The Rise of the Sunbelt and the Decline of the Northeast* (New York: Praeger, 1978), 44–47. The dates indicate the peak period of the phenomena in question and are not meant to be inclusive. For example, increasing urbanization has occurred from the first census and these dates represent the most important periods.

3. For example, beginning in the 1970s two seemingly simultaneous trends are occurring on a smaller scale: (1) movement back to small and intermediate-sized towns and (2) gentrification movement back into the central cities.

4. Numerous works in U.S. demographic history and historical geography were consulted and are listed in the Bibliography. See especially Robert D. Mitchell and Paul A. Groves, eds., *North America, The Historical Geography of a Changing Continent* (Totowa, N.J.: Rowman & Littlefield, 1987); Conrad Taeuber and Irene Taeuber, *The Changing Population of the United States* (New York: John Wiley, 1958); David Ward, ed., *Geographic Perspectives on America's Past* (New York: Oxford University Press, 1979); Michael Greenwood, *Migration and Economic Growth in the United States* (New York: Academic Press, 1981); Ralph H. Brown, *Historical Geography of the United States* (New York: Harcourt, Brace & Company, 1948).

5. Three other cases of interstate urban expansion should be noted: (1) the expansion of Philadelphia across the Delaware River into southwestern New Jersey; (2) the growth of Chicago into northwestern Indiana; and (3) the expansion of St. Louis across the Mississippi River into Illinois.

Political Impact

For a member of Congress, power is manifested in many ways, such as membership in a political party, seniority, membership in the party leadership, important committee positions, and media recognition and prestige. Likewise, as discussed in Part 1, a state's political power is made up of the sum of the above items, especially as manifested in the size of its congressional delegation. Although a state's delegation can be, and usually is, divided into different political parties, ideologies, and high and low seniority members, it is the size of a state's delegation that counts. This is especially so in the presidential electoral college where the winner-take-all rule is in effect. The larger a state's delegation, the larger a state's potential influence in a political party, in forming a particular policy or ideological stance, or in having a member selected as a powerful committee chair or simply to be on an important committee. Although party membership and political ideology play a strong role in roll-call voting, members of the U.S. Congress have more independence in voting decisions than members in any national democratic legislative body in the world.[6] When local, district, state, or regional circumstances warrant, senators or representatives are free to vote the way they believe or that is expedient. Historically, many state delegations have caucused, irrespective of party or ideology, so members can keep posted on issues of state and regional concern.[7]

Large powerful states and the development of regional and sectional blocs by neighboring states have had a determining role in congressional roll-call voting and the passage of critical legislation, in swinging congressional elections and party control of the House and Senate, and, of course, in presidential elections. The decennial shifting of political power from one region to another, and the growth and decline of large dominant states, have had a profound effect on American political history.[8]

Congressional Roll-Call Voting

The passage, or in some cases blockage, of legislation that has shaped American political, social, and economic development is replete with examples of the influence of large powerful states and the coalition of regional interests.[9] When party and ideological influences break down, they are oftentimes replaced by regional or sectional interests.[10] Regional voting had its origins in the Continental Congress and the Congress of the Confederation and has been present throughout the two-hundred-year history of the U.S. Congress.[11]

Political Parties

A sectional party structure was the basis of American politics and greatly influenced the political control of the House and Senate for approximately one hundred years. The rise of sectional parties actually occurred in the mid 1850s with the demise of the Whig-Democrat party system. In the 1856–1857 elections to the Thirty-fifth Congress, a strictly northern Republican party arose winning over one-third of the House. By the 1858–1859 elections the northern Republicans captured nearly half of the House.[12] After Reconstruction the Democrats and Republicans were sectional parties. The Democrats had a solid southern base, with some support in the swing Border states and central northern cities. The Republicans had a solid northern base. As states were admitted along the northern tier they had a strong Republican heritage, which added to the Republican numbers in Congress, especially the Sen-

6. In the European-style parliamentary system the voting is virtually always by party. In the U.S. Congress both senators and representatives are somewhat independent by comparison. Aage R. Clausen, *How Congressmen Decide* (New York: St. Martin's Press, 1973).

7. Ibid., 162–165.

8. Frederick Jackson Turner, *Sections in American History* (New York: Henry Holt, 1931); Wilbur R. Jacobs, ed., *America's Great Frontiers and Sections* (Lincoln: University of Nebraska Press, 1969); V. O. Key, *Politics, Parties, and Pressure Groups* (New York: Thomas Y. Crowell, 1964); Joel Silbey, ed., *The Congress of the United States 1789–1989*, vol. 5, *The United States Congress in a Transitional Era, 1800–1841: The Interplay of Party, Faction and Section* (New York: Carlson, 1991).

9. Kenneth C. Martis, *The History of Natural Resources Roll Call Voting in the United States House of Representatives: An Analysis of the Spatial Aspects of Legislative Voting Behavior* (Ann Arbor, Mich.: University Microfilms, 1976); Richard F. Bensel, *Sectionalism and American Political Development, 1880–1980* (Madison: University of Wisconsin Press, 1984).

10. See, for example, Barbara Deckard and John Stanley, "Party Decomposition and Region: The House of Representatives, 1945–1970," *Western Political Quarterly* 27 (June 1970): 249–264. There are several good maps illustrating regional roll-call votes: for a 1958 vote dealing with a western water issue, see Kenneth C. Martis, *The Historical Atlas of United States Congressional Districts* (New York: Free Press, 1982), 21; for a 1980 vote dealing with fuel subsidies, see Bensel, *Sectionalism*, 297; for a 1893 vote on silver, see Clifford L. Lord, *Atlas of Congressional Roll Call: An Analysis of Yea-Nay Votes* (Newark, N.J.: Works Progress Administration, 1941); for several votes on tariff, see H. R. Smith and J. F. Hart, "The American Tariff Map," *Geographical Review* 55:327–346; for thirty-six roll-call voting maps on different issues, see C. O. Paullin and J. K. Wright, *Atlas of Historical Geography of the United States* (New York: American Geographical Society, 1932), plates 113–123.

11. Clifford L. Lord, ed., *The Atlas of Congressional Roll Calls for the Continental Congresses 1777–1781 and the Congresses of the Confederation 1781–1789* (Cooperstown, N.Y.: New York State Historical Association, 1943).

12. Kenneth C. Martis, *The Historical Atlas of Political Parties in the United States Congress: 1789–1989* (New York: Macmillan, 1989), 111–113.

ate. It was not until the political party realignment of the 1930s that widespread permanent Democratic inroads were made in much of the rural North. Although the parties traded control of the House and Senate for much of the one hundred years after the Civil War, the breakdown of the sectional-based congressional elections probably did not occur significantly in the South until 1964.[13]

Presidential Elections

Sectional voting in American presidential elections is legendary. From the first competitive presidential election in 1796, between John Adams and Thomas Jefferson (North vs. South), to the last competitive election in 1976, between Jimmy Carter and Gerald Ford (East vs. West), the regional nature of voting is apparent.[14] The regional structure of the electoral college vote is most noticeable in the one-hundred-year period of sectional parties discussed above. One of the most notable examples of regional voting patterns occurred in the 1896 presidential election. In this election the West united with the Democratic South over the silver issue.[15] However, the combined West and South electoral vote was far less than the more populous Northeast, and Republican William McKinley defeated Democrat, silverite, and populist William Jennings Bryan.

Conclusion

State, regional, and sectional influences have affected: (1) congressional roll-call voting and legislation, (2) party power bases and party control of Congress, and (3) the election of the president. Because of these profound influences on U.S. history, it is important to understand fully the state, regional, and sectional shifts in power generated by the decennial census apportionments. The following four case studies discuss significant political power shifts in apportionment and American political history. The first study examines western expansion from 1790–1850 and its effect on the original thirteen states and the changing political agenda of the day. The second study analyzes the steady drop in House apportionment of the slave states relative to that of the northern states and its effect on politics, congressional legislation, and the coming of the Civil War. The third study examines the influence of a growing urban industrial society on congressional power and the nonapportionment of the 1920s. Finally, the contemporary Sunbelt migration is discussed in light of both long-term trends and recent apportionments. These case studies, in combination with the decade analyses in Part 2, help interpret and explain the maps in this atlas and make the geographical trends of shifting state power in the United States more understandable.

13. Kenneth C. Martis, "Sectionalism and the United States Congress," *Political Geography Quarterly* 7 (April 1988): 99–109.

14. See the electoral college election maps in numerous sources: Congressional Quarterly, *Guide to U.S. Elections* (Washington, D.C.: Congressional Quarterly, 1985), 272–311; Hammond, *United States History Atlas* (Maplewood, N.J.: Hammond, 1984), U59–U62. For color maps by county for each presidential election from 1789–1928, see Paullin and Wright, *Atlas,* plates 102–111.

15. S. L. Jones, *The Presidential Election of 1896* (Madison: University of Wisconsin Press, 1964); J. R. Hollingsworth, *The Whirligig of Politics* (Chicago: University of Chicago Press, 1963); J. Clark Archer and Peter J. Taylor, *Section and Party* (Chichester: Research Studies Press, 1981), 129–134.

Original and New States

1790–1850 Apportionments

It was vain for the old States to expect to retain forever their present relative representation; that of the new states must of course increase.

Rep. Richard W. Thompson, Indiana, *Congressional Globe*,[16] Apportionment Debate, April 1842

The westward expansion of population is the dominant long-term geographic trend in U.S. demographic history. The first European settlements in North America were isolated pockets along the Atlantic coast. Throughout the 1600s and 1700s, American settlement moved westward across the coastal plain into the Piedmont and eventually into the valleys of the Appalachians. To control the Americans, British colonial policy inhibited settlement beyond the highlands into the trans-Appalachian West. In the 1783 Treaty of Paris recognizing American independence, the British relinquished all claims to lands up to the Mississippi River (see the configuration of the United States in Maps 1A and 1B in Part 2). At its inception, the new American state had boundaries that made it already physically larger than England and most other European nations.

Independence allowed unencumbered migration to those wishing to claim land and settle in the trans-Appalachian West. Even during the 1780s, the Congress of the Confederation wrestled with the questions of state land claims, western lands grants, land surveys, and land sales. During the Constitutional Convention of 1787 western lands were again a subject of contention. The small coastal states with no western land claims insisted that the trans-Appalachian area be ceded to the new federal government. The states with western land claims eventually ceded their claims to the federal government, the Constitution was adopted, and the fate of westward expansion lay with the policies of the new U.S. government. Even though there were some political and philosophical misgivings about the ability to have a democratic government in such a large country, policies were adopted that called for land in the West to be surveyed, sold to private individuals to provide revenue for the government, settled, and eventually organized as new states to enter the Union. The original states, the larger of which had significant areas of unsettled lands away from the coast, were allowed to retain control of and sell the lands within their own new boundaries east of the Appalachian highlands.

The first trans-Appalachian "frontier" state to be admitted to the Union was Kentucky in June 1792. The area of Kentucky was long claimed by Virginia and actually was the Second District of Virginia in the First Congress.[17] The 1790 census recorded 68,705 whites already in Kentucky.[18] Since Kentucky is mentioned specifically in the 1792 apportionment act, it is included on the 1790 apportionment maps (see Maps 1A and 1B). The second trans-Appalachian state, Tennessee, was admitted in June 1796. North Carolina originally claimed the area now called Tennessee, which was designated as the 5th District of North Carolina during the First Congress. Because of their origins as claimed and settled areas of original states, both Kentucky and Tennessee were also allowed to retain state control of the land within their boundaries. However, all other continental states entering the Union were to be first owned, controlled, surveyed, and sold by the federal government as public domain lands.[19] The process of American settlement and establishment of local and territorial governments preceded entry into the Union.

The original states understood that the admission of new trans-Appalachian states would dilute their political power in the U.S. Congress and in the election of the president. As the frontier of American settlement pushed westward in the 1800s, and more western states entered

16. U.S. Congress, House, *Congressional Globe,* 27th Cong., 2d sess., 1842, 436.

17. Martis, *Atlas of Districts,* 50.

18. Lawrence F. Schmeckebier, *Congressional Apportionment* (Washington, D.C.: Brookings Institution, 1941), 227.

19. Texas was also made an exception because of a short period of independent status in the late 1830s and early 1840s.

Table 3-2. Original and New States, 1790–1850

Original Atlantic Coast States	New Trans-Appalachian States
New England	Northwest
Maine[a]	Ohio (1803)
New Hampshire	Indiana (1816)
Massachusetts	Illinois (1818)
Connecticut	Michigan (1837)
Rhode Island	Wisconsin (1848)
Vermont[b]	Great Plains
Middle Atlantic	Iowa (1846)
New York	Southwest
New Jersey	Tennessee (1796)
Pennsylvania	Louisiana (1812)
Border	Mississippi (1817)
Delaware	Alabama (1819)
Maryland	Arkansas (1836)
South	Florida (1845)[c]
Virgina	Texas (1845)
North Carolina	Border
South Carolina	Kentucky (1792)
Georgia	Missouri (1821)
	Pacific Coast
	California (1850)

[a]*Maine was a part of Massachusetts until 1820; therefore, it is treated and counted as an original state.*

[b]*Since Vermont, admitted in 1791, is not a trans-Appalachian state, it is also treated and counted in the statistics as an origingal Atlantic Coast state.*

[c]*Since Florida is a new state, admitted in 1845, it is treated and counted as a new trans-Appalachian state.*

the Union, the original states became more acutely aware of the power and needs of the new states. As the West grew, it became a new functional region, bringing its own political and economic agenda to the U.S. Congress.[20] This agenda was not only different, but many times in conflict with the interests of the original coastal states.

This section examines the shift in state power from the original states to the western states over the 1790 to 1850 apportionments. The original states are defined here as the "original Atlantic Coast" states and include Maine and Vermont.[21] The western states are defined as the "new trans-Appalachian" states and include Florida (see Table 3-2). This section will review the demographic trends, discuss the numerous factors behind western expansion, and analyze the resultant changing regional and sectional power structure in Congress and the electoral college.

Patterns of Population Geography

The population expansion into the trans-Appalachian West was not always a consistently moving frontier of American settlement.[22] Pockets of settlement jumped ahead of the frontier to occupy areas of exceptional agricultural land and flat floodplains along rivers. Town sites at river junctions, fords, mountain passes, and other transportation routes were claimed and settled by individual and corporate land speculators. Areas of poorer agricultural land, thickets, swamps, and marshes were settled later. Of course, some marginal and mountainous land was never settled. In addition to spatial variations, settlement also varied temporally, slowing down in times of war or depression, speeding up in times of low land prices or peace.

Nor was the West uniform in its physical geography and settlement pattern. The Northwest was settled mainly by a population migrating westward from the northern Atlantic Coast states. The physical geography of soil and climate of the Northwest generally lent itself to densely populated small family farms, which would eventually be linked to the Northeast by an extensive transportation system. The Southwest was settled mainly by a population migrating westward from the southern coastal states. The climate of the Southwest lent itself not only to poor white migrants but also to the expansion of the slavery cotton plantation system across the Deep South and up the Mississippi River valley. The Northwest states entered the Union as free states and the Southwest states entered the Union as slave states. Although the western states as a group had much in common, they also evolved intraregional differences on some key issues. Eventually the slavery issue, a common heritage, and commercial ties linked the political and economic agenda of the Northwest and Northeast. These same issues eventually linked the political and economic agenda of the Southwest and Southeast (see the next case study on free and slave states).

Since the West in the 1790–1850 period was made up of two somewhat different areas, the Northwest and Southwest, a number of different variables explain westward expansion. Some of these variables were

20. Frederick Jackson Turner, *Rise of the New West 1819–1829* (New York: Harper & Brothers, 1906); Andrew R. L. Clayton, "'Separate Interests' and the Nation-State: The Washington Administration and the Origins of Regionalism in the Trans-Appalachian West," *Journal of American History* 79 (June 1992): 39–67.

21. See note to Table 3-2.

22. James E. Davis, *Frontier America 1800–1840* (Glendale, Calif.: Clark, 1977); Ray A. Billington, *Westward Expansion* (New York: Macmillan, 1974); Malcolm J. Rohrbough, *The Trans-Appalachian Frontier* (New York: Oxford University Press, 1978); Nelson Klose, *American Frontier* (Lincoln: University of Nebraska Press, 1964); Robert D. Mitchell, ed., *Appalachian Frontiers* (Lexington: University of Kentucky Press, 1991).

Table 3-3. Factors of Westward Migration, 1790–1850

National Trends

High internal birthrate
Improvements in transportation and communication technology
Expansion of the transportation network
Movement from subsistence farming to commercial farming
Increasing European immigration

Pull Factors To the Trans-Appalachian West	Push Factors From the Atlantic Coast	Pull Factors To the Trans-Appalachian West	Push Factors From the Atlantic Coast
Economic		**Technology**	
Relatively inexpensive farmland	Relatively expensive farmland	Transportation developments	
Available farmland	Unavailable farmland	Road construction/national roads	
Wealth accumulation possibilities	Exploitive industrial labor practices	Rivers/steamboats	
Demand for agricultural products:		Canal construction/Erie Canal	
Corn/wheat		Railroads	
Cotton/tobacco		Agricultural implement improvement	
Physical Environment		**Social**	
High-amenity farmland	Low-amenity farmland	Advertising	Class immobility
High soil fertility	Rocky soils	Land companies	
Flat land	Hilly topography	Canal companies	
Plentiful precipitation	Soil depletion/erosion	Railroad companies	
Adequate growing season		Glamor/romance factor	
Natural resources		Frontier/independent spirit/trailblazing	
Great Lakes		Religious freedom	
River system			
		Demographic	
Government Policy		Immigration patterns (1840s–1850s)	High birthrates/household size
Amerindian policy			High-density farmland
Tribal treaties			High-density cities
Indian removal			Increased life expectancy
Frontier army garrisons			
Slavery policy			
Land grant policy			
Land sales policy			
Relatively inexpensive			
Credit purchase			
Small plots			
Preemption			
Sale to actual settlers			
Nationalism, Manifest Destiny, and expansionism			
Purchase of trans-Mississippi lands			
Exploration and survey			
Military force			
Florida			
Texas			
Oregon			
Internal improvements policy			

common to both areas, some acted as stronger forces in one region, and some were unique to one area. Table 3-3 lists a number of factors that partially explain the migration of population westward in the first decades of U.S. history. This table outlines both national trends and regional "push" (from the Atlantic Coast states) and "pull" (to the West) factors that influenced western migration.

Factors of Population Change

National Trends

The two engines that powered westward expansion were the expropriation of Native American lands for settlement and a rapidly expanding population to the fill these lands. The U.S. birthrate in the early 1800s was exceedingly high.[23] In the 1840s and 1850s this internal increase was augmented by an enormous increase in foreign immigration.[24] As the urban population grew, there was an increasing internal and international demand for agricultural products. This demand allowed the original frontier subsistence farmer to switch to commercial farming. The commercial farming and growing industrial sector needed a national system of transportation and communication. The West slowly became an integral part of the growing national economic engine.

Economic

The single most important factor that allowed western expansion was the appropriation of Native American land. This land was good for agriculture and was sold by the government at a relatively inexpensive price. In the East, yeoman farmers typically had numerous children and tended relatively small increasingly unproductive plots. Local land for their children to farm was undesirable, expensive, or unavailable. As the demand for agricultural products increased, the possibility of settling in the West, owning land, supporting a family, and possibly selling the land later for a profit was alluring. Economic choices in the old states were limited. In this era, the frontier increasingly meant opportunity rather than mere survival.

23. In 1800, there were an estimated 55 live births per 1,000 white women. Comparable data for blacks are not available. In the late 1960s, total live births averaged 17 per 1,000 women across the United States.
24. Taeuber and Taeuber, *Changing Population,* 53.

Physical Environment

Some of the most fertile farmland in the world is found in the Mississippi River valley, the Midwest, the Great Plains, and California. The Mississippi River system is one of the largest in the world, and the Great Lakes are the largest area of surface freshwater in the world. The climate, soil, flatness, and natural transportation system combined eventually to make the above regions the breadbasket of America and much of the world. The desire of early Americans to acquire, exploit, and profit from western farmland and numerous other valuable frontier natural resources was compelling. The environmental resources of the West contrasted sharply with the conditions in the coastal areas. In New England, low-amenity farmland lost out to western products in the 1820s and 1830s as the Erie Canal provided cheap water transportation through the mountains. In the South, cotton and tobacco depleted soil, and soil erosion made virgin western lands appealing. The frontier West helped produce an American national psyche with the feeling of limitless natural resources and unbounded optimism.

Government Policy

Numerous government policies ensured continued westward growth of the American Republic to the Pacific. Growing American nationalism was fueled by dreams of Manifest Destiny and expansionism.[25] Of course, the indigenous population of Amerindians fought European expansion into their lands from the 1600s. Once Americans flooded into the trans-Appalachian West after the Revolution, a new round of Indian wars, treaties, and land acquisition took place. The infamous Indian Removal Act of 1830 was just one in a series of government actions of disdain, disregard, genocide, and removal of the original inhabitants.

Once Native American land was secured for the federal public domain the government could grant or sell the land. Generous land sales policies in large blocks were always lobbied for by large eastern corporate speculators. However, as the number of western states increased in Congress, land sales became more geared to the actual settlers, smaller and smaller sales price, and smaller plots with generous credit. Even squatters who surged ahead of the surveyed lands were eventually treated kindly by the federal government, allowing them to keep their claimed land. This favorable preemption policy in turn encouraged more squatting.

The policies that were probably most influential in transforming the trans-Appalachian West from a frontier subsistence economy into a commercial economy were the internal transportation improvement projects of the government. Federal money was spent improving coastal navigation and eastern roads; and as the western states entered the Union they demanded a share of improvement funds. These funds mostly took the form of government subsidies for road construction, river navigation, canal construction, and eventually railroad construction. As transportation improved, westward migration became easier, the population increased, and the more numerous western representatives in turn demanded an even larger share of internal improvements. The increased demand for improved land increased the value of these properties and local landholders and commercial interests profited. The trans-Appalachian West, both North and South, pressed vigorously in Congress for cheap land prices and continued internal improvement projects in their region.

Technology

The engineering improvements in transportation technology also expanded in the early nineteenth century. Road construction techniques improved. These same techniques were applied to canal construction. The completion of the Erie Canal in 1825 not only irrevocably changed the Northwest region but also was an engineering feat recognized worldwide. The development of the steam engine with its application to steamboats and eventually to the railroad also occurred during this period. River navigation improvements, later with locks and dams, enabled flatbottomed steamboats to go far into the interior on the tributaries of the Mississippi River.

Social

The American frontier was a harsh, dangerous, and uncomfortable place. The frontier was also a place of independence, renewal, spirit, equality, property, and hope for its Euro-American settlers. At the very edge of frontier settlement many times were poor individuals for whom the class system of the East promised only poverty, exploitation of labor, and social immobility. The individual pioneer spirit coupled with a na-

25. Major L. Wilson, *Space, Time, and Freedom: The Quest for Nationality and the Irrepressible Conflict 1815–1861* (Westport, Conn.: Greenwood Press, 1974), 94–117.

tional spirit of Manifest Destiny and expansionism helped shape a western society that offered social mobility, free public education, and the hope of an egalitarian frontier democracy.

Shifts in State, Regional, and Sectional Political Power

Expansion of the New Trans-Appalachian States

In the period from 1792 to 1850, sixteen new trans-Appalachian states were admitted into the United States.[26] Through this long period the West expanded, changed, and expanded again several times. The decade-by-decade admission of states is as follows:

1790s: Kentucky (1792) and Tennessee (1796)
1800s: Ohio (1803)
1810s: Louisiana (1812), Indiana (1816), Mississippi (1817), Illinois (1818), and Alabama (1819)
1820s: Missouri (1821)
1830s: Arkansas (1836) and Michigan (1837)
1840s: Florida (1845), Texas (1845), Iowa (1846), and Wisconsin (1848)
1850: California

Between the period 1812 and 1821 alone, six states entered the Union making a total of nine western states. This rapid increase in regional power was especially noticeable in the Senate, where the West now controlled eighteen out of forty-eight seats (37.5 percent).

By the 1820 apportionment, nine new states were allocated 22 percent of the House of Representatives. In each apportionment from 1790 through 1820, all new trans-Appalachian states gained in seats and percentage of representation (see Maps 1A and 1B through 4A and 4B in Part 2). However, in the 1830 apportionment, Kentucky and Louisiana, both settled early in western expansion, lost relative representation (see Map 5B). The frontier of expansion had already passed these areas and relatively greater population increases were occurring in areas further west. Since the House was reduced in size in 1840, rather than expanded, as had been the case in the previous five apportionments, both Kentucky and Tennessee received an actual reduction in delegation size. This was the first time a trans-Appalachian state lost actual representation. In

1840, however, the other nine new states all gained representatives while virtually all the original Atlantic Coast states lost seats.[27] In addition, the 1840 apportionment registered a spectacular increase in the size of western states representation in the House from 28 percent in 1830 to 37 percent in 1840, the second largest single western percentage increase in this period (see Table 3-4).

By the 1840s the American frontier was well beyond the Mississippi River. Americans were venturing into Oregon, California, Texas, and into northwest Iowa and Wisconsin. The 1850 apportionment map displays a remarkable geographical pattern of representation change in the older trans-Appalachian states (see Map 7A). A band of states stretching from Ohio and Kentucky to Tennessee and Alabama did not gain seats. All these states registered no change in their delegation or, in the case of Tennessee, a loss of a seat.[28] The frontier of settlement had gone beyond these areas further west, even to the Pacific Coast. The peak settlement stage has passed in these older trans-Appalachian states. Interestingly, as time went on the fervor for certain western policies in this region began to change. For example, these states no longer pressed for internal improvements, and sometimes they began to act and vote in Congress like Atlantic Coast states. This geographical pattern of older trans-Appalachian western states beginning to lose relative representation as newer western states entered the Union continued in 1860 (see Map 8A), and some aspects of this pattern were apparent through the second half of the nineteenth century.

Decline of the Original Atlantic Coast States

As early as the passage of the Northwest Ordinance in 1787, the original states understood and encouraged the formation of new states in the trans-Appalachian West. The original states' proportion in the House would, of course, be reduced over time. Although the decennial apportionment battles in Congress centered on the small-state versus large-state ratio debate, as new states entered the Union and the population

26. Vermont was admitted in 1791 and is considered an Atlantic Coast state, see note to Table 3-2.

27. Delaware had one seat and, of course, remained unchanged; Rhode Island had two seats and remained the same.

28. In the 1860 apportionment this geographic pattern is repeated with all four states losing seats; plus in the adjacent West, Mississippi and Indiana have no gain in seats for the first time (see Maps 7A and 8A).

Table 3-4. Apportionment for Original and New States, 1790–1850

Original Atlantic Coast States	Census Apportionment						
	1790	1800	1810	1820	1830	1840	1850
New England							
Maine[a]				7	8	7	6
New Hampshire	4	5	6	6	5	4	3
Massachusetts	14	17	20	13	12	10	11
Connecticut	7	7	7	6	6	4	4
Rhode Island	2	2	2	2	2	2	2
Vermont[b]	2	4	6	5	5	4	3
Subtotal	29	35	41	39	38	31	29
Middle Atlantic							
New York	10	17	27	34	40	34	33
New Jersey	5	6	6	6	6	5	5
Pennsylvania	13	18	23	26	28	24	25
Subtotal	28	41	56	66	74	63	63
Border							
Delaware	1	1	2	1	1	1	1
Maryland	8	9	9	9	8	6	6
Subtotal	9	10	11	10	9	7	7
South							
Virginia	19	22	23	22	21	15	13
North Carolina	10	12	13	13	13	9	8
South Carolina	6	8	9	9	9	7	6
Georgia	2	4	6	7	9	8	8
Subtotal	37	46	51	51	52	39	35
Total Seats	103	132	159	166	173	140	134
Percentage	98%	94%	88%	78%	72%	63%	57%

New Trans-Appalachian States	Census Apportionment						
	1790	1800	1810	1820	1830	1840	1850
Northwest							
Ohio (1803)			6	14	19	21	21
Indiana (1816)				3	7	10	11
Illinois (1818)				1	3	7	9
Michigan (1837)						3	4
Wisconsin (1848)							3
Subtotal			6	18	29	41	48
Great Plains							
Iowa (1846)							2
Subtotal							2
Southwest							
Tennessee (1796)		3	6	9	13	11	10
Louisiana (1812)				3	3	4	4
Mississippi (1817)				1	2	4	5
Alabama (1819)				3	5	7	7
Arkansas (1836)						1	2
Florida (1845)[c]							1
Texas (1845)							2
Subtotal		3	6	16	23	27	31
Border							
Kentucky (1792)	2	6	10	12	13	10	10
Missouri (1821)				1	2	5	7
Subtotal	2	6	10	13	15	15	17
Pacific Coast							
California (1850)							2
Subtotal							2
Total Seats	2	9	22	47	67	83	100
Percentage	2%	6%	12%	22%	28%	37%	43%

[a]Maine was a part of Massachusetts until 1820; therefore, it is treated and counted as an original state.
[b]Since Vermont, admitted in 1791, is not a trans-Appalachian state, it is also treated and counted in the statistics as an original Atlantic Coast state.

[c]Since Florida was admitted in 1845, it is treated and counted in the new trans-Appalachian category.

expanded westward most of the Atlantic Coast states had a stake in encouraging an ever-increasing size of the House. The increase in size would at least ameliorate their actual loss of seats. Of course, the House did expand in size from 1790 onward, except for the reduction in 1840, to the present size of 435 in 1910.

The apportionment of 1790 was the first based on actual national census figures. Using 1790 as the base, no Atlantic Coast state lost seats until 1820 because of the increase in House size from 101 seats in 1790 to 154 in 1820. In 1820, however, Virginia, Connecticut, Vermont, and Delaware all lost one seat.[29] In spite of the House's further increase to 160 seats in 1830, Virginia, Maryland, Massachusetts, and New Hampshire all lost seats.

The reduction in the House size in 1840 resulted in a sharp decrease in representation for the Atlantic Coast states. Thirteen of the fifteen states lost delegation size, while all the new states, except the old settled areas of Kentucky and Tennessee, gained delegation size. Maps 6A and 6B illustrate one of the most stark geographic patterns in U.S. apportionment history. The old versus new, East versus West, state power shift is shown vividly in the 1840 maps. In 1850 there was a small increase in the size of the House from 223 to 234, and this only after a supplemental apportionment bill was passed. The stark geographic pattern of representation losses was repeated in 1850 (see Maps 7A and 7B). All the original Atlantic Coast states lost or registered no change in seats except two, and only one gained in proportional strength. This pattern of eastern percentage loss in congressional power carries on through most of the second half of the nineteenth century (see Maps 8A and 8B through 11A and 11B).

Although actual losses of seats were kept to a minimum until 1840, the original states lost relative strength in Congress from the beginning. Statistically, of course, only the original states initially made up 100 percent of Congress; and it was obvious that when more states were added, the original percentages had to fall. However, the statistics in Table 3-4 show how far original representation fell during this period. Using the 1790 apportionment as the base, the maps illustrating the change in power for 1800, 1810, 1820, and 1830 show a consistent reduction in

---

29. Although several small states recorded no change in 1800 and 1810 (see Maps 2A and 3A).

state power of the Atlantic Coast states (see Maps 2B through 5B). New York is a notable exception throughout this period. New York had a large unsettled western frontier and developed a strong base of state-supported internal improvements, including beginning construction of the Erie Canal in 1817. All of this enabled New York City and upstate New York cities to flourish. The few other original states that avoided relative reductions from 1800 to 1830 usually were larger states with unsettled areas. Almost all the small original states lost percentage power in almost all of the apportionments from 1800 through 1850. In 1840 and 1850 all Atlantic Coast states, large and small, lost power except Rhode Island in 1840 and Massachusetts in 1850.[30]

The relative power of western population expansion, the perplexities of the apportionment formula, and the use of relative statistics are all illustrated by the original states in this period. For example, even though Massachusetts experienced textile and other industrialization beginning in the 1820s and 1830s, the state still lost seats in the House over those two decades. The explosive 35 percent population growth rate in the 1840s, driven mostly by the arrival of immigrant labor, garnered Massachusetts one additional seat in 1850 and a relative percent increase, virtually the only small Northeast state to accomplish this in the nineteenth century. The addition of new states and exponential growth rates on the frontier made it statistically difficult for old states to register a real increase in representation.

Rise of the West: Political Power, Sectionalism, and Intraregional Differences

The rise of the trans-Appalachian West in the early 1800s replaced the original North and South divisions that existed at the beginning of the Republic and created a new tripartite sectional system of North, South, and West. Even though the 1820s through the mid 1850s was not a time of strong sectional political parties, it was a period of sectional roll-call voting patterns in Congress on many issues.[31] In addition, this period was a time of strong sectional political power increase by the West. Each section had its own economic and political agenda. In some cases one section would form a coalition with another section, and on some issues there would even be intrasectional differences. The reapportionment growth of the West in the early 1800s thrust that section's agenda more and more on the national political scene.

The issue of slavery was a contentious issue from the founding of the Republic (see the next case study on free and slave states). Three other issues of primary importance on the national domestic agenda from the mid 1820s through the mid 1840s were public land sales, internal transportation improvements, and the import tariff. Each was related to the other. Low-priced lands necessitated a high tariff to generate government revenue. A high tariff protected the expanding manufacturing base of the North but made goods purchased by southerners and westerners more expensive. A high tariff, however, enabled the price of the land to be kept low. Low-priced western land encouraged migration that decreased eastern and southern land values and political strength. Low-priced western land also drew upon the cheap supply of surplus labor, especially in the expanding northern industrial base. In Congress and in the nation, each piece of legislation was weighed carefully by each section with respect to its particular sectional economic, political, and demographic impact. Whatever the issue, however, the resources of the West and growing western political influence played a critical role in the ability of each section to satisfy its agenda.[32]

The rise of a strong western presence in Congress after the 1810 and 1820 apportionments brought clear sectional policy stances for at least the next two decades. These stances for each section were in the following order of importance:

North: (1) high tariff
         (2) high-priced public lands
         (3) internal improvements

South: (1) low tariff
         (2) no internal improvements at federal expense
         (3) high-priced public lands

West: (1) low-priced public lands.[33]

On the remaining issues of the day the West was split. Not only were there strong differences over slavery, but the Northwest wanted (2) internal improvements and (3) a high tariff, while the Southwest wanted (2)

---

30. Again Delaware remained the same with one representative.

31. Thomas B. Alexander, *Sectional Stress and Party Strength: A Study of Roll-Call Voting in the United States House of Representatives, 1830–1860* (Nashville, Tenn.: Vanderbilt University, 1967); Martis, *Roll Call Voting*, 44–144.

32. Martis, *Roll Call Voting*, 69–70.

33. Raynor G. Wellington, *Political and Sectional Influences of Public Lands 1829–1842* (Boston: Riverside Press, 1914), 9.

a low tariff and (3) internal improvements. Again, as each particular piece of legislation came before Congress the national party and ideological alignments many times broke down over sectional needs, and within the West these needs differed somewhat.

Conclusion

The rise of the trans-Appalachian West changed the political, economic, social, and demographic landscape of the United States. By 1850 new western states controlled 43 percent of the House and 52 percent of the Senate and were a powerful force in Congress and the presidential elections. This change is clearly shown on the 1800 through 1850 apportionment maps, and, in fact, on the apportionment maps for most of the nineteenth century.

In the 1840s and 1850s the issue of slavery began to dominate almost every other issue before Congress and the nation. In the same period, the Northeast began to reevaluate its economic relationship with the Northwest. These regions began to view each other as complementary areas exchanging natural resources and agricultural products for manufactured goods. The Northeast slowly came to accept the position that western internal improvements and even low-priced public land aided linkages between the two regions. The issue of slavery further unified the North, and eventually in the mid 1850s a strictly northern antislavery Republican party arose. The melding of the Northeast and the Northwest and the Southeast with the Southwest over slavery slowly evolved over the antebellum period. In the first fifty years of American history, census statistics and apportionment results were looked upon as a large-state versus small-state, or original state versus new state, or North versus South versus West phenomenon. Increasingly, the apportionment results were watched for their effects on the free-state versus slave-state apportionment balance and its resultant effects on state and sectional political power and the overriding issue of the day, the abolition or continuation of slavery in the South.

Free and Slave States

1790–1860 Apportionments

> The South, which provided the Union with four Presidents, which now knows that federal power is slipping from it, which yearly sees its number of representatives in Congress falling and that of the North and West rising—the South, whose men are ardent and irascible, is getting angry and restless.
>
> Alexis de Tocqueville, *Democracy in America*,[34] 1835

> If the bill should pass in its present form, and no provisions made for fractional representation, it would operate injuriously upon one section of the Union—the Southern and Southwestern States.
>
> Rep. Jacob Thompson, Mississippi, *Congressional Globe*,[35] Apportionment Debate, June 1842

In November 1860 Abraham Lincoln of Illinois, the nominee of the strictly northern antislavery Republican party, was elected president of the United States. In a four-way race Lincoln received a plurality of 39.8 percent of the popular vote, but received 180 electoral votes, 59.4 percent of the electoral college, enough to win the presidency easily. Within weeks a South Carolina secession convention voted to separate from the Union. Within months the remaining Deep South states seceded and the Civil War began.

The Civil War is considered by many the single most important event

34. Alexis de Tocqueville, *Democracy in America*, ed. J. P. Mayer and Max Lerner (New York: Harper & Row, 1966), 350.
35. U.S. Congress, House, *Congressional Globe*, 27th Cong., 2d sess., 1842, 626.

**Table 3-5. Slave and Free States,
1790–1860**

Southern Slave States	Northern Free States
Deep South	New England
Virginia	Maine
North Carolina	New Hampshire
South Carolina	Massachusetts
Georgia	Connecticut
Tennessee (1796)	Rhode Island
Louisiana (1812)	Vermont (1791)
Mississippi (1817)	
Alabama (1819)	Middle Atlantic
Arkansas (1836)	New York
Florida (1845)	New Jersey
Texas (1845)	Pennsylvania
Border	Old Northwest
Delaware	Ohio (1803)
Maryland	Indiana (1816)
Kentucky (1792)	Illinois (1818)
Missouri (1821)	Michigan (1837)
	Wisconsin (1848)
	Great Plains
	Iowa (1846)
	Minnesota (1858)
	Kansas (1861)[a]
	Pacific Coast
	California (1850)
	Oregon (1859)

[a]*Kansas was included in the report called for by the apportionment act enabling the 1860 census; therefore, it is included in this table.*

in U.S. history. One of the most troublesome worries of southerners in the decades before the Civil War was the gradual erosion of slave state and southern regional power in the House of Representatives, the Senate, and the presidential electoral college. The South is defined here as the "southern slave states"—that is, the states in which slavery was legal. This includes the Border states of Delaware, Maryland, Kentucky, and Missouri. The North is defined as the "northern free states" where by 1787 slavery was illegal. Table 3-5 enumerates the states in each section, provides their regional subcategory, and gives the date of each state's entry into the Union. The terms North/free states and South/slave states are used interchangeably throughout this case study.

Table 3-6 indicates the South was in relative parity with the

Table 3-6. Slave State Representation from Constitutional to 1860 Apportionment

	Constitutional Apportionment	1790	1800	1810	1820	1830	1840	1850	1860
Deep South seats	23	37	49	57	67	75	66	66	61
Border South seats	7	11	16	21	23	24	22	24	24
Total southern representation	30	48	65	78	90	99	88	90	85
Percentage of representation from Deep South	35%	35%	35%	31%	31%	31%	30%	28%	25%
Percentage of representation from Border South	11%	11%	11%	12%	11%	10%	10%	10%	10%
Total percentage of representation from southern states	46%	46%	46%	43%	42%	41%	40%	38%	35%

North at the beginning of the Republic. However, beginning with the census of 1810 the South consistently lost power at each apportionment. By 1860 the Southerners realized the census would show them to be just a third of the nation. Even more worrisome for the southern leadership, a large percentage of this third lived in Border states that had close economic ties with the North. The 1860 census allotted only one fourth of the House and electoral college to the Deep South slave states of Alabama, Arkansas, Florida, Georgia, Louisiana, Mississippi, North Carolina, South Carolina, Tennessee, Texas, and Virginia. Because of the changing composition of state and regional power in Congress and the electoral college, Republican Abraham Lincoln could lose all of the Border and Deep South states and still easily win the presidency.

Antebellum censuses show a significant difference in population growth rates of slave versus free states, especially beginning in the 1840s. This section will review changing sectional strength for the period 1790 through 1860. It will review the demographic trends, discuss the numerous factors contributing to faster northern growth, and analyze the resultant changing state, regional, and sectional power structure in Congress and the electoral college.

Patterns of Population Geography

The previous case study on western expansion demonstrated that the western states grew considerably faster than the coastal states. However, within the West, the Northwest states eventually grew somewhat faster

Table 3-7. Factors of Population Growth for Slave and Free States, 1790–1860

Expansion Factors for Northern Free States	Retardation Factors for Southern Slave States
Physical Environment	
High-amenity farmland	Soil depletion/erosion
High soil fertility	
Natural resources	
Great Lakes	
Natural harbors	
Economic	
Available farmland	Slavery
Wealth accumulation possibilities	Plantation dominance of best farmland
Commercialization of family farm	Rural agricultural economy
Demand for agricultural products produced by family farm	Lack of marketing infrastructure
Industrialization/urbanization	
Commercial economy/capital accumulation	
Transportation developments	
Roads/canals/railroads	
Cycle of growth	
Government Policy	
Tariff	
Land sales policy	
Relatively inexpensive	
Credit purchase	
Small plots	
Preemption	
Sale to actual settlers	
Internal improvements policy	
Technology	
Agricultural implement improvement benefits family farm	Cotton gin revives slavery system
"Yankee ingenuity"	
Industrial machines	
Social	
Advertising	Class immobility
Land companies	Conservative, rural, aristocratic, class society
Canal companies	
Railroad companies	
Education system	
Business/entrepreneurial culture	
Demographic	
Immigration patterns (1840s–1850s)	

than the Southwest states.[36] Even more importantly, urbanization and industrialization were beginning to flourish in the northeastern states, but not in the southeastern states, and this industrial growth made up for relative losses of population and decennial apportionment by the Northeast.[37] The uneven development of the North and South in the antebellum era has numerous causes.[38] Table 3-7 lists a number of factors that partially explain the relative growth of the North compared to the lagging development of the South.

Factors of Population Change

Physical Environment

The physical geography of the Northwest allowed a more intensive, sustained, and expansive growth of family farms than did the Southwest. The exceptional soil, especially on the glacial till, drained marshland, and dryer grassland, enabled high productivity for high-demand crops such as wheat and corn. This region also had an abundance of mineral, forest, and other natural resources that enhanced growth and economic diversity. The Great Lakes served as a natural route of cheap water transportation of goods to the growing northern cities and the great natural harbors of the coast. This was especially true after the opening of the Erie Canal in the 1820s. In comparison with the soils of the Northwest, neither northeastern nor southeastern soils are particularly good, however the larger amount of leaching rainfall and erosion in the South and the depletion of soil nutrients by cotton and tobacco added an additional burden across the Deep South.

36. Harry N. Scheiber, *The Old Northwest* (Lincoln: University of Nebraska Press, 1969); Brian Page and Richard Walker, "From Settlement to Fordism: The Agro-Industrial Revolution in the American Midwest," *Economic Geography* 67 (October 1991): 281–315; Billington, *Westward Expansion*, 279–332; Rohrbough, *Trans-Appalachian Frontier*, 289–346. See also general references in footnote 22.

37. Michael Kraus, *The United States to 1865* (Ann Arbor: University of Michigan Press, 1969), 390–410. See the next case study on rural and urban places, especially the general references in footnote 43.

38. Wendell H. Stephenson and E. Merton Coulter, eds., *A History of the South* (Baton Rouge: Louisiana State University Press): vol. 4, Thomas P. Abernethy, *The South in the New Nation 1789–1819* (1961); vol. 5, Charles S. Sydnor, *The Development of Southern Sectionalism* (1948); vol. 6, Avery O. Craven, *The Growth of Southern Nationalism* (1953). Clement Eaton, *A History of the Old South* (London: Macmillan, 1966).

Economic

The institution of slavery itself has been suggested as a major reason for lagging economic development of the South.[39] While many very large and medium-sized plantations accumulated great wealth from the slavery system, the South as a region suffered from the economic, cultural, and social demands of slavery. Large plantations dominated the best southern farmland, and wealth was concentrated in a small elite. This elite was rural, conservative, and aristocratic, and a rigid class society developed. Cotton dominated the southern economy, as it did the national economy, but in the South a stagnant rural agricultural economy evolved. Although it could produce and harvest cotton, the South lacked the infrastructure to fabricate and market goods from its staple crop.

The North, on the other hand, evolved a dynamic changing economy in both in the Northwest and Northeast regions. With vast Native American lands becoming available, millions moved to the highly productive agricultural land of the Northwest. The Northwest farmland allowed a continuous dense settlement pattern on 160- or 320-acre plots. As these family farms moved from subsistence to commercial farming, northwestern farmers were able to accumulate capital, especially in good economic times.

During this same period the Northeast was beginning the process of industrialization. Starting with the textile industry in Massachusetts and broadening into all types of manufacturing activity, the North joined western Europe in the Industrial Revolution. A commercial economy developed with vast capital accumulation that could be reinvested in northern agricultural products and in the development of the natural resources of the Northwest. European and American private capital was also invested, along with public internal improvement funds, in developing a transportation system linking the two northern regions. A cycle of growth emerged, between these two regions and between the North and the world in general. This cycle allowed the absorption by both the northwestern frontier and northern industrial cities of the large internal increase in population and well as vast immigration from Europe in the 1840s and 1850s. The Northeast was beginning to participate in the world economy as manufacturer while the South participated as a supplier of agricultural goods.

Government Policy

The federal government encouraged westward expansion by its land and internal improvement policies. Land policies were continually liberalized with respect to price, credit, size, sale to actual settlers, and preemption. The ultimate northern liberal reform came at the beginning of the Civil War with the passage of the Homestead Act and the granting of free land to individuals after a period of settlement and improvement.

Since the physical geography of high-amenity farmland drew a proportionally larger number of settlers to the Northwest, internal improvements were proportionally greater in this region. By 1860 a great system of roads, canals, and railroads linked the North, while the South relied on the Mississippi River system for much of its transportation.

Import tariff legislation was always an economic flashpoint between northeastern and southern interests. A high tariff hurt the South not only in retaliatory cotton tariffs in Europe but also in the increased cost of imported manufactured goods. A high tariff protected the budding northern industries from English/European competition. Over the long term, federal tariff policies helped the North and hurt the South.

Technology

The advance of the Industrial Revolution and engineering techniques in such areas as cotton textile machines and iron production fueled northern industrial expansion. A reputation of "Yankee ingenuity" in the industrial sector became known worldwide. Even the development of farm machinery, such as the plow and grain reaper, seemed to help the North more than the South. The invention of the cotton gin was undoubtedly a boon to the cotton South. However, if the gin was a major cause of the revitalization of slavery, and if slavery was not only a moral evil but an economic drag for the South as a whole, then even this invention, it could be argued, helped retard the South.

39. Eugene D. Genovese, *The Political Economy of Slavery* (New York: Vintage, 1967); John A. Garraty, *The American Nation* (New York: Harper & Row, 1966), 332–336.

Social

There is no doubt that a commercial, capitalist, entrepreneurial culture developed in the North. This eventually spread to and enveloped the commercial farming sector. The conservative aristocratic southern leadership almost seemed to frown upon the spreading entrepreneurial ways. A fixed southern society allowed little class mobility, even among poor whites.

In the Northwest a widespread democratic frontier spirit developed. This community spirit manifested itself in many ways, such as the development of a universal free education system. The commercial farmers in good times accumulated capital, stimulating a banking system and allowing taxes to be levied for roads and public schools. The literacy level of working-class whites in the North was greater than whites in the South on the eve of the Civil War.

Demographic

Birthrates in the entire United States were high throughout this period. However, beginning in the 1840s and through the 1850s, a great surge of overseas migration added to the national population. Irish, English, and German immigrants came by the tens of thousands. Like immigrants to every country in any era these immigrants were drawn to the places of greatest opportunity, in this case in the northern industrial cities and the northwestern frontier. The 1850 and 1860 apportionments alone reduced southern representation by 5 percent to 35 percent of the House (see Table 3-6). Natural increase, immigration, and interregional migration had transformed the North into the dominant economic, cultural, educational, industrial, and population core of the United States. The North had a political and social agenda that not only was different from the South but threatened the very pillar on which the slave society was based.

Shifts in State, Regional, and Sectional Political Power

The division of the House in the original Constitution gave 46 percent of the members to the slave states (see Table 3-6). The Deep South made up 35 percent of the total and the Border South 11 percent. The 1790 and 1800 census apportionments reported the same sectional percentage even though individual state's proportion differed. During this early period the apportionment showed relative equality between the North and South.

The 1810 apportionment showed a 3 percent drop in southern representation. All of this came from the Deep South. A 1 percent decline continued in the 1820, 1830, and 1840 apportionments. As the cotton culture expanded and somewhat revitalized the Deep South, these losses came mostly from the Border South. The 1850 apportionment shows a 2 percent drop and the 1860 apportionment a 3 percent drop in slave state representation, the largest in this period. Table 3-6 indicates that over the 1790–1860 period, the Border South remained somewhat stable while the Deep South dropped from 35 percent to 25 percent.

Table 3-8 enumerates individual state changes, which reveal much about the general sectional trend. New York after the first census was allocated ten seats. Remarkably, this is the same as North Carolina and only two more than Maryland! However, New York registered phenomenal growth in the next forty years, quadrupling its delegation to forty in 1830. On the other hand, in 1830 North Carolina had only increased its delegation from ten to thirteen in spite of a more than doubling of the size of the House. Similarly, in 1830 Maryland still had eight representatives, the same as after the first census.

New York's rise is attributable to a number of factors. First, it had a large upstate and western frontier available for settlement. The Hudson River and Mohawk River valleys provided an easy access into the interior and an outlet for northwestern products. The great harbor at New York City helped make the port the largest shipping and commercial center of North America. In the 1810 census New York surpassed Philadelphia as the largest city in the United States. An aggressive state government pushed internal improvements and, with private support, began construction of the Erie Canal in 1817. The completion of the canal in 1825 created an inexpensive water transportation route from the Great Lakes at Buffalo, across the Appalachian Mountains by way of the Mohawk Valley to Albany, and then south on the Hudson River to New York and the ocean. This was the only rapid and cheap crossing of the Appalachian Mountain chain along the entire East coast of the United States. This made New York City the funnel into which western products met the eastern markets and world commerce. New York's position as

Table 3–8. Apportionment for Slave and Free States, 1790–1860

Census Apportionment

Northern Free States	1790	1800	1810	1820	1830	1840	1850	1860
New England								
Maine				7	8	7	6	5
New Hampshire	4	5	6	6	5	4	3	3
Massachusetts	14	17	20	13	12	10	11	10
Connecticut	7	7	7	6	6	4	4	4
Rhode Island	2	2	2	2	2	2	2	2
Vermont (1791)	2	4	6	5	5	4	3	3
Subtotal	29	35	41	39	38	31	29	27
Middle Atlantic								
New York	10	17	27	34	40	34	33	31
New Jersey	5	6	6	6	6	5	5	5
Pennsylvania	13	18	23	26	28	24	25	24
Subtotal	28	41	56	66	74	63	63	60
Old Northwest								
Ohio (1803)			6	14	19	21	21	19
Indiana (1816)				3	7	10	11	11
Illinois (1818)				1	3	7	9	14
Michigan (1837)						3	4	6
Wisconsin (1848)							3	6
Subtotal			6	18	29	41	48	56
Great Plains								
Iowa (1846)							2	6
Minnesota (1858)								2
Kansas (1861)[a]								1
Subtotal							2	9
Pacific Coast								
California (1850)							2	3
Oregon (1859)								1
Subtotal							2	4
Total Seats	57	76	103	123	141	135	144	156

Southern Slave States	1790	1800	1810	1820	1830	1840	1850	1860
Deep South								
Virginia	19	22	23	22	21	15	13	11
North Carolina	10	12	13	13	13	9	8	7
South Carolina	6	8	9	9	9	7	6	4
Georgia	2	4	6	7	9	8	8	7
Tennessee (1796)		3	6	9	13	11	10	8
Louisiana (1812)				3	3	4	4	5
Mississippi (1817)				1	2	4	5	5
Alabama (1819)				3	5	7	7	6
Arkansas (1836)						1	2	3
Florida (1845)							1	1
Texas (1845)							2	4
Subtotal	37	49	57	67	75	66	66	61
Border								
Delaware	1	1	2	1	1	1	1	1
Maryland	8	9	9	9	8	6	6	5
Kentucky (1792)	2	6	10	12	13	10	10	9
Missouri (1821)				1	2	5	7	9
Subtotal	11	16	21	23	24	22	24	24
Total Seats	48	65	78	90	99	88	90	85

[a]Kansas was included in the report called for by the 1860 apportionment act; therefore, it is included in this table.

the prime city of North America and its future financial and corporate dominance was influenced by its original geographic location. New York is the only original Atlantic Coast state to register actual and proportional gains in representation in the first five apportionments (see Maps 1A and 1B through 5A and 5B in Part 2).

The slow population increase of Maryland, on the other hand, is understandable. In the colonial days the lush Chesapeake Bay region attracted numerous early settlers. However, Maryland was a small state with virtually no easily accessible interior. Maryland registered a proportional loss in representation in every apportionment from 1790 through 1850 (see Maps 1B–7B). The relative stagnation of other larger southern states in the period is explained by additional causes.

While North Carolina started even with New York in House seats, Table 3-8 shows Virginia was the dominant state power in Congress after the first census. In 1790 it was assigned 19 of the 105 House seats, by far the largest delegation. By 1830 the Virginia delegation had grown by only two in part due to a large, but somewhat impenetrable western Appalachian plateau portion of the state. The decline of tidewater Virginia in the early 1800s is typical of coastal North Carolina and much of the coastal South.[40] Although the planters blamed the tariff, southern land was worn out by tobacco and cotton cultivation, which in some areas had been farmed since the 1600s. When the Revolution and the Louisiana Purchase opened up the trans-Appalachian West to new cotton-growing areas, the new plantations became more productive than the old coastal ones. Even the old aristocratic plantation families could not stem the tide of both depleted land and competition from the Mississippi River valley and the Southwest. The westward migration not only included cotton plantations, but also the purchase of slaves from the tidewater region, especially after the end of slave importation in 1808, and the migration of poor whites westward. This movement west brought stagnation to the tidewater as illustrated by a sharp drop in land values. Although similar events occurred in the New England states, industrialization eventually ameliorated some of these losses.

The reduction in the total size of the House in 1840 acutely points out the decline of the South in the federal government. Even though the entire section's proportion only dropped 1 percent, the Virginia delega-

40. Turner, *Rise of the New West*, 50–66.

tion was down to fifteen seats, out of an original nineteen, and North Carolina fell to nine seats out of an original ten. In addition, many of the southern representatives were now from upland mountain districts that had less concern about plantation/slave problems. The industrialization and immigration of the 1840s and 1850s virtually bypassed the South, and the 1850 and 1860 apportionments sharply reduced the section's House membership by 2 percent and 3 percent, respectively.

Although the trans-Appalachian Southwest grew, it grew somewhat slower than the trans-Appalachian Northwest. Nine new slave states entered the Union between 1796 and 1845 and were counted in the 1850 apportionment. Eight new free states entered the Union before the 1850 apportionment and seven of these were trans-Appalachian. The 1850 apportionment was basically the last pre-Civil War apportionment. In 1850, for example, the nine new southern slave states had a combined total of forty-eight seats.[41] These forty-eight seats were 53 percent of the slave state total. In 1850, the seven new free states west of the Appalachians had a combined total of fifty-two seats. These fifty-two seats were only 36 percent of the free state total. This points out not only a slightly bigger gain by the Northwest over the Southwest, but also a considerable decline in the original coastal slave states with respect to both the South as a whole and with respect to the Northeast.

Eleven new free states were included in the 1860 apportionment, ten of these being west of the Appalachians (see Table 3-5). In 1860 the gap in the apportionment numbers of the Southwest versus the Northwest became much greater, fifty trans-Appalachian slave state members versus sixty-nine trans-Appalachian free state members. Ohio with nineteen members in 1860 was allocated the same representation as Alabama, Mississippi, Louisiana, and Arkansas combined.

Conclusion

The decline of the influence of the South in the first seventy years of U.S. history is a classic case study of regional decline in congressional and presidential power. This regional unbalance took power away from the South and made it difficult to stem the tide of tariff, land, and internal improvement legislation in Congress, to influence the election of the president, and eventually to stop the abolition of slavery.

The congressional apportionment maps in this period show a general decline in all the eastern states both North and South. However, two important statistical points from Tables 1-1, 1-2, and 1-3 (see Part 1) must be considered. First, the relative decline in northeastern representation was significantly less than southeastern representation. Second, the relative growth of the Northwest outstripped the relative growth of the Southwest for this period. These two factors allowed the Northeast and Northwest to increase their strength in Congress. When the two regions united around the Republican party in the mid 1850s, they were able to dominate U.S. politics.

41. Florida, which had one member in both 1850 and 1860, is included as a new slave state (see note to Table 3-2).

Rural and Urban Places

1870–1930 Apportionments and the 1920 Nonapportionment

To leave the House at its present membership would . . . take away from 11 states 12 representative districts and transfer those districts to large cities in other states—new districts made up mainly by reason of the increase in large alien populations. . . . One of the greatest dangers that confront the Republic to-day is the tendency of the large cities to control the American Congress. . . .

Rep. Ira G. Hersey, Maine, *Congressional Record,*[42]
Apportionment Debate, January 1921

The 1920 census was the first in U.S. history to report that over half of the population lived in urban places.[43] The 1920s was the only decade in U.S. history in which constitutionally mandated congressional reapportionment did not take place. These two events are related. Although the urban-rural conflict was just one among many reasons for the nonapportionment of the 1920s, the shifting political power from the rural agricultural states to urban industrial states is probably the most important.[44]

Patterns of Population Geography

In every decade in U.S. history, from the first census up until the Great Depression of the 1930s, the urban proportion of the U.S. population steadily increased. The 1790 census reported that the new American nation of nearly four million was 5 percent urban and 95 percent rural. On the eve of the Civil War in 1860, the population had risen to more than thiry-one million with 25 percent being urban residents. By the 1920 census the country had more than one hundred and five million people with over 50 percent living in urban places.

**Table 3–9. Size of Urban Places in the United States,
1870–1930**

City Size	1870	1880	1890	1900	1910	1920	1930
1 million or more		1	3	3	3	3	5
500,000 to 999,999	2	3	1	3	5	9	8
250,000 to 499,999	5	4	7	9	11	13	24
100,000 to 249,999	7	12	17	23	31	43	56
50,000 to 99,999	11	15	30	40	59	76	98

Source: *U.S. Department of Commerce, Bureau of the Census,* Historical Statistics of the United States: Colonial Times to 1970 *(Washington, D.C.: Government Printing Office, 1975), Part 1, 11.*

More and more these urban dwellers were living in large urban conglomerations not just in small town America. Much of rural America viewed these larger cities as filled with ethnic groups with foreign languages and customs, corrupt urban political machines, and communities with industrial and, worse, moral pollution. Table 3-9 summarizes urban size and population figures from 1870 through 1930 censuses. These cities were larger and more complex than any other in American history. They were manufacturing places with heavy industry, not simply commercial towns whose purpose was to transport, mill, and process agricultural and natural resource products. The Western world was changing from a mercantile commercial economy to an industrial economy and America was a significant part of this change.

The American agricultural regions, states, and representatives from rural congressional districts of the 1920s realized that these and other

42. U.S. Congress, House, *Congressional Record,* 66th Cong., 3d sess., 1921, 1640.

43. An urban place is defined as a population of 2,500 or more. See the following for the various demographic histories, definitions, and changing definitions of urban/metropolitan: David Ward, "Population Growth, Migration and Urbanization, 1860–1920," in Robert D. Mitchell and Paul A. Groves, eds., *North America, The Historical Geography of a Changing Continent* (Totowa, N.J.: Rowman & Littlefield, 1987), 299–320; E. L. Ullman, "Regional Development and the Geography of Concentration," *Papers and Proceedings of the Regional Science Association* 4 (1958): 179–198; M. O. Shapiro, "Filling Up America: An Economic-Demographic Model of Population Growth and Distribution in the Nineteenth-Century United States," in J. P. McKay, ed., *Industrial Development and the Social Fabric,* vol. 8 (Greenwich, Conn.: 1986); Taeuber and Taeuber, *Changing Population,* 112–146; Michael Conzen, "The Maturing Urban System in the United States 1840–1910," in David Ward, ed., *Geographic Perspectives,* 253–274; Greenwood, *Migration and Economic Growth*; Kenneth Jackson and Stanley Schultz, eds., *Cities in American History* (New York: Knopf, 1972).

44. For the most recent and complete work on this event, see Charles W. Eagles, *Democracy Delayed: Congressional Reapportionment and the Urban-Rural Conflict in the 1920s* (Athens, Ga.: University of Georgia Press, 1990).

long-term economic, social, and demographic trends had political consequences. In 1890 the census reported the frontier of arable land settlement was closed. In the decade of the 1890s, industrial output figures clearly show America becoming the top manufacturing nation in the world. The stoppage of foreign immigration in 1914 because of the beginning of World War I in Europe precipitated a massive internal migration from rural America to industrial cities to fill the growing industrial need for workers, especially in increased war-related production. The crushing agricultural depression after World War I put agricultural states and regions into another of repeated cycles of downward spirals. Representatives from out-migration rural districts, and agricultural states and regions in general, saw district, state, and regional congressional power shifting from rural areas to urban areas. Table 3-10 lists a number of factors that partially explain the relatively rapid growth of urban places compared to rural areas around the turn of the century.

Factors of Population Change

National and International Trends

The development of an industrial urban economy in the United States parallels trends in the larger world. Under British colonial policy, the American colonies were to be exporters of agricultural products and natural resources to England and importers of manufactured products from England. American independence brought the freedom to develop the Republic's own manufacturing sector. Of course, America was dependent on Europe for much of its manufactured products for many decades. As the Industrial Revolution spread to North America, an industrial, capitalist U.S. economy transformed the previous agricultural-based commercial mercantile economy.

Physical Environment

The natural resource base of the United States allowed it to become the most powerful industrial nation in the world. Within its boundaries the United States had all the requisite resources for industrialization and the resultant urbanization. For example, Appalachia had one of the great coal reserves in the world, while Minnesota had one of the great iron ore deposits of the world. Since textiles and iron and steel are the bases of in-

Table 3-10. Factors of Rural to Urban Migration, 1870–1930

National and International Trends

Industrial revolution
Commercial mercantile to industrial capitalist economy
Development of a world economy

Pull Factors to Cities	Push Factors from Rural Areas
Physical Environment	
Natural resources	Soil depletion/erosion
Coal, iron ore, forests, petroleum	Marginal lands
Great Lakes/rivers	Droughts/pests/crop diseases
Natural harbors	
Technology	
Machine age—fossil fuel power substituting	Mechanization of agriculture/labor
human/animal power	surplus
Communication advancement	
Telegraph/telephone/wireless	
Transportation advances	
Railroads/streetcar/automotive	
Sanitation/public health	
Water supply/sewage/medical	
Electricity	
Elevator	
Economic	
Industrial employment	Profitability of small farm
Factory system/mass production	Southern sharecropping system
Large domestic market	Agricultural overproduction and lower
Expanding foreign market	farm prices
Efficiencies of concentration	
High internal labor demand (post-1914)	
Recruitment of labor	
Transportation developments	
Railroads/highways	
Cycle of growth	
Government Policy	
Protective tariff	Monetary policy—rural debt/credit
Exploitation of public domain resources	
Laissez-faire capitalism	
Labor/resources/pollution	
Banking system	
Demographic	
Immigration patterns (to 1914)	Closing of the frontier (1890)
Relatively high birthrates	
Lengthening of life span	
Social	
Business/entrepreneurial culture	Southern black segregation and
Glamor/romance of cities	oppression
Consumer culture	

dustrialization, America had the raw materials to build, supply, and then export these basic items. In the twentieth century, as transportation and energy needs began to rely on petroleum, the Gulf Coast and interior oil fields were among the largest known in the world and made America a petroleum exporter up to the 1960s. The large waterway transportation system linked the natural resource and agricultural areas into one vast economic unit.

Some resource problems pushed farmers from the land. Soil depletion and erosion were rampant, especially in the South. Some marginal lands were occupied in the Great Plains and the West during the last period of frontier settlement. In these and in other areas, marginal farmers, usually indebted, periodically were pushed off the land by droughts, crop failures, pests, and diseases.

Technology

Continuing scientific discoveries and human inventiveness brought on the machine age. Industrial machines powered by fossil fuels worked faster, more consistently, and more cheaply than humans and animals. In communications technology the telegraph, telephone, and wireless tied together complex systems of suppliers and markets. The expanding network of railroads, and within the cities, streetcars and later automobiles and trucks greatly improved means of transportation. Scientific advancements in medicine, sanitation, and public health allowed millions of people to live in close proximity. Electricity not only provided domestic light and consumer appliances but ran new industrial machines and removed the need to locate near sites of water or steam power. The simple application of electricity to the elevator allowed buildings to reach new heights with "skyscrapers" further increasing urban density.

The application of industrial machines on the farm (tractors, reapers, threshers) not only reduced manual labor, but also allowed significantly fewer individuals to produce more goods. This produced the problem of surplus labor in rural districts. Farm size began to increase as the number of farmers decreased. Large families were no longer needed to run farms. This surplus population migrated to cities in search of economic opportunity.

Economic

Technical advances in iron and steel, textiles, metal fabricating, and electronics allowed the construction of large industrial facilities employing thousands of individuals in a mass production factory system. The growing American market consumed these industrial products at an increasing pace. America changed from a net importer to a net exporter of manufactured goods. This industrial growth demanded more labor than could be supplied internally and millions of European immigrants flooded America in the 1890s through 1914. This further increased the product demand from the internal U.S. market, which demand continued the cycle of growth.

Although industrial wages and working conditions were many times abysmal, the farm economy went through numerous recessions and depressions. The settlement and cultivation of all possible arable land and farm mechanization generated vast overproduction from the fertile U.S. soil and climate. Overproduction meant lower commodity prices. Many farmers fell into debt, often to buy machinery, and went bankrupt. Farms were sold into ever larger and sometimes more efficient sizes. The small family farm began its slow demise.

In the South the special land tenure system of sharecropping emerged after the Civil War. Rural blacks generally were agricultural workers without land. Southern white landowners offered families and individuals the right to work their land with the payment of keeping and selling a share of the crop. Most of the time the share was not enough to provide for a family, especially in bad years. Sharecroppers also went into debt and were trapped in a seemingly endless cycle of poverty and obligation. Both black and white sharecroppers were lured north by recruiters, rumors, and relatives, all telling of the new life and the promise of economic opportunity.

Government Policy

The levying of a tax on imported industrial goods was the general long-term policy of the United States until recent decades. The tariff policy was designed to protect the American manufacturers from foreign competition and foster national industrialization. Although this made goods generally more expensive for the consumer, it encouraged industrial and urban growth to the extent that, by the turn of the century, America was the leading manufacturing country in the world. As large-scale capitalism arose, the government continued a laissez-faire attitude with respect to industrial corporations. Wholesale exploitation of labor, the public domain, and privately held natural resources did indeed accrue capital, but at widespread individual and environmental harm. Various monetary and banking policies, such as the gold standard, hit the poor and indebted classes especially hard.[45] These policies directly or indirectly affected the debt-ridden poor farmer and increased rural-to-urban migration.

Demographic

Immigration has always been the one of the most salient features of the American experience. The decades of 1890s and 1900s were the peak period of immigration in American history. The millions of immigrants not only increased U.S. population, but almost all headed for the industrial cities, especially after the closing of the frontier.

By 1890 virtually all of the arable land in the United States was settled. The frontier was always thought of as a safety valve for excess population and the hope for the landless and poor. With no frontier to move onto, the farm children of the 1890s and 1900s had just one place to go—the city. Relatively high birthrates for the period ensured a steady supply of migrants. The cutting off of the European immigrant labor supply in 1914 and the World War I industrial boom significantly increased this flow northward to the cities, much of it coming from the rural South, Great Plains, and Midwest.

Social

Cities meant many things to many people. At the turn of the century, cities were looked upon as both dens of iniquity and towers of opportunity and hope. For many rural youth the city was the rejection of the drudgery of farm life and the anticipation of the excitement and glamor of urban bright lights. Other than a growing textile industry on the Carolina Piedmont, most of the South was a lagging region that produced little economic opportunity during this period. Appalachian and southern whites began a fifty-year trend of northward migration beginning in the mid 1910s through the mid 1960s. Southern blacks joined in the flow for all of the above reasons, and with the added incentive of escaping segregation, and economic, political, and social oppression. Many felt the northern cities could only improve their condition of endless discrimination.

Shifts in State, Regional, and Sectional Political Power

The massive growth of urban America in the late nineteenth and early twentieth centuries is explained by numerous variables. Urban expansion occurred in all sections, but the majority of this growth was concentrated in the industrial cities along the lower Great Lakes and the Northeast. This region became known as the American Manufacturing Belt. The belt stretched from southern New England and the Middle Atlantic states westward along the lower Great Lakes and Ohio River valley as far west as Milwaukee and Chicago.[46] The size of the House delegation of the Manufacturing Belt states became enormous. In 1930, for example, the largest four state delegations in the nation were from this region: New York (forty-five seats), Pennsylvania (thirty-four seats), Illinois (twenty-seven seats), and Ohio (twenty-four seats). Of the forty-eight states, just these four states composed 30 percent of Congress.

Although the growth of northern manufacturing has a long history, the Manufacturing Belt boom is depicted on the national apportionment maps only after the closing of the frontier in 1890. The 1870, 1880, and 1890 maps of House seat changes reflect the final expansion of the United States to the Pacific coast (see Maps 9A–11A in Part 2). The 1900, 1910, and 1930 seat change maps show relative growth in the large industrial northern states (see Maps 12A, 13A, and 14). These maps show that with the increasing size of the House from 1870 through 1910 virtually no state lost seats. The 1890 map of seat change (Map 11A) reflects a classic nineteenth-century apportionment pattern—most western states gain seats while most of the areas east of the Mississippi have no change. However, the 1900 and 1910 seat apportionments (Maps 12A and 13A) illustrate the first significant break up of this historical apportionment pattern—that is, some states in the West and Great Plains receive no additional seats and some industrial states in the Northeast receive an

45. See references listed in footnote 15.
46. Stephen S. Birdsall and John W. Florin, *Regional Landscapes of the United States and Canada* (New York: John Wiley, 1992), 127–154.

increase in seats. Some of these industrial state gains are substantial: in 1900, New York and Illinois added three seats and Pennsylvania and New Jersey added two; in 1910 there were six new seats in New York, four in Pennsylvania, and two in Illinois, Massachusetts, and New Jersey. While the western states simultaneously received increases, the booming Manufacturing Belt of the Northeast is clearly outlined on Maps 12A and 13A.

This pattern is illustrated to some extent again on Map 14 portraying the 1930 apportionment. In 1930 Michigan had an increase of four seats; New York, Ohio, and New Jersey each had two; Connecticut had one; and Illinois registered no change. This is the last extensive large gain by the Northeast states in U.S. history. The Great Depression of the 1930s created heavy losses in the Manufacturing Belt and the 1940 apportionment map (Map 15) clearly outlines this pattern. Although many of these areas boomed again in World War II and the postwar period, the 1940 map was a precursor of the future apportionment patterns of this region (see the next case study on the Sunbelt and Snowbelt).

Maps 9B–13B illustrate the relative growth in congressional strength for 1870 through 1910. These percentage change maps give a more detailed picture of the patterns discussed above. The 1870, 1880, and 1890 percentage change maps again illustrate the expansion of the West to the Pacific and the end of the frontier of settlement. This relative growth clearly shows the western half of the nation increasing and the eastern half decreasing. The positive pattern in the South in 1870 and in 1880 reflects the count of African-Americans as whole individuals rather than three-fifths as in the previous censuses. The 1890 apportionment illustration (Map 11B) is the last clear strictly West versus East expansion map in U.S. history.

In 1900 some Great Plains and western states lost relative strength or had no change and some eastern states gained relative strength.[47] This was a departure from the long-term pattern. New York held its own, a statistically significant achievement for a large delegation state, and neighboring New Jersey and Connecticut gained from New York City suburbanization and industrialization. West Virginia gained strength as a small state with an increase in population because of increasing timber for urban construction, and especially coal production, fueling the heavy industries of the North. The southern state that industrialized first, North Carolina, mostly by way of cotton textiles, also had a positive gain in three of the four apportionments from 1900 through 1940. In 1910 four northeastern states registered a gain and three had no change. And, as stated above, in 1930 five northern states made substantial gains. In 1930 and throughout most of this period, California (aided substantially by Los Angeles and San Francisco), Texas (oil boom towns), and Florida (vacation, retirement, and land boom) also recorded gains. These states had steady growth for most of their history and were the anchors of the contemporary postindustrial pattern (see the next case study on the Sunbelt and Snowbelt). It is also important to note the areas of losses in 1900, 1910, and 1930. Large areas of the South, Great Plains, and rural Midwest had substantial out-migration to the northern cities and to the other growth areas.

Although the Manufacturing Belt does not show up on the apportionment maps as a consistently unified region of growth, its real and relative increases break the century-old historical pattern of continuous western relative increase and continuous eastern relative decrease. Some of the growth of the cities in the Manufacturing Belt derived from intrastate migration, intraregional migration, and natural increase, but much of this growth was from immigration and interregional migration. During this period the Manufacturing Belt cities, and cities in general, established themselves as a force influencing the reapportionment of House power both nationally and within states. Table 3-11 illustrates the increase of high-density congressional districts from 1870–1930. This table gives the number of high-density districts at each apportionment as a fraction of the total number of districts in each state.

Nonapportionment of the 1920s

The 1920s was the only decade in American history in which the House and electoral college were not reapportioned according to population changes. The reasons for this are numerous and complex. The size of the House increased at every apportionment since the beginning of Congress, except in 1840. There were physical limitations of the House

47. Industrial development is concentrated in six or seven northern states. Even after the explosive immigration of the 1890s and 1900s, the northern states as a whole did not keep up with the relative growth of the West (see tables of regional differences in the 1900 and 1910 decades in Part 2). Intraregional migration from the rural and agricultural areas of the North account for part of this, as does the continued large relative growth of the West.

Table 3-11. High-Density House Districts in Relation to Total House Districts, 1870–1930[a]

	1870	1880	1890	1900	1910	1930
California	1/4	1/6	1/7	1/8	3/11	10/20
Colorado					1/4	1/4
Georgia						1/10
Illinois	3/19	4/20	7/22	10/25	10/27	10/27
Kentucky	1/10	1/11	1/11	1/11	1/11	1/9
Maryland	2/6	2/6	2/6	2/6	2/6	2/6
Massachusetts	6/11	6/12	7/13	7/14	9/16	11/15
Michigan	1/9	1/11	2/12	2/12	2/13	5/17
Minnesota			1/7	1/9	2/10	2/9
Missouri	2/13	2/14	2/15	3/16	3/16	5/13
Nebraska						1/5
New Jersey	3/7	3/7	3/8	4/10	6/12	7/14
New York	12/33	15/34	17/34	20/37	26/43	26/45
Ohio	3/20	3/21	3/21	3/21	4/22	5/24
Oregon					1/3	1/3
Pennsylvania	7/27	7/28	8/30	14/32	18/36	19/34
Rhode Island	1/2	1/2	1/2	1/2	1/3	1/2
Tennessee						1/9
Texas						3/21
Washington						1/6
Wisconsin		1/9	1/10	1/11	2/11	2/10
High-Density House Districts/ Total House Districts	42/293	47/322	56/357	70/394	91/435	115/435
Percent High-Density Districts in House	14%	15%	16%	18%	21%	26%

[a]*Measurements for high-density congressional districts taken from Kenneth C. Martis,* The Historical Atlas of United States Congressional Districts: 1789–1983 *(New York: Free Press, 1982). A high-density district is defined as a small district that encompasses one county or less with a large city within its boundaries, or two counties with the majority of the district population from a large city. The count of districts was made at the end of each decade to ensure all redistricting for the decade had been completed. The Congress used in each decade is : 1870 (Forty-seventh); 1880 (Fifty-second); 1890 (Fifty-seventh); 1900 (Sixty-second); 1910 (Sixty-seventh); 1930 (Seventy-seventh).*

chamber to hold even the 435 seats allotted in 1910. However, the apportionment debate centered not only on practical gains and losses of congressional seats and power but also on serious social and political feelings and demographic questions that cut to the heart of a changing America.

The apportionment debate began as usual after the report of the 1920 census data. The basic controversy centered on two propositions: (1) expand the House once more to accommodate all states and ensure no losses of seats; or (2) fix the House size at 435 and reapportion accordingly. The debate began in 1921 and lasted virtually the entire decade. Many of the arguments used were as old as the Republic with respect to the size of the House and political representation (see Part 1).

Those arguing for an increased size of the House put forth the following rationale:

1. The recent enfranchisement of women meant an increase in the size of the average constituency and the need for more representatives.

2. More representatives would better serve democracy since they could be located closer to their constituents.

3. More representatives would keep power from being concentrated in the hands of a few.

4. The mathematical formula was generally unfair.

5. The census figures were inaccurate, especially in rural areas.

6. The nation was disrupted by World War I and an accurate count was not made.[48]

Those arguing for keeping the size of the House at 435 and for passing an apportionment bill immediately put forth the following rationale:

1. More representatives would lessen the efficiency of the House operation.

2. More representatives would decrease the amount of debate time for all.

3. More representatives would incur additional cost.

4. There should be fair redistribution of representatives and districts.

5. The American people and media supported reapportionment.

6. The Constitution mandated action on reapportionment every ten years.

One argument to increase the size of the House or to delay apportionment was new to the debate or at least was brought up in a consistent and vitriolic way as never before in American history. This argument concerned the growth of the city and its influence on American politics and culture. In the floor debate, the urban-rural conflict was brought out, usually by fearful rural representatives, as one significant theme. City values were corrupting fundamental native "American" religious and moral life. City bosses were corrupting American political life. Cites were filled with immigrants wishing to repeal prohibition. Cities were filled with immigrants wishing to repeal the new restrictive immigration laws. The hostility toward the city brought out the fear of changing economic, cultural, social, demographic, and technological realities of twentieth-century America.

An analysis of roll-call voting on the various apportionment bills suggests that the representatives from states likely to lose seats wanted an increased House size or have no apportionment at all. These states were usually rural agricultural states (see Maps 13A and 14). Representatives from states likely to increase in seats favored fixing the size of the House and passing an apportionment bill. These states usually had urban industrial areas and other growing areas. The states that had no change in seats were critical. Rural "no change" states seemed to vote against reapportionment, especially from the Democratic rural South. Urban "no changers" tended to support reapportionment, many from the Republican Northeast.[49]

In spite of the constitutional and legal questions involved, Congress did not pass an apportionment bill after the census. The 1922 elections were held with the same numbers given to each state in 1910. Throughout the 1920s apportionment was debated on and off with the same forces in the House and Senate aligning and blocking passage of a bill. As the time for a new census came near sentiment arose to once again make apportionment automatic with the census as in 1850 and 1860. With President Herbert Hoover's support, a bill was passed in 1929 to incorporate apportionment in the census with automatic calculations based on a House fixed at 435 seats. This system of automatic reapportionment has been in effect since that time.

48. Eagles, *Conflict,* 33–62; Schmeckebier, *Apportionment,* 120–124.
49. Eagles, *Conflict,* 85–115.

Conclusion

The two most famous census reports in American history were released after the 1890 and 1920 counts. The 1890 report announced the closing of the American western frontier. This ended a sustained movement that began in the 1600s. This momentous event focused American thought on such issues as the meaning of the frontier in American history and the limits of natural resources.

The second census report that grabbed the attention of the American public came as a result of the 1920 census. It reported that for the first time the United States was more urban than rural. Although the rural to urban movement is one of the major trends in all of American demographic history, the passing of this threshold focused American thought on what kind of nation it had been and what kind of nation it would become. In addition, this trend had geopolitical consequences both within states and between states. The massive industrialization and urbanization in the 1890s through late 1920s brought increased power to urban areas in all regions, but especially states in the Northeast Manufacturing Belt. This produced the first noticeable change in the long-term trend of positive percentage gain in the frontier western states and relative losses in the eastern portions of the country.

The Great Depression of the 1930s brought economic disaster to the Manufacturing Belt with losses in population and congressional seats. Although some Northeast industrial areas prospered in the 1940s and 1950s, America was moving from an industrial society to a postindustrial society. The industrial core declined with this movement. Manufacturing in a postindustrial society was decentralized and produced an entirely different range of products with a totally different set of constraints. Competition in the world economy in the modern era even brought deindustrialization to America and the Manufacturing Belt suffered further. These new economic realities again had vast demographic and political consequences in shifting state and regional political power. The next section discusses the specifics of the new regional geopolitics within the United States and the rise of a new region, the Sunbelt.

Sunbelt and Snowbelt

1970–1990 Apportionments

The decennial population count affects political power and money. As a result, the census and its uses garner substantial controversy. It's no secret that population growth in the Northeast-Midwest region failed to keep pace with the rest of the nation. . . .

Northeast-Midwest Congressional Coalition, founded 1976

The . . . Representatives and . . . Senators from the South and Southwest look to the Congressional Sunbelt Caucus to rise above party lines and state boundaries to bring a reasoned analysis of issues before Congress from a regional perspective. They also use the Sunbelt Caucus to build consensus and advocate regional interests in an increasingly complex federal policy process.

Congressional Sunbelt Caucus, founded 1981

Westward migration is one of most significant features of American demographic history. In the last thirty years this migration pattern has been augmented by a movement to the southern states. This movement to certain areas of the South has reversed decades of southern out-migration. In addition, the nature of American society and the forces affecting American migration have changed. For these and other reasons the general tide of the population from the North and Northeast to the South and Southwest in the last thirty years has been termed by demographers, population geographers, and the popular media as the "Sunbelt" move-

Table 3-12. Sunbelt and Snowbelt States, 1970–1990

Apportionment Sunbelt	Apportionment Snowbelt
Southern/Southwestern/Pacific Coast Tier	Northern Tier
South	New England
Virginia	Maine
North Carolina	New Hampshire
South Carolina	Vermont
Georgia	Massachusetts
Florida	Rhode Island
Alabama	Connecticut
Mississippi	
Tennessee	Middle Atlantic
Arkansas	New York
Louisiana	New Jersey
Texas	Delaware
Oklahoma	Maryland
	Pennsylvania
Southwest	
New Mexico	Border
Arizona	West Virginia
Colorado	Kentucky
Utah	Missouri
Nevada	
	Midwest
Pacific Coast	Ohio
California	Michigan
Oregon	Indiana
Washington	Illinois
Hawaii	Wisconsin
	Great Plains
	Minnesota
	Iowa
	North Dakota
	South Dakota
	Kansas
	Nebraska
	Mountain
	Wyoming
	Montana
	Idaho
	Alaska

ment.[50] The term Sunbelt first describes the southern tier of the United States where the climate is subtropical and winter is conducive to outdoor leisure activities. However, the term has taken on many different meanings and, of course, numerous other variables account for this demographic phenomena. The complementary term "Snowbelt" is used to describe the northern region.

This atlas uses the apportionment maps of 1970, 1980, and 1990 (Maps 18–20 in Part 2) to define an "apportionment Sunbelt"—that is, a tier of states along the southern half of the United States that includes the Pacific Coast states. The Sunbelt is also called the "southern/southwestern/Pacific Coast tier." The "apportionment Snowbelt" is all the states in the northern half of the country up to those that border the Pacific Coast. The Snowbelt is also called the "northern tier." Both of these terms for both of these divisions are used interchangeably. Table 3-12 lists the states in each category and their regional subdivisions. This section reviews the demographic shifts, discusses the many variables behind Sunbelt/Snowbelt changes, and analyzes the resultant changing regional power structure in Congress and the electoral college.

Patterns of Population Geography

Population geographers and demographers universally agree the Sunbelt is not a homogeneous area of economic growth and in-migration. Numerous counties in the South and West have recorded significant economic decline and out-migration. The term "sunspots" of growth may better describe the phenomenon at hand, especially in the South.[51] The Sunbelt is an area of many places with spectacular growth relative to the U.S. average, but with some areas of stagnation and even decline. Even though the Sunbelt is not a ubiquitous band of growth across the southern tier of the United States, on a sectional level the congressional apportionment maps for the House of Representatives show a noteworthy increase in political power.

Since the Sunbelt encompasses three vastly different regions—the South, Southwest, and Pacific Coast—and has areas of both growth and

50. Bruce J. Schulman, *From Cotton Belt to Sunbelt* (New York: Oxford University Press, 1991); Larry Sawers and William K. Tabb, eds., "Urban Development and Regional Restructuring, an Overview," in *Sunbelt/Snowbelt: Urban Development and Regional Restructuring* (New York and Oxford: Oxford University Press, 1984); Weinstein and Firestine, *The Rise of the Sunbelt.*
51. Thomas A Lyson, *Two Sides to the Sunbelt* (New York: Praeger, 1989).

Table 3-13. Factors of Sunbelt Migration, 1960–1990

National and International Trends

Movement from industrial to postindustrial society
Disintegration of the small family farm
Increase in national wealth and growth of the middle class
Retirement programs—private and social security
Lifestyle changes

Pull Factors To the South and Southwest/Pacific	Push Factors From the North and Northeast
Economic	
Lower wages	High labor wages/benefits
"Right-to-work" laws	High union membership
Lower taxes	High state and local taxes
Lower cost of living	Oil industrial facilities
Housing costs/land values	
Utilities/heating	
New branch plants	
Social	
Retirement	Disintegration of urban infrastructure
Advertising/promotion	Crime
Glamor/romance factor	
Physical Environment	
Pleasant winter climate	Harsh winter climate
Scenery	
Atlantic and Gulf coasts	
Southwest desert	
Rocky Mountains	
Pacific Coast	
Technology	
Air conditioning	
Interstate highway system	
Communication revolution	
High-tech industries	
Aerospace	
Computers/software	
Electronics	
Biotechnology	
Tourism	
Health	
Government Policy	
Defense facilities	
Aerospace installations	
Research and development funding	
Demographic	
Southern returnees	Crowding/high-density cities
Recent immigration patterns	
Birthrates	

decline, many different variables are responsible for Sunbelt seat gains in the House. Table 3-13 lists a number of variables that partially explain this phenomenon. This table outlines both national and international variables and regional "push" (from the North and Northeast) and "pull" (to the South and Southwest/Pacific Coast) factors that have influenced Sunbelt migration. Some of these variables are common to all areas of the Sunbelt, some act stronger in one region, and some are unique to one area.

Factors of Population Change

National and International Trends

American society has gone through vast structural changes since the end of World War II. The heavy industry-based society of the recent past relied on large fixed facilities close to natural resources and markets. In contrast, the postindustrial society contains a large service sector and has high-technology industries, such as electronics, computers, software, and biotechnology, which can locate in numerous, preferably desirable, locations.

Since the 1940s the wealth and educational attainment of American society has grown allowing freedom of travel, choice of job location, leisure time, and the ability to retire to enticing environments. The maturation of the baby boom generation brought significant lifestyle changes with certain material and environmental desires. The United States is part of a world economy that has both usurped its industrial role and helped drive the postindustrial changes. These and other trends allow population shifts from the traditional northern Manufacturing Belt and small farm agricultural areas to the South and Southwest/Pacific Coast.

Economic

Numerous economic factors fueled Sunbelt growth. Industrial wages were higher in the North where there was a history of union organization. In the South unionism was not widespread. Indeed, to lure industry from the North, southern states passed so-called "right-to-work" laws of various types that hindered union organization. Beginning in the 1950s, many industrial concerns either opened branch plants in the South or closed their northern plants and moved South outright.[52] This was encouraged in many cases by the sheer age of many northern industrial plants. In addition to high wages, most northern and midwestern states had progressive work rules and benefit laws that industrial employers found burdensome. Social benefits and educational systems of the North were also progressive, prompting high state personal and corporate income taxes and local real estate taxes. Many of these so-called "business climate" factors encouraged industry to relocate or establish themselves in the South or Southwest.

Social

Most of the large industrial cities of the North had their surge of development around the turn of the century. Many of these "old" northern cities now have a physical infrastructure (highways, sewage systems, bridges, school buildings) in deteriorating condition. With suburbanization in the 1950s and 1960s, many northern cities, like Detroit, were left with an elderly and poor African-American population. These conditions not only led to further deterioration, encouraging more white flight to the suburbs, but also flight to the Sunbelt for employment or retirement.[53]

In the 1950s and 1960s retirement and second home communities sprang up across the Southwest and South. Land sale promotions touting communities in places like Florida and Arizona helped to change the perception of retirement in the Sunbelt. These promotions pitched such points as low land/house costs, pleasant winters, and general environmental amenities.

Physical Environment

Climate is one of the main reasons population has shifted to the southern tier/Pacific Coast in the postindustrial era. The pleasant winters allow outdoor activities. The dry climate of the Southwest and mild win-

---

52. This trek to the South for cheap labor continued into the 1980s, for example, with the location of new American and foreign auto assembly plants outside the traditional auto/manufacturing region. However, this search for cheap labor led many of these same concerns overseas and across the border into Mexico. This may lead to both possible job losses in the Southwest border region or possible job gains from crossborder development that positively affects the U.S. side.

53. "Northeast Continues Slip as West and South Grow," *New York Times,* January, 13 1992, A10.

ter in Florida have lured many simply because of health concerns. The magnetism of the topographic grandeur of the American West and Pacific Coast has also enticed millions.[54] These combined attributes have spawned an extensive tourist industry that, in many Sunbelt states, is the first or second largest income producer.

Technology

The development of central air conditioning and its widespread use in homes and businesses made large-scale migration to the desert Southwest possible. The same can undoubtedly be said for the summer in the Deep South. This simple technological innovation has irrevocably changed the ability to live comfortably along the southern tier.

The desert Southwest has also developed because of one of the most intricate water delivery systems in the world. Dams were constructed beginning in the early part of this century to deliver irrigation water to allow an agriculture economic base to develop. Later dams provided cheap hydroelectric power that benefited the region. In the postindustrial era, this water more and more is being used for urban and industrial development, which, of course, could not occur in the desert under natural conditions.

The telecommunications revolution has also allowed the disbursement of industrial and service operations away from the northern manufacturing core and traditional locations of corporate headquarters. Beginning with the modernization of the long-distance telephone system, all the way to facsimile machines, satellite communication, and computer networking, telecommunications have allowed branch operations to locate in cheap labor markets and have enabled the relocation or establishment of businesses in the Sunbelt.

The interstate highways system has also enabled the linking of the Sunbelt with the traditional Manufacturing Belt. Branch plants can be located in the South or West and be a day or two from the major plant or the still significant markets of the Northeast. The rise of the trucking industry and the corresponding deterioration of the American railroad system has allowed further geographical dispersal of the manufacturing facilities, probably to the benefit of the Sunbelt.

Government Policy

Many have argued that federal government politics have been central to Sunbelt growth.[55] For year-round outdoor training, the need for coastal ports, and other purposes many military bases are located in the southern and western states.[56] For much of this century, the power of southern senators and representatives with powerful committee chairs has been legendary.[57] Other aspects of the military industrial complex also have a history of southern-tier location, such as the initial location of the aircraft industry in California. As aerospace development followed aircraft, the federal government located many of these facilities in California, Texas, and Florida. As other high-tech industries, such as computers and electronics, followed aircraft and aerospace, the location of these facilities in the growth-pole states further accelerated their economic fortunes. Furthermore, a great percentage of federal research and development funds went to these facilities, nearby universities, and Sunbelt government research laboratories.[58]

Demographic

Foreign immigration has always been a factor in regional U.S. population growth. Immigrants locate in states where economic conditions provide opportunities. This was true in the 1890s in the northern industrial cities and is true in recent years with respect to the Sunbelt. Latin Americans have dominated recent immigration to the United States. Both legal and illegal Mexican immigration is the largest Latin component and all of the Southwest border states have experienced this influx.[59] Asian immigration has also been strong to the Pacific Coast states.

Internal migration also follows economic opportunity. In addition to

54. Michael J. Greenwood et al., "Migration, Regional Equilibrium and the Estimation of Compensating Differentials," *American Economic Review* 81 (December 1991): 1382.

55. For example, Michael I. Luger argues that federal tax policies have benefited many of the growth areas of the Sunbelt states in his article "Federal Tax Incentives as Industrial and Urban Policy," *Sunbelt/Snowbelt,* 201–231.

56. Weinstein and Firestine, *The Rise of the Sunbelt,* 23–24.

57. Merle Black and Earl Black, "The South in the Senate: Changing Patterns of Representation on Committees," in Robert P. Steed, Lawrence W. Moreland, and Tod A. Baker, eds., *The Disappearing South? Studies in Regional Change and Continuity* (Tuscaloosa and London: University of Alabama Press, 1990).

58. E. Soja, *Post-Modern Geographies* (London: Verso, 1989), Chapter 12.

59. Niles Hansen, *The Border Economy* (Austin: University of Texas Press, 1981); Rogelio Saenz, "Mexican-American Interstate Migration Flows Along Arizona, California, Colorado, New Mexico and Texas," *Sociology and Social Research* 73 (April 1989): 153.

western migration, in recent decades migration flows have also been from the North to the South, a reversal of historical twentieth-century migration patterns. Many of these migrants are southern returnees, both black and white, going back to home roots. Although some of these returnees are retirees, many returned because of deteriorating conditions in the North and opportunities in the new South.[60]

Shifts in State, Regional, and Sectional Political Power

Background to the Sunbelt Era: 1940–1960 Apportionments

The large cities of the Northeast and lower Great Lakes were the original core of American industrialization. The Manufacturing Belt received vast European immigration, especially from the 1890s through 1914, and received vast rural to urban migration, especially from the 1890s through 1920s and 1940s through 1960s. During the above periods the larger northeastern industrial states were able to keep pace with the West and other high percentage growth areas (see previous case study). The congressional reapportionment statistics of 1900, 1910, and 1930 show the major states in the Manufacturing Belt with gains or holding their own. This was a departure from the patterns of nineteenth-century apportionments. However, even in the boom period not all states in the region could keep pace with percentage growth in other areas (see Maps 12A and 12B through 13A and 13B).

The Great Depression of the 1930s hit the industrial sector particularly hard. The 1940 apportionment map (Map 15) vividly illustrates the broad band of losses along the Manufacturing Belt, plus losses in the Midwest farm and Great Plains dust bowl states. World War II defense production brought life to the heavy industries of the North, but the 1950 census apportionment (Map 16) shows only one industrial state, Michigan, gaining one seat. One Border state, Maryland, also gained one seat, but this is largely attributable to suburbanization from the wartime expansion of Washington, D.C., and the federal government. In spite of the war, the Manufacturing Belt states of Pennsylvania and New York lost three seats and two seats, respectively. The giant winner in the 1950 census was California with a gain of seven seats. The Pacific war theater, aircraft and other defense-related industries, and the unmatched climate discovered by thousands of service personnel continued the extraordinary growth of California in this century. While some industrial areas of the Northeast grew, they did not keep pace with rapid growth in other areas.

There was a postwar boom in the late 1940s and 1950s because of latent consumer demand and because the United States was still the undisputed industrial leader of the world. In 1960 Michigan and Ohio each gained a seat because of the automobile boom. Maryland gained another seat from Washington, D.C., suburbanization. New Jersey also gained a seat through an intraregional transfer by way of suburbanization from New York City and Philadelphia. Six other Manufacturing Belt states, however, lost ten seats to more than cancel the gains.[61] The gains of Michigan, Ohio, Maryland, and New Jersey are historic, because since 1960 no northern-tier state has increased its congressional delegation! Throughout the 1940–1960 period California, Florida, and Texas show up on the map as centers of apportionment increases.

Northern Decline

In the seven reapportionments since the House size was fixed at 435 seats (1930–1990), only six of the twenty-nine northern states have gained seats in a decennial census. In the same period, virtually every northern-tier state with more than one House seat has registered a net decline in representation (see Maps 14–20). Table 3-14 delineates that in the last three Sunbelt apportionments, 1970–1990, sixteen northern-tier states have lost a combined total of forty-four seats. All forty-four seats, of course, have been transferred to the Sunbelt.

Southern Reversal

In the seven reapportionments since the House size was fixed at 435 seats, 1930–1990, the states of the South (see Table 3-12) have reversed their fortunes in House reapportionment (see Maps 14–20). In the four reapportionments from 1930 through 1960, each of the southern states,

60. For an examination of the phenomena of blacks returning to the South, see John Cromartie and Carol B. Stack, "Reinterpretation of Black Return and Nonreturn Migration to the South, 1975–1980," *The Geographical Review* 79 (July 1989): 297.

61. Joseph H. Turek, "The Northeast in a National Context: Background Trends in Population, Income, and Employment," in Harry W. Richardson and Joseph H. Turek, eds., *Economic Prospects for the Northeast* (Philadelphia: Temple University Press, 1985), 28–65; Daniel H. Garnick, "The Northeast States in National Context," in Benjamin Chinitz, ed., *The Declining Northeast* (New York: Praeger, 1978), 145–159.

Table 3-14. Apportionment Change for Sunbelt and Snowbelt States, 1970-1990

Apportionment Snowbelt
Northern Tier

	1970	1980	1990	Total
New England				
Maine	0	0	0	0
New Hampshire	0	0	0	0
Vermont	0	0	0	0
Massachusetts	0	-1	-1	-2
Rhode Island	0	0	0	0
Connecticut	0	0	0	0
Subtotal	0	-1	-1	-2
Middle Atlantic				
New York	-2	-5	-3	-10
New Jersey	0	-1	-1	-2
Delaware[a]	0	0	0	0
Maryland	0	0	0	0
Pennsylvania	-2	-2	-2	-6
Subtotal	-4	-8	-6	-18
Border				
West Virginia	-1	0	-1	-2
Kentucky	0	0	-1	-1
Missouri	0	-1	0	-1
Subtotal	-1	-1	-2	-4
Midwest				
Ohio	-1	-2	-2	-5
Michigan	0	-1	-2	-3
Indiana	0	-1	0	-1
Illinois	0	-2	-2	-4
Wisconsin	-1	0	0	-1
Subtotal	-2	-6	-6	-14
Great Plains				
Minnesota	0	0	0	0
Iowa	-1	0	-1	-2
North Dakota	-1	0	0	-1
South Dakota	0	-1	0	-1
Kansas	0	0	-1	-1
Nebraska	0	0	0	0
Subtotal	-2	-1	-2	-5
Mountain				
Wyoming[a]	0	0	0	0
Montana	0	0	-1	-1
Idaho	0	0	0	0
Alaska[a]	0	0	0	0
Subtotal	0	0	-1	-1
Total Change	**-9**	**-17**	**-18**	**-44**

Apportionment Sunbelt
Southern/Southwestern/Pacific Coast Tier

	1970	1980	1990	Total
South				
Virginia	0	0	1	1
North Carolina	0	0	1	1
South Carolina	0	0	0	0
Georgia	0	0	1	1
Florida	3	4	4	11
Alabama	-1	0	0	-1
Mississippi	0	0	0	0
Tennessee	-1	1	0	0
Arkansas	0	0	0	0
Louisiana	0	0	-1	-1
Texas	1	3	3	7
Oklahoma	0	0	0	0
Subtotal	2	8	9	19
Southwest				
New Mexico	0	1	0	1
Arizona	1	1	1	3
Colorado	1	1	0	2
Utah	0	1	0	1
Nevada[a]	0	1	0	1
Subtotal	2	5	1	8
Pacific Coast				
California	5	2	7	14
Oregon	0	1	0	1
Washington	0	1	1	2
Hawaii	0	0	0	0
Subtotal	5	4	8	17
Total Change	**9**	**17**	**18**	**44**

[a]Denotes states that have one representative in 1960.

except Louisiana and the growth-pole states of Texas and Florida, lost a House seat at least once. Beginning in 1914, and intensifying during World War II and the postwar industrial boom, black and white migration was significant from the rural South to the urban North (and West) into the 1960s.[62]

In the last three Sunbelt apportionments only two of the twelve southern states recorded a net loss of seats: Alabama (one in 1970) and Louisiana (one in 1990).[63] In recent decades black and white migration has even reversed and shows a net flow from the North to the South.[64] In the 1990 apportionment, Virginia, North Carolina, and Georgia gained one seat to go along with the seven additional members from Texas (three seats) and Florida (four seats). In the last three apportionments these five southern states have gained a combined total of twenty-one seats with a net gain of nineteen for the region.

Western Expansion

In the seven reapportionments since the House size was fixed at 435 seats, 1930–1990, none of the Southwest/Pacific Coast states (see Table 3-12) has lost a seat.[65] California led the way throughout this period with an enormous gain of forty-one seats. From 1970–1990 all Southwest/Pacific Coast states (except Hawaii) gained House members. In fact, just in 1980 (Map 19) all eight of the continental states gained seats. Over the last three apportionments the nine Southwest/Pacific Coast states have gained a combined total of twenty-five seats.

Sunbelt Growth Poles: California, Texas, and Florida

Three states have recorded extraordinary growth rates in the twentieth century: California, Texas, and Florida (see Table 3-14). Each has grown for somewhat different reasons and surged in different time periods. However, they all have several characteristics in common. Two geographic characteristics are important. First, they are all physically large in size: Texas is the second largest state; California is the third largest; and Florida is the twenty-second largest, but the second largest state east

---

62. Daniel M. Johnson and Rex R. Campbell, *Black Migration in America, A Social Demographic History* (Durham, N.C.: Duke University Press, 1981), 71–101.
63. Tennessee lost a seat in 1970, but gained it back in 1980.
64. See footnotes 58 and 59.
65. Of the total eleven continental western states (both Sunbelt and northern tier) only one state in all of American history, Montana in 1990, has ever lost a seat.

Table 3-15. Sunbelt and Snowbelt Representation, 1960-1990

	Seats				Percent of House			
	1960	1970	1980	1990	1960	1970	1980	1990
Snowbelt Total	260	251	234	216	59.8%	57.7%	53.8%	49.7%
Southwest/								
Pacific Coast	63	70	79	88	14.5%	16.1%	18.2%	20.2%
South	112	114	122	131	25.7%	26.2%	28.0%	30.1%
Sunbelt Total	175	184	201	219	40.2%	42.3%	46.2%	50.3%

of the Mississippi River. In addition, these three growth-pole states are also along the southern tier and generally possess pleasant winter climates.

Since California entered the Union in 1850, it has increased its House delegation in every census. California is the only state in U.S. history to achieve this sustained political power growth. Since Texas entered the Union in 1845, it has increased its number of seats in every census except 1940.[66] Since Florida entered the Union in 1845 it has increased its House delegation in every census except three—1860, 1880, and 1890—and has sustained the largest percentage increase of the growth-pole states in the 1930–1990 reapportionments.[67]

In the 1970, 1980, and 1990 apportionments, California gained fourteen seats (five, two, and seven, respectively) for a total delegation of fifty-two, Texas gained seven (one, three, and three, respectively) for a total delegation of thirty, and Florida gained eleven (three, four, and four, respectively) for a total delegation of twenty-three. These three states account for 72.7 percent of all the Sunbelt increase during this period. In the 1990s the three growth-pole states have a combined total of one hundred and five seas, nearly one-quarter of the entire House of Representatives. For the Sunbelt as a whole, Table 3-15 indicates the region has increased its representation in the House from 40.2 percent in 1960 to a majority 50.3 percent in 1990. The South has increased its representation by 4.4 percent and the Southwest/Pacific Coast by 5.7 percent since 1960.

Conclusion

There are many ways to explain the shifting of congressional and electoral state power to the Sunbelt. These explanations are not all applicable to all areas of the Sunbelt. Land values tend to be high in the Pacific

Coast states while low in many areas of the Southwest and South. While the climate of Los Angeles is still delightful, air pollution, crowding, cost of housing, long-distance commuting, and urban deterioration is similar to that experienced by some northern cities. The long-term trend, however, is for continued westward migration of the American population, stabilization, and growth in many areas of the South, with a resultant continued growth of congressional and presidential power in California, Texas, and Florida along with the rest of the southern tier of the United States.

66. The dust bowl drought of the 1930s severely affected the northern and northern panhandle Texas agricultural counties. Also, although Texas increased its delegation by two in 1910 its relative strength remained unchanged (see Maps 13A and 13B).

67. The following table lists the gain in seats for the three growth-pole states from the 1930 to 1990 apportionments:

	1930 Seats	1990 Seats	Percent Gain
Florida	5	23	360%
California	20	52	160%
Texas	21	30	43%

Reference Material

Bibliography and Index

Bibliography

"Advantage Shifts to G.O.P. in 1992 Redistricting Battle." *New York Times,* December 30, 1991.

Alexander, Thomas B. *Sectional Stress and Party Strength: A Study of Roll-Call Voting in the United States House of Representatives, 1830–1860.* Nashville, Tenn.: Vanderbilt University, 1967.

Archer, J. Clark, and Peter J. Taylor. *Section and Party.* Chichester, UK: Research Studies Press, 1981.

Baker, Gordon E. *The Reapportionment Revolution.* New York: Random House, 1966.

Barringer, Felicity. "Census Count of People Abroad Gives Massachusetts' Seat in Congress to Washington." *New York Times,* January 5, 1991.

———— "Census Revisions Would Widen Political Gains of 3 Big States." *New York Times,* June 14, 1991.

Bell, Rudolf M. *Party and Faction in American Politics: The House of Representatives, 1789–1801.* Westport, Conn.: Greenwood Press, 1973.

Bensel, Richard F. *Sectionalism and American Political Development, 1880–1980.* Madison: University of Wisconsin Press, 1984.

Biggar, Jeanne C. "The Sunning of America: Migration to the Sunbelt." *Population Bulletin* 34 (1979): 22.

Billington, Ray A. *Westward Expansion.* New York: Macmillan, 1974.

Birdsall, Stephen S., and John W. Florin. *Regional Landscapes of the United States and Canada.* New York: John Wiley, 1992.

Black, Merle, and Earl Black. "The South in the Senate: Changing Patterns of Representation on Committees." In *The Disappearing South? Studies in Regional Change and Continuity,* edited by Robert P. Steed, Lawrence W. Moreland, and Tod A. Baker. Tuscaloosa: University of Alabama Press, 1990.

Bogue, Donald J. *The Population of the United States.* Glencoe, Ill.: Free Press, 1959.

Brown, Ralph H. *Mirror for Americans: Likeness of the Eastern Seaboard.* New York: George Grady Press, 1943.

———— *Historical Geography of the United States.* New York: Harcourt, Brace & Company, 1948.

Carson, Gerald, and Bernard A. Weisberger. "The Great Countdown." *American Heritage* 7 (November 1989): 5–21.

Cayton, Andrew R. L. "'Separate Interests' and the Nation-State: The Washington Administration and the Origins of Regionalism in the Trans-Appalachian West," *Journal of American History* 79 (June 1992): 39–67.

Clausen, Aage R. *How Congressmen Decide.* New York: St. Martin's Press, 1973.

Common Cause. *Toward a System of "Fair and Effective Representation."* Washington, D.C.: Common Cause, 1977.

Congressional Quarterly. *Guide to U.S. Elections.* Washington, D.C.: Congressional Quarterly, 1985.

Conzen, Michael. "The Maturing Urban System in the United States 1840–1910." In *Geographic Perspectives on America's Past,* edited by David Ward. New York: Oxford University Press, 1979.

Cromartie, John, and Carol B. Stack. "Reinterpretation of Black Return and Nonreturn Migration to the South, 1975–1980." *Geographical Review* 79 (July 1989): 297.

Davidson, Chandler, ed. *Minority Vote Dilution.* Washington, D.C.: Howard University Press, 1984.

Davis, James E. *Frontier America 1800–1840, A Comparative Demographic Analysis of the Frontier Process.* Glendale, Calif.: Arthur H. Clark Company, 1977.

Deckard, Barbara, and John Stanley. "Party Decomposition and Region: The House of Representatives, 1945–1970." *Western Political Quarterly* 27 (June 1970): 249–264.

Dempsey, M. W. *Daily Telegraph Atlas of the United States of America.* London: Nomad Publishers, 1986.

de Tocqueville, Alexis. *Democracy in America*. Edited by J. P. Mayer and Max Lerner. New York: Harper & Row, 1966.

Eagles, Charles W. *Congressional Reapportionment and Urban-Rural Conflict in the 1920s*. Athens: University of Georgia Press, 1990.

Eaton, Clement. *A History of the Old South*. London: Macmillan, 1966.

Encyclopedia of Congress. New York: Simon & Schuster, 1993, s.v. "gerrymandering" by Kenneth C. Martis.

Gannett, H. *Statistical Atlas of the United States Based Upon the Results of the Eleventh Census*. Washington, D.C.: Government Printing Office, 1896.

Garnick, Daniel H. "The Northeast States in National Context." In *The Declining Northeast*, edited by Benjamin Chinitz. New York: Praeger, 1978.

Garraty, John A. *The American Nation*. New York: Harper & Row, 1966.

Genovese, Eugene D. *The Political Economy of Slavery*. New York: Vintage, 1967.

Greenwood, Michael J. *Migration and Economic Growth in the United States*. New York: Academic Press, 1981.

Greenwood, Michael J., Gary Hunt, Dan S. Rickman, and George I. Treyz. "Migration, Regional Equilibrium and the Estimation of Compensating Differentials." *American Economic Review* 81 (December 1991): 1382.

Grofman, Bernard, ed. *Political Gerrymandering and the Courts*. New York: Agathon Press, 1990.

Hammond. *United States History Atlas*. Maplewood, N.J.: Hammond, 1984.

Hansen, Niles. *The Border Economy*. Austin: University of Texas Press, 1981.

Haub, Carl. "Census: 248,709,873 U.S. Residents." *Population Today* (February 1991).

———. "The Top 10 Findings from the 1990 Census (So Far...)." *Population Today* (July/August 1991).

Hicks, John D., George E. Mowry, and Robert E. Burke. *A History of American Democracy*. Boston: Houghton Mifflin, 1970.

Hilliard, Sam B. *Atlas of Antebellum Southern Agriculture*. Baton Rouge: Louisiana State University Press, 1984.

Hollingsworth, J. R. *The Whirligig of Politics*. Chicago: University of Chicago Press, 1963.

Jackson, Kenneth, and Stanley Schultz, eds. *Cities in American History*. New York: Knopf, 1972.

Jacobs, Wilbur R., ed. *America's Great Frontiers and Sections*. Lincoln: University of Nebraska Press, 1969.

Johnson, Daniel M., and Rex R. Campbell. *Black Migration in America, A Social Demographic History*. Durham, N.C.: Duke University Press, 1981.

Jones, S. L. *The Presidential Election of 1896*. Madison: University of Wisconsin Press, 1964.

Key, V. O. *Politics, Parties, and Pressure Groups*. New York: Thomas Y. Crowell, 1964.

Klose, Nelson. *American Frontier*. Lincoln: University of Nebraska Press, 1964.

Kraus, Michael. *The United States to 1865*. Ann Arbor: University of Michigan Press, 1969.

Lehne, Richard. "Population Change and Congressional Representation." In *Commission on Population Growth and the American Future*, edited by A. E. Keir Nash. Washington, D.C.: Government Printing Office, 1972.

Lord, Clifford L. *Atlas of Congressional Roll Call: An Analysis of Yea and Nay Votes*. Newark, N.J.: Works Progress Administration, 1941.

———., ed. *The Atlas of Congressional Roll Calls for the Continental Congresses 1777–1781 and the Congresses of the Confederation 1781–1789*. Cooperstown, N.Y.: New York State Historical Association, 1943.

Lyson, Thomas A. *Two Sides to the Sunbelt*. New York: Praeger, 1989.

Martis, Kenneth C. *The History of Natural Resources Roll Call Voting in the United States House of Representatives: An Analysis of the Spatial Aspects of Legislative Voting Behavior*. Ann Arbor, Mich.: University Microfilms, 1976.

———. *The Historical Atlas of United States Congressional Districts: 1789–1983*. New York: Free Press, 1982.

———."Sectionalism and the United States Congress." *Political Geography Quarterly* 7 (April 1988): 99–109.

———. *The Historical Atlas of Political Parties in the United States Congress: 1789–1989*. New York: Macmillan, 1989.

Meinig, D. W. *The Shaping of America*. Vol. 1, *Atlantic America, 1492–1800*. New Haven, Conn.: Yale University Press, 1986.

Mitchell, Robert D., ed. *Appalachian Frontiers*. Lexington: University of Kentucky Press, 1991.

Mitchell, Robert D., and Paul A. Groves, eds. *North America, The Historical Geography of a Changing Continent*. Totowa, N.J.: Rowman & Littlefield, 1987.

Page, Brian, and Richard Walker. "From Settlement to Fordism: The Agro-Industrial Revolution in the American Midwest." *Economic Geography* 67 (October 1991): 281–315.

Passel, J. S. "What Census Adjustment Would Mean." *Population Today* (June 1991).

Patterson, John H. *North America*. New York: Oxford University Press, 1984.

Paullin, C. O., and J. K. Wright. *Atlas of Historical Geography of the United States*. New York: American Geographical Society, 1932.

Plane, David A. "Age-composition and Change and the Geographical Dynamics of Intermigration in the United States." *Annals of the Association of American Geographers* 82 (March 1992): 64–85.

Ragsdale, Bruce A., ed. *Origins of the House of Representatives: A Documentary Record*. Washington, D.C.: Government Printing Office, 1990.

Rogers, A., and J. Watkins. "General Versus Elderly Interstate Migration and Population Redistribution in the United States." *Research on Aging* 9 (1987): 483–529.

Rohrbough, Malcolm J. *The Trans-Appalachian Frontier*. New York: Oxford University Press, 1978.

Saenz, Rogelio. "Mexican-American Interstate Migration Flows Along Arizona, California, Colorado, New Mexico and Texas." *Sociology and Social Research* 73 (April 1989): 153.

Sawers, Larry, and William K. Tabb, eds. "Urban Development and Regional Restructuring, an Overview." In *Sunbelt/Snowbelt: Urban Development and Regional Restructuring.* New York: Oxford University Press, 1984.

Sayre, Wallace S., and Judith H. Parris. *Voting for President: The Electoral College and the American Political System.* Washington, D.C.: Brookings Institution, 1970.

Scheiber, Harry N. *The Old Northwest.* Lincoln: University of Nebraska Press, 1969.

Schmeckebier, Lawrence F. *Congressional Apportionment.* Washington, D.C.: Brookings Institution, 1941.

Schnell, George A., and Mark S. Monmonier. *The Study of Population: Elements, Patterns, Processes.* Columbus, Ohio: Charles E. Merrill, 1983.

Schulman, Bruce J. *From Cotton Belt to Sunbelt.* New York: Oxford University Press, 1991.

Schwab, Larry M. *The Impact of Congressional Reapportionment and Redistricting.* Landam, Md.: University Press of America, 1988.

Shapiro, M. O. "Filling Up America: An Economic-Demographic Model of Population Growth and Distribution in the Nineteenth-Century United States." Vol. 8 of *Industrial Development and the Social Fabric,* edited by J. P. McKay. Greenwich, Conn.: JAI Press, 1986.

Silbey, Joel H., ed. *The Congress of the United States 1789–1989.* 10 vols. New York: Carlson, 1991. Vol. 5, *The United States Congress in a Transitional Era, 1800–1841: The Interplay of Party, Faction and Section.*

Smith, Howard R., and John F. Hart. "The American Tariff Map." *Geographical Review* 45 (July 1955): 327–346.

Smith, S. K., and H. H. Fiskind. "Elderly Migration into Rapidly Growing Areas." *Review of Regional Studies* 15 (March 1985): 11–20.

Soja, Edward. *Postmodern Geographies.* London: Verso, 1989.

Stephenson, Wendell H., and E. Merton Coulter, eds. *A History of the South.* 10 vols. Baton Rouge: Louisiana State University Press, 1943–1961. Vol. 4, *The South in the New Nation 1789–1819,* by Thomas P. Abernethy. Vol. 5, *The Development of Southern Sectionalism,* by Charles S. Sydnor. Vol. 6, *The Growth of Southern Nationalism,* by Avery O. Craven.

Taeuber, Conrad, and Irene Taeuber. *The Changing Population of the United States.* New York: John Wiley, 1958.

Turek, Joseph H. "The Northeast in a National Context: Background Trends in Population, Income, and Employment." In *Economic Prospects for the Northeast,* edited by Harry W. Richardson and Joseph H. Turek. Philadelphia: Temple University Press, 1985.

Turner, Frederick Jackson. *Rise of the New West 1819–1829.* New York: Harper & Brothers, 1906.

———. "The Significance of the Frontier in American History." *Wisconsin Magazine of History* 3 (March 1925): 255–280.

———. *Sections in American History.* New York: Henry Holt, 1931.

Ullman, Edward L. "Regional Development and the Geography of Concentration." *Papers and Proceedings of the Regional Science Association* 4 (1958): 179–198.

USA Today, June 8, 1992.

U.S. Congress. *The Debates and Proceedings of the Congress of the United States, Second Congress: October 24, 1791 to March 2, 1793.* Washington, D.C.: Gales and Seaton, 1849.

U.S. Congress. *Biographical Directory of the United States Congress 1774–1989.* Washington, D.C.: Government Printing Office, 1989.

U.S. Congress. House. *Congressional Globe.* 27th Cong., 1842.

U.S. Congress. House. *Congressional Record.* 66th Cong., 3d sess., 1921.

U.S. Department of Commerce. Bureau of the Census. *Historical Statistics of the United States: Colonial Times to 1970.* Washington, D.C.: Government Printing Office, 1975.

U.S. Department of Commerce. Bureau of the Census. "Projections of the Population of the United States by Age and Sex: 1970 to 2000." *Current Population Reports* ser. P-25, no. 470. Washington, D.C.: Government Printing Office, 1973.

U.S. Department of Commerce. Bureau of the Census. *1980 Census of Population.* Vol. 1, *Characteristics of Population.* Washington, D.C.: Government Printing Office, 1984.

United States Population Data Sheet. 9th ed. Washington, D.C.: Population Reference Bureau, Inc., 1991.

Vining, David, R. Pallone, and D. A. Plane. "Recent Migration Patterns in the Developed World: A Clarification of Some Differences Between Our and IIASA's Findings." *Environment and Planning A* 13 (1981): 243–250.

Ward, David. "Population Growth, Migration and Urbanization, 1860–1920." In *North America, the Historical Geography of a Changing Continent,* edited by Robert D. Mitchell and Paul A. Groves. Totowa, N.J.: Rowman & Littlefield, 1987.

———., ed. *Geographic Perspectives on America's Past.* New York: Oxford University Press, 1979.

Weinstein, Bernard L., and Robert E. Firestine. *Regional Growth and Decline in the United States: The Rise of the Sunbelt and the Decline of the Northeast.* New York: Praeger, 1978.

Wellington, Raynor G. *Political and Sectional Influences of Public Lands 1829–1842.* Boston: Riverside Press, 1914.

Wilson, Major L. *Space, Time, and Freedom: The Quest for Nationality and the Irrepressible Conflict, 1815–1861.* Westport, Conn.: Greenwood Press, 1974.

Zagarri, Rosemarie. *The Politics of Size.* Ithaca, N.Y.: Cornell University Press, 1987.

Index

For states, year of U.S. admission is in parentheses.